TIGER & BUNNY THE MOVIE
The Beginning
SIDE A

ART BY **TSUTOMU OONO**

PLANNING/STORY **SUNRISE**

ORIGINAL SCRIPT **MASAFUMI NISHIDA**

ORIGINAL CHARACTER AND HERO DESIGN **MASAKAZU KATSURA**

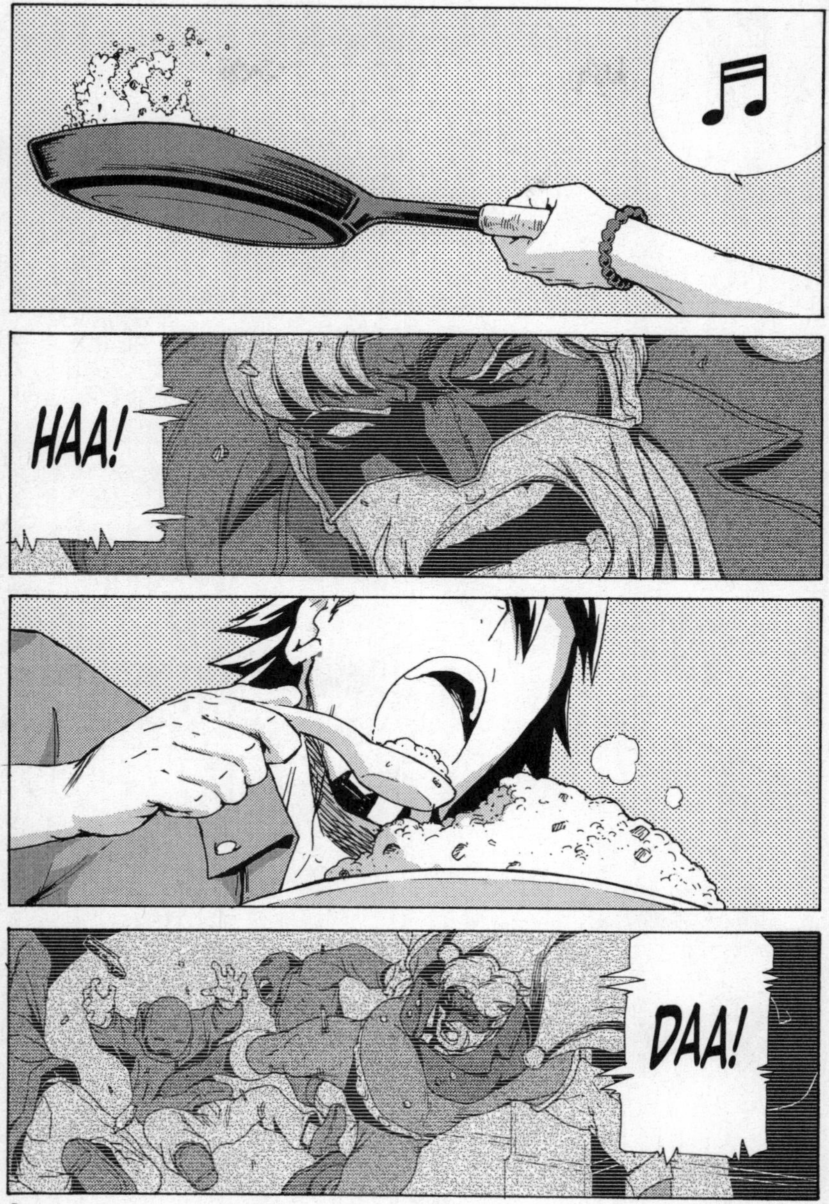
♬
HAA!
DAA!

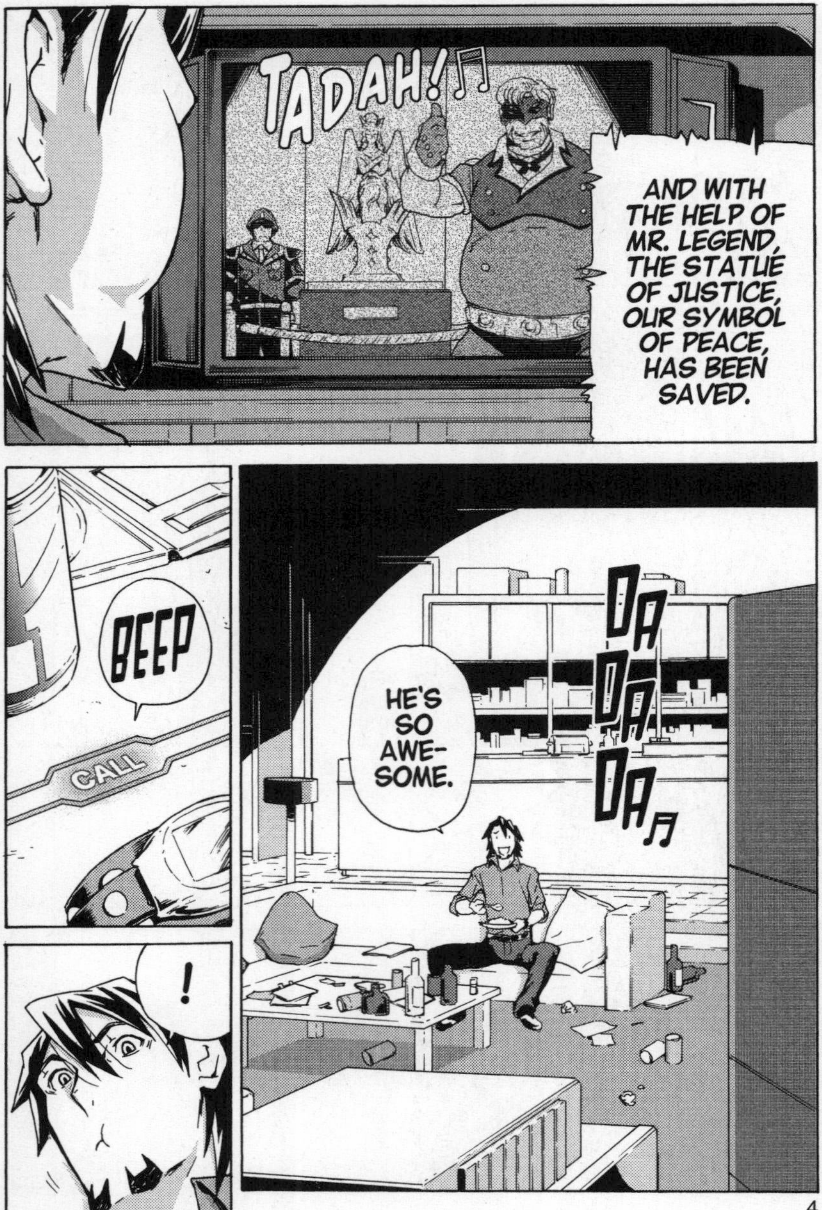
AND WITH THE HELP OF MR. LEGEND, THE STATUE OF JUSTICE, OUR SYMBOL OF PEACE, HAS BEEN SAVED.
TADAH!♫
DA DA DA DA♫
HE'S SO AWE-SOME.
BEEP
CALL
!

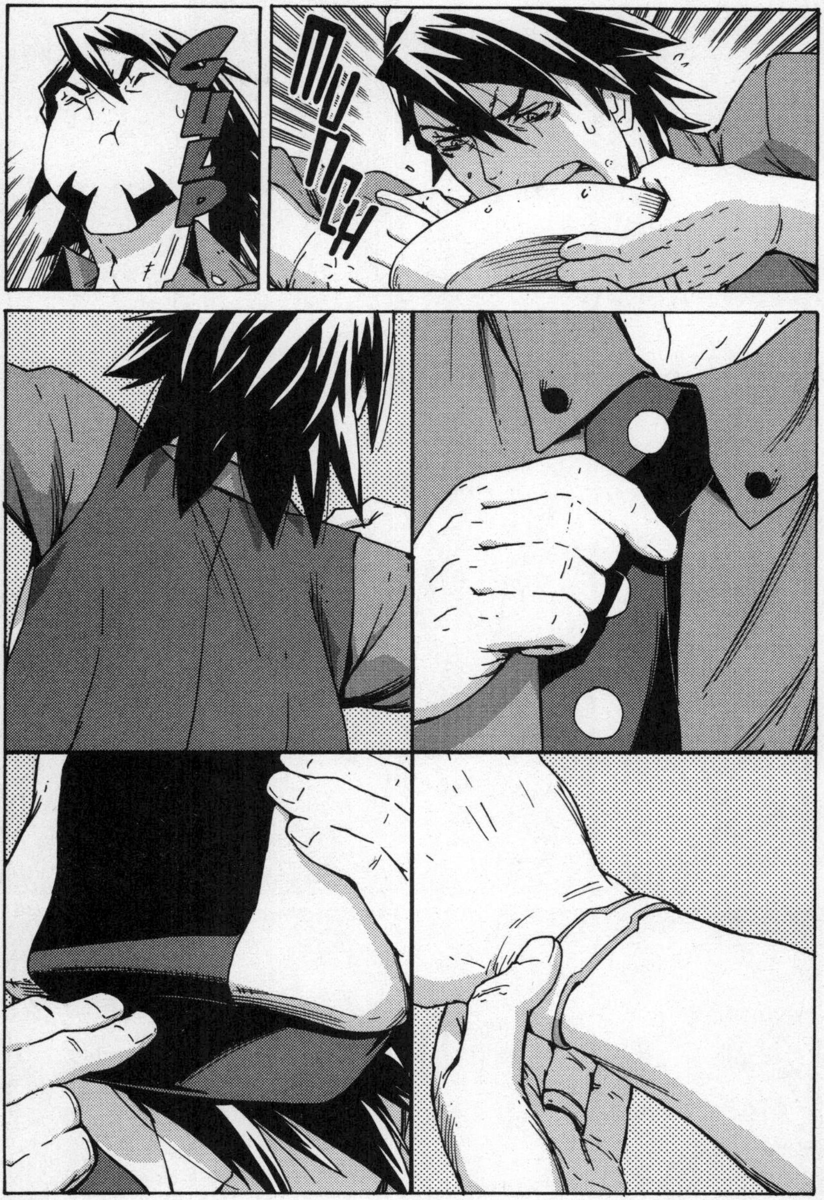
MUNCH
GULP

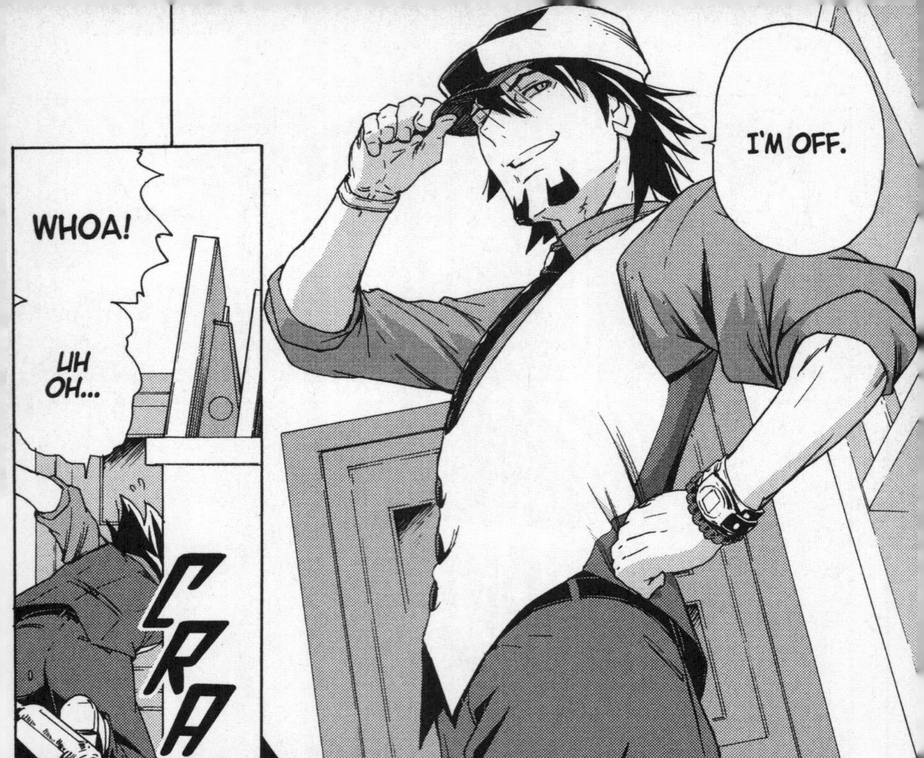
I'M OFF.
WHOA!
UH OH...
CRASH
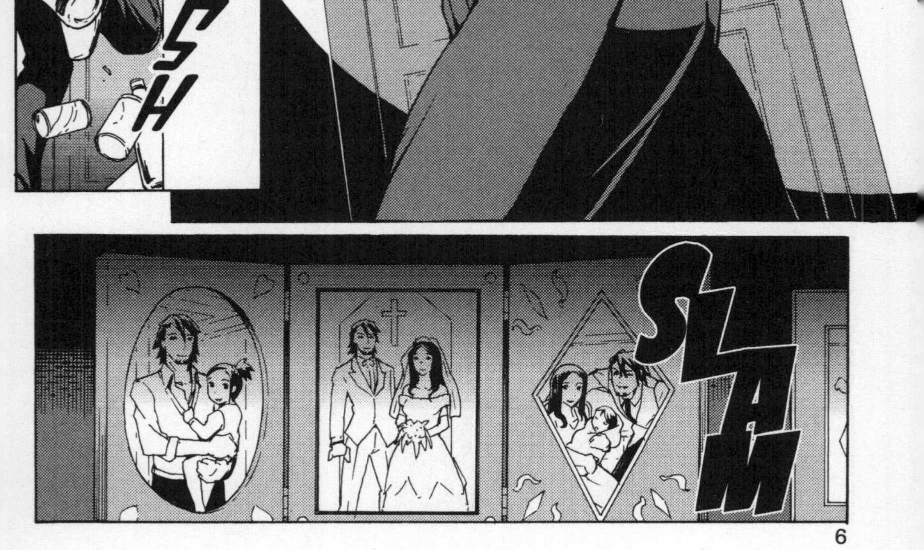
SLAM

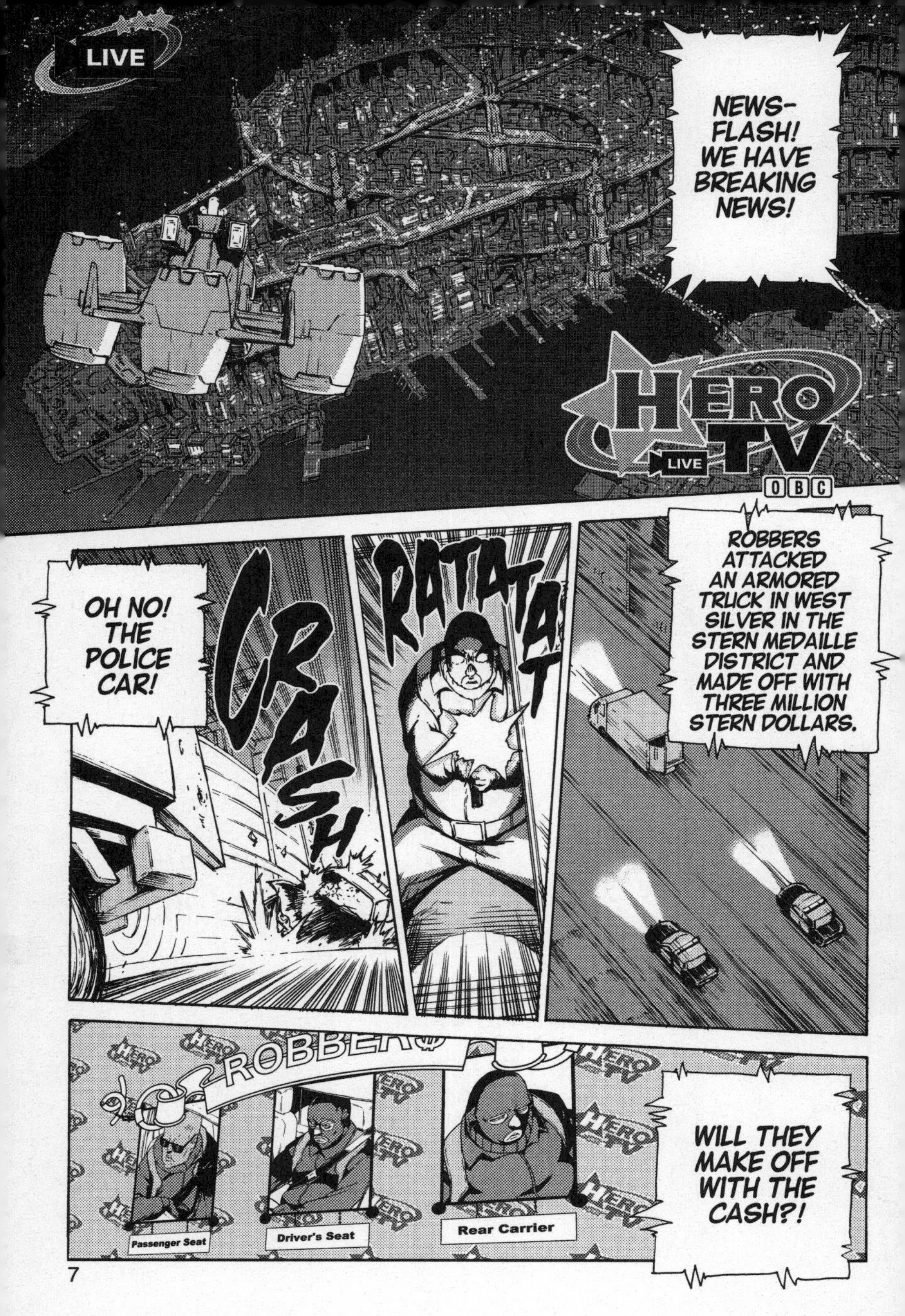
LIVE
NEWS-FLASH! WE HAVE BREAKING NEWS!
HERO TV
LIVE
OBC
ROBBERS ATTACKED AN ARMORED TRUCK IN WEST SILVER IN THE STERN MEDAILLE DISTRICT AND MADE OFF WITH THREE MILLION STERN DOLLARS.
RATATATAT
CRASH
OH NO! THE POLICE CAR!
WILL THEY MAKE OFF WITH THE CASH?!
ROBBER$
Rear Carrier
Driver's Seat
Passenger Seat

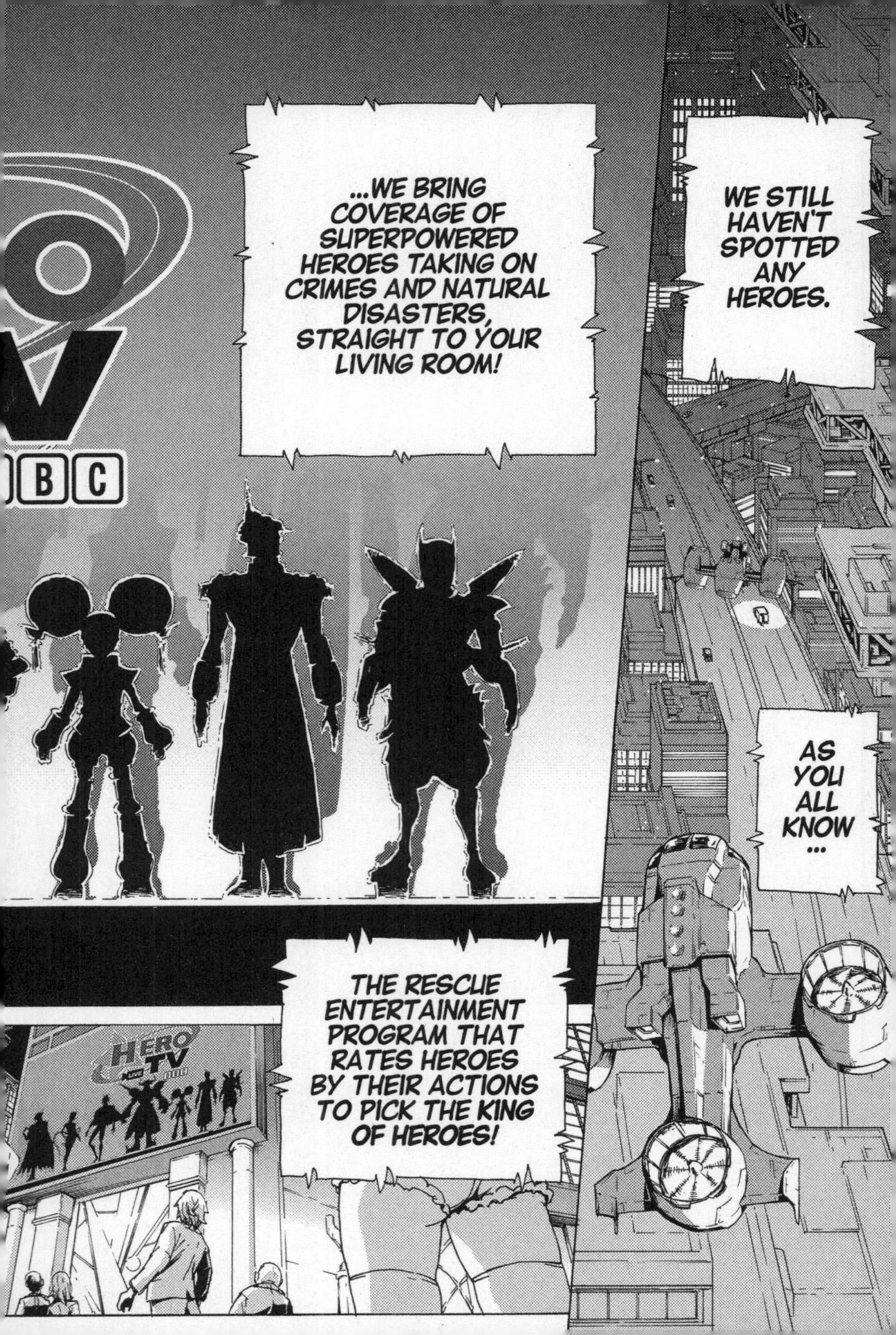
WE STILL HAVEN'T SPOTTED ANY HEROES.
AS YOU ALL KNOW...
...WE BRING COVERAGE OF SUPERPOWERED HEROES TAKING ON CRIMES AND NATURAL DISASTERS, STRAIGHT TO YOUR LIVING ROOM!
B C
THE RESCUE ENTERTAINMENT PROGRAM THAT RATES HEROES BY THEIR ACTIONS TO PICK THE KING OF HEROES!
HERO TV
LIVE

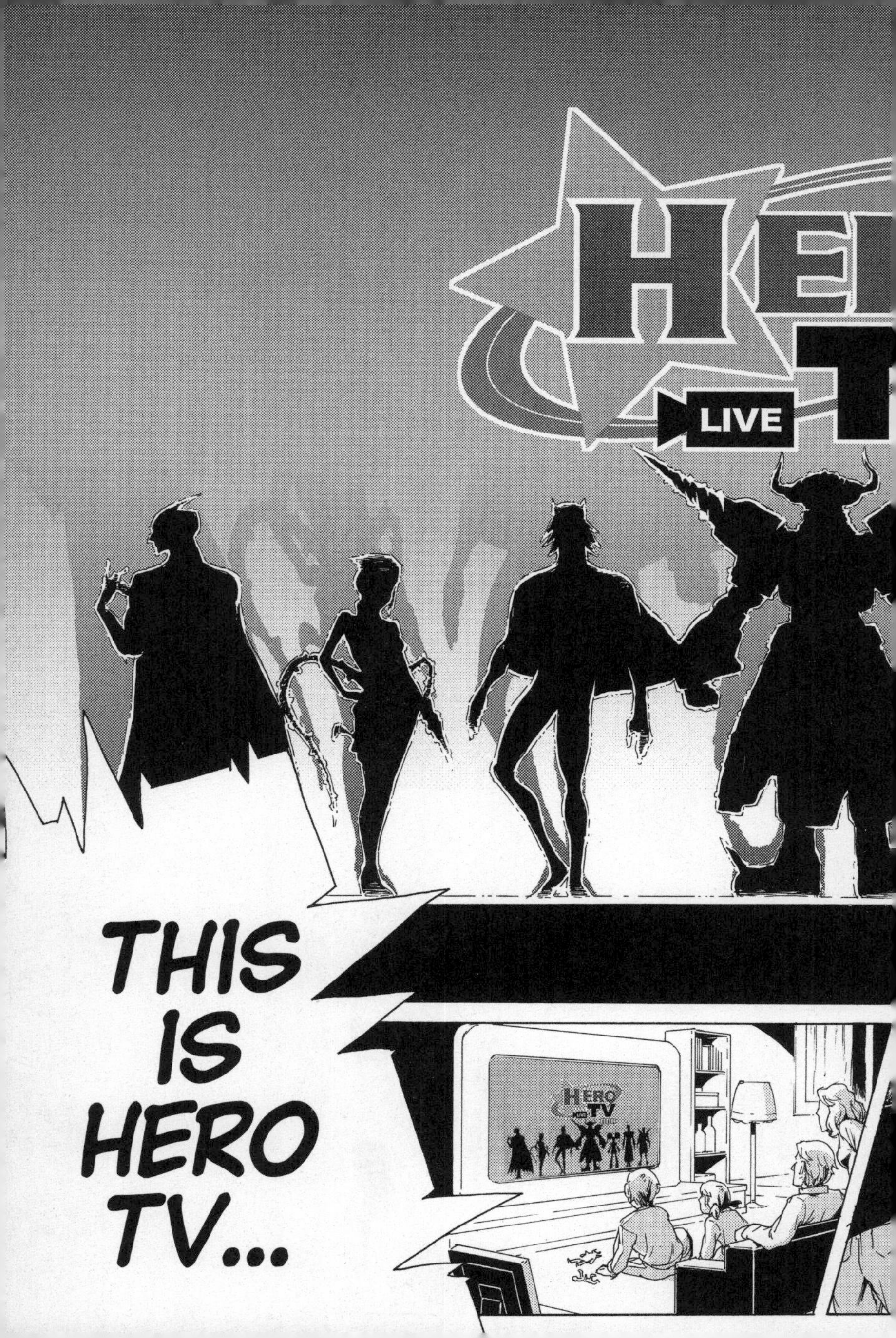
LIVE
THIS IS HERO TV...

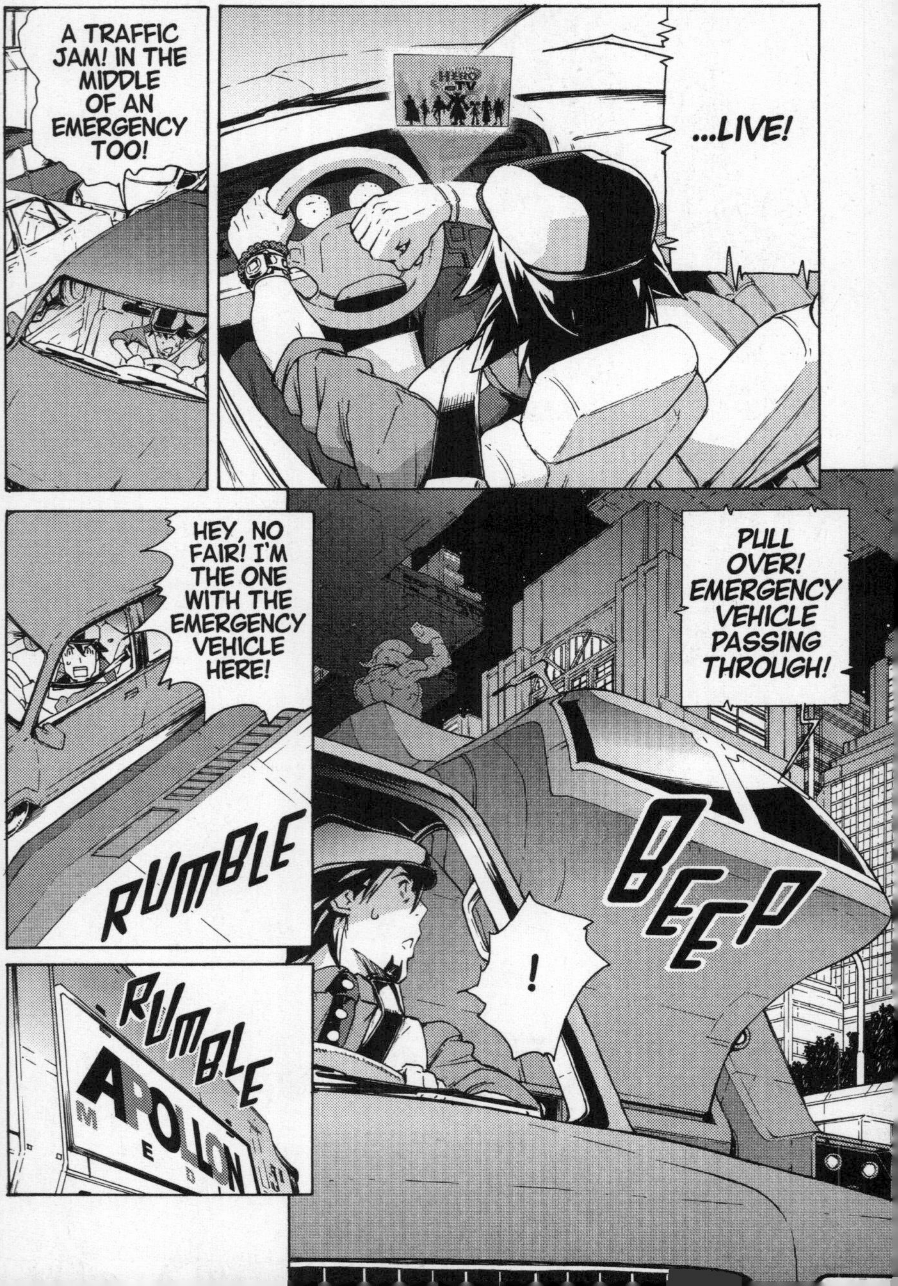
HERO TV
...LIVE!
A TRAFFIC JAM! IN THE MIDDLE OF AN EMERGENCY TOO!
PULL OVER! EMERGENCY VEHICLE PASSING THROUGH!
BEEP
!
HEY, NO FAIR! I'M THE ONE WITH THE EMERGENCY VEHICLE HERE!
RUMBLE
RUMBLE
APOLLON
MED

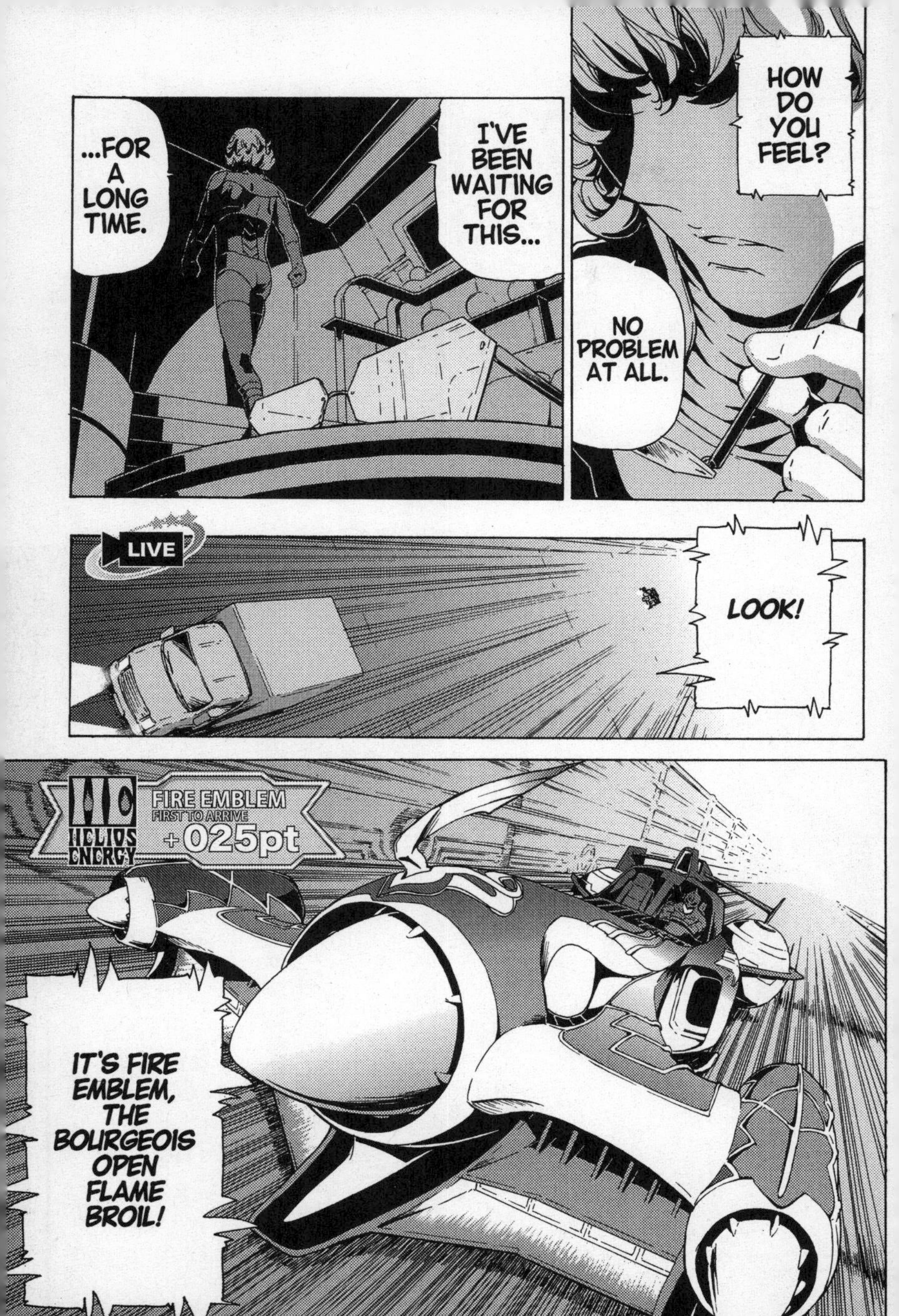
HOW DO YOU FEEL?
NO PROBLEM AT ALL.
I'VE BEEN WAITING FOR THIS...
...FOR A LONG TIME.
LIVE
LOOK!
HELIOS ENERGY
FIRE EMBLEM
FIRST TO ARRIVE
+025pt
IT'S FIRE EMBLEM, THE BOURGEOIS OPEN FLAME BROIL!

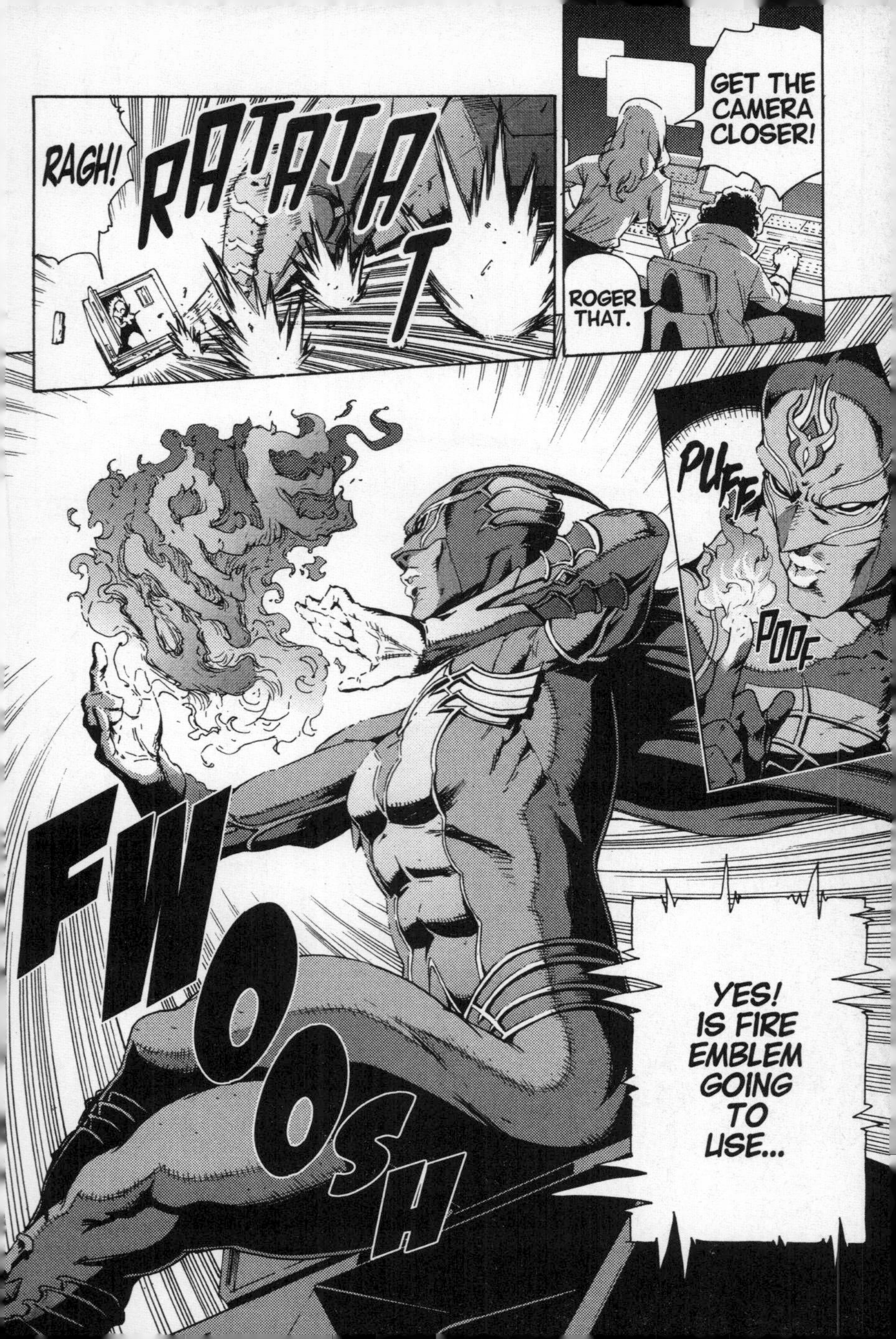
GET THE CAMERA CLOSER!
ROGER THAT.
RAGH!
RATATATAT
PUFF
POOF
FWOOSH
YES! IS FIRE EMBLEM GOING TO USE...

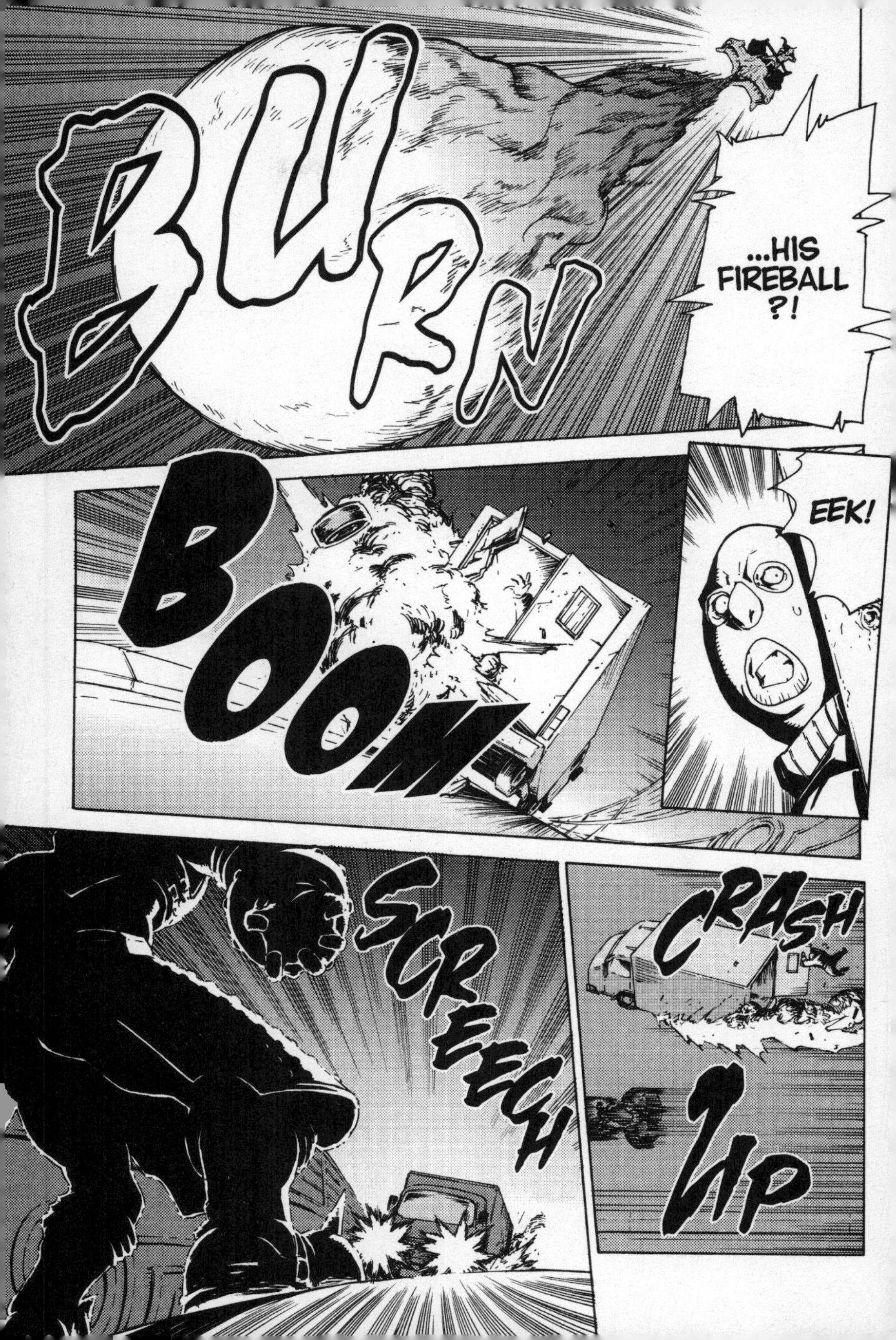
...HIS FIREBALL ?!
BURN
EEK!
BOOM
CRASH
ZIP
SCREECH

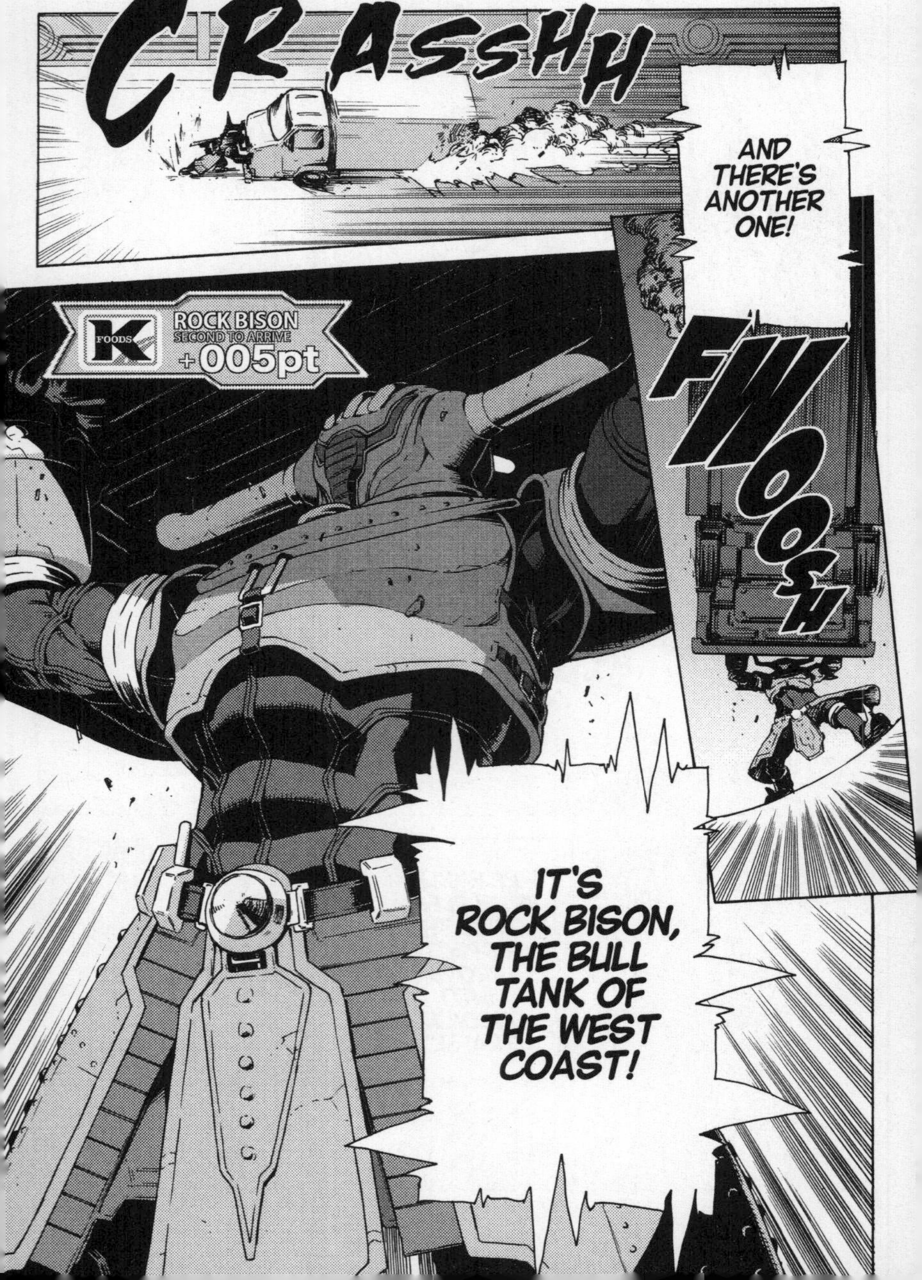
CRASSHH
AND THERE'S ANOTHER ONE!
FWOOOSH
ROCK BISON
SECOND TO ARRIVE
+005pt
K FOODS
IT'S ROCK BISON, THE BULL TANK OF THE WEST COAST!

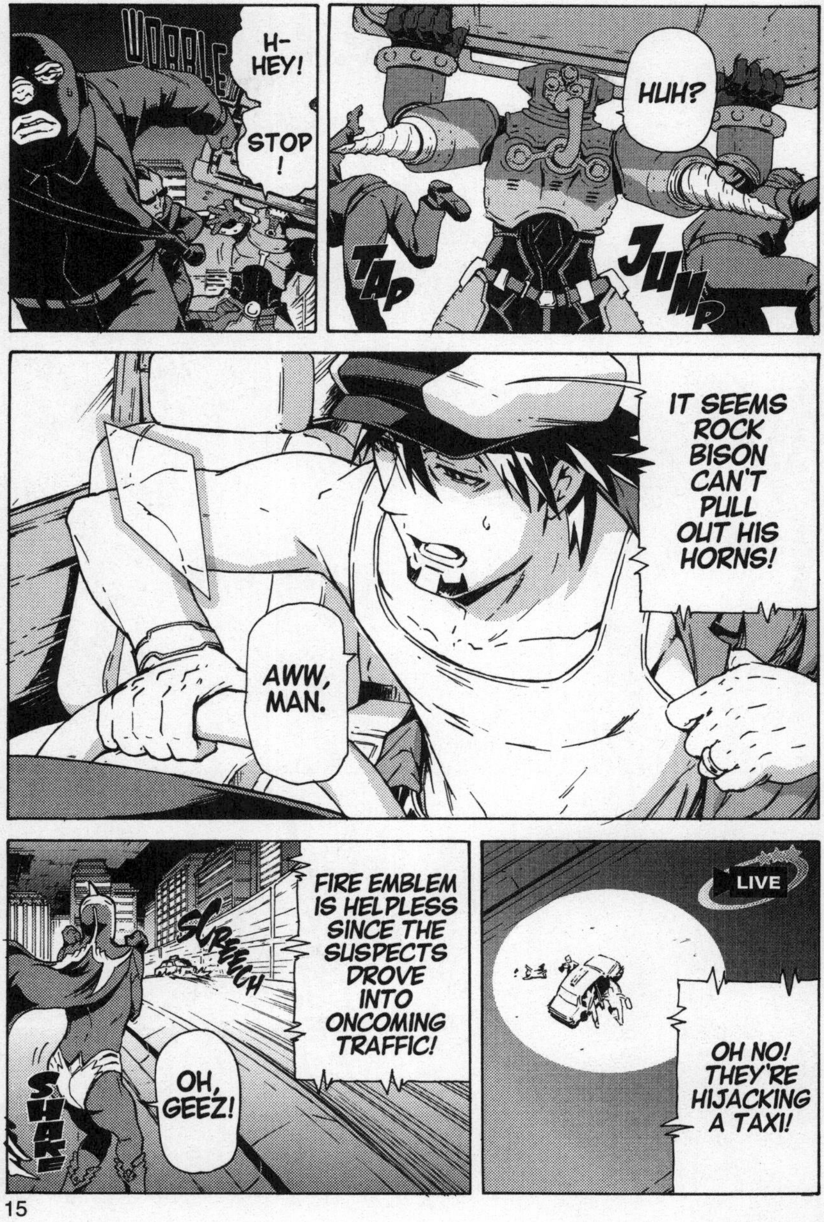
HUH?
JUMP
TAP
H-HEY!
WOBBLE
STOP!
IT SEEMS ROCK BISON CAN'T PULL OUT HIS HORNS!
AWW, MAN.
LIVE
OH NO! THEY'RE HIJACKING A TAXI!
FIRE EMBLEM IS HELPLESS SINCE THE SUSPECTS DROVE INTO ONCOMING TRAFFIC!
SCREECH
OH, GEEZ!
SHAKE

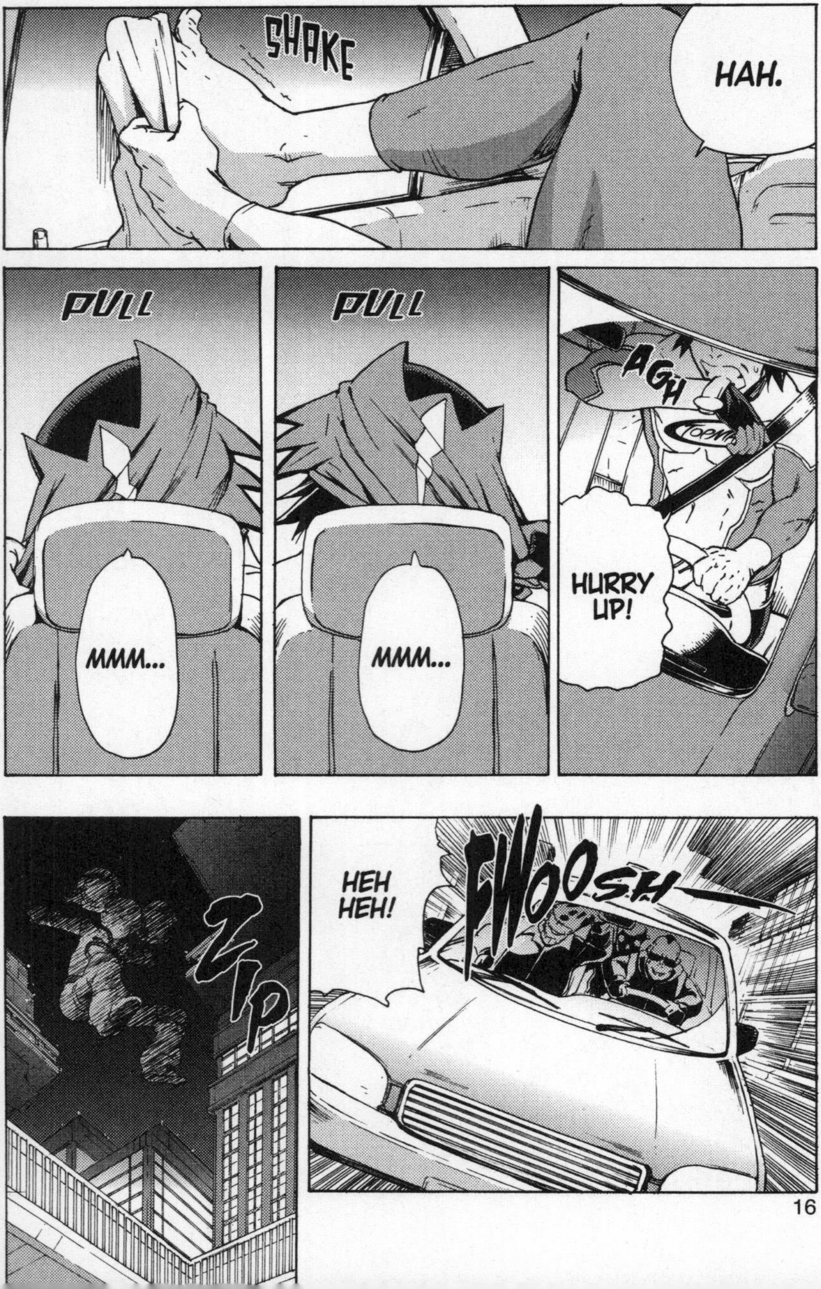
SHAKE
HAH.
AGH
HURRY UP!
PULL
MMM...
PULL
MMM...
FWOOSH
HEH HEH!
ZIP

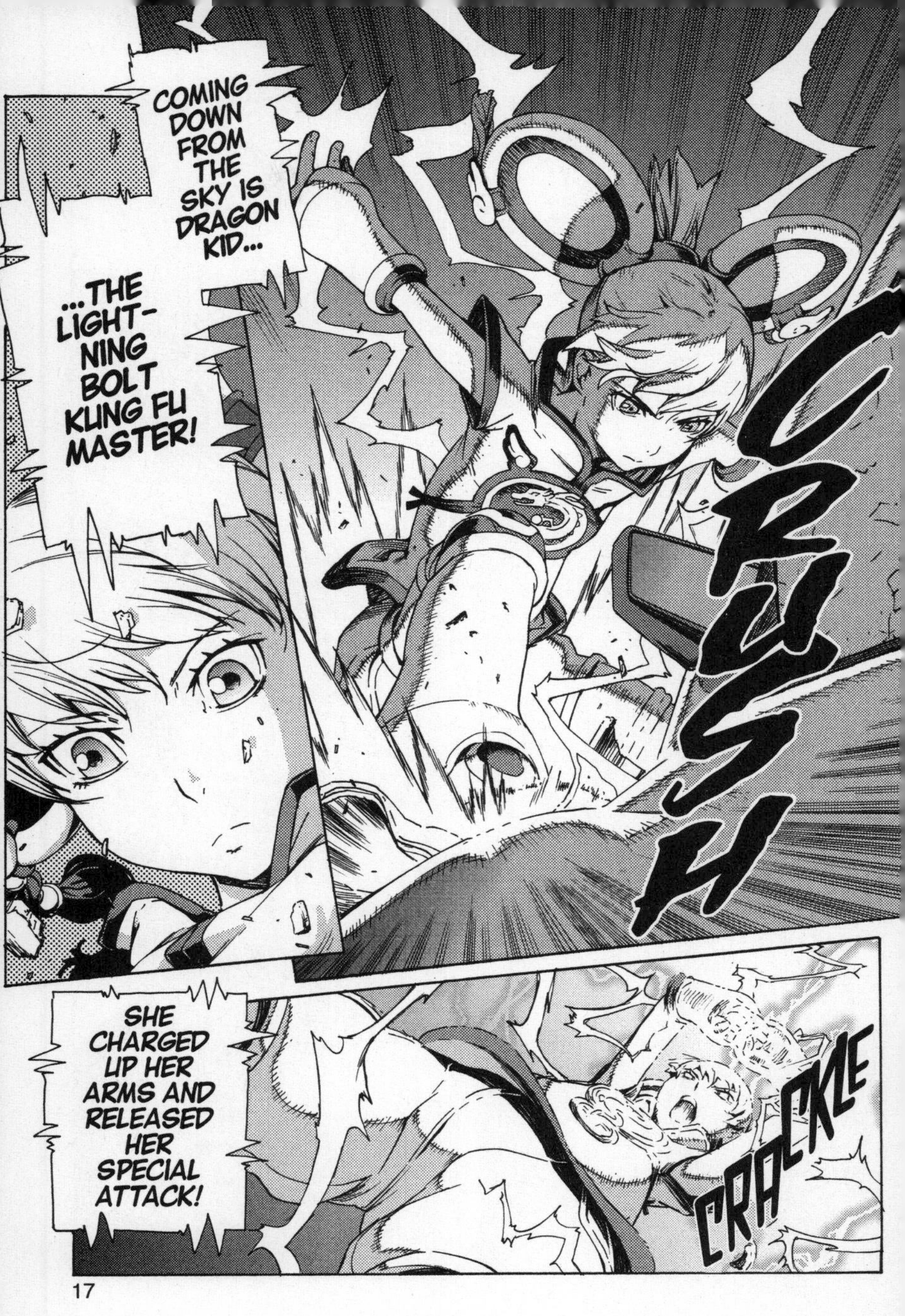
COMING DOWN FROM THE SKY IS DRAGON KID...
...THE LIGHTNING BOLT KUNG FU MASTER!
CRUSH
SHE CHARGED UP HER ARMS AND RELEASED HER SPECIAL ATTACK!
CRACKLE

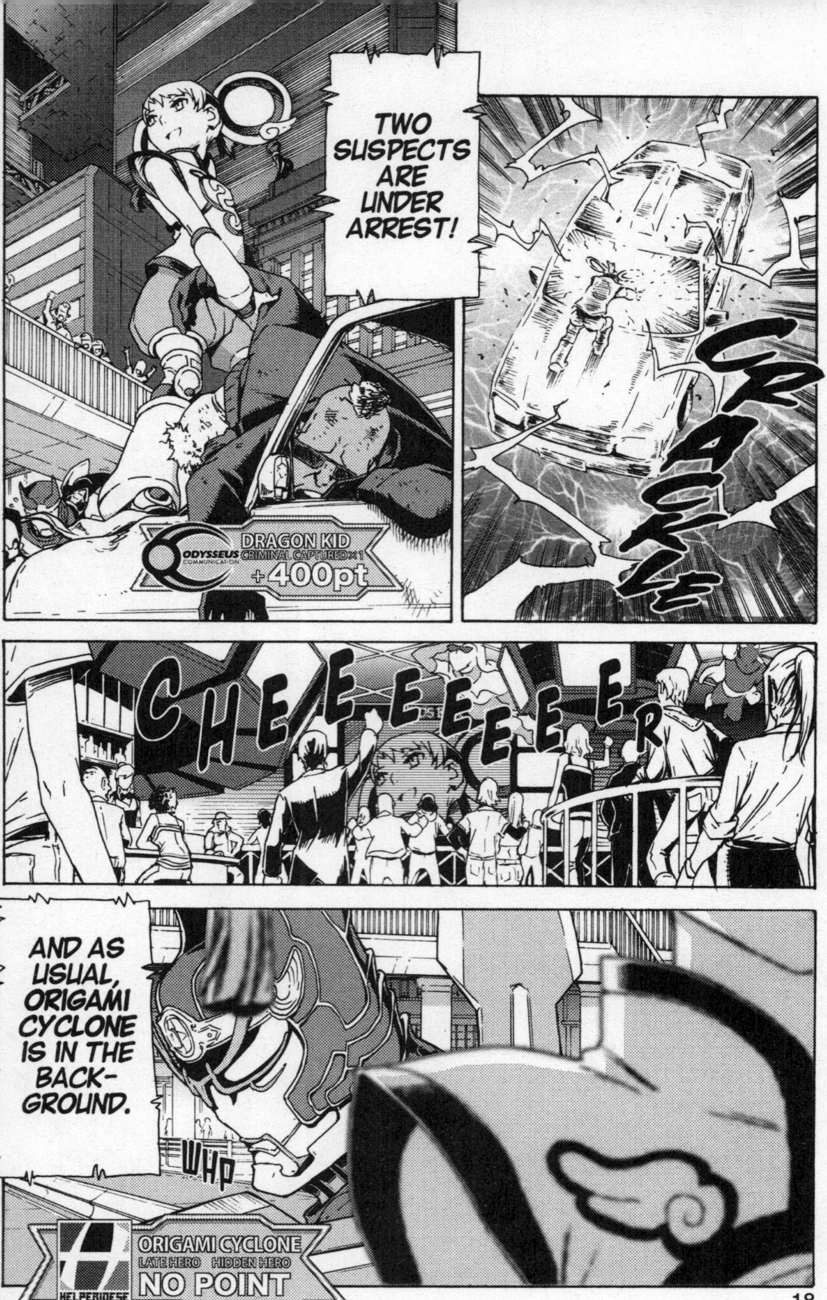
CRACKLE
TWO SUSPECTS ARE UNDER ARREST!
ODYSSEUS COMMUNICATION
DRAGON KID
CRIMINAL CAPTURED ×1
+400pt
CHEEEEEEER
AND AS USUAL, ORIGAMI CYCLONE IS IN THE BACK-GROUND.
WHP
HELPERIDESE FINANCE
ORIGAMI CYCLONE
LATE HERO HIDDEN HERO
NO POINT

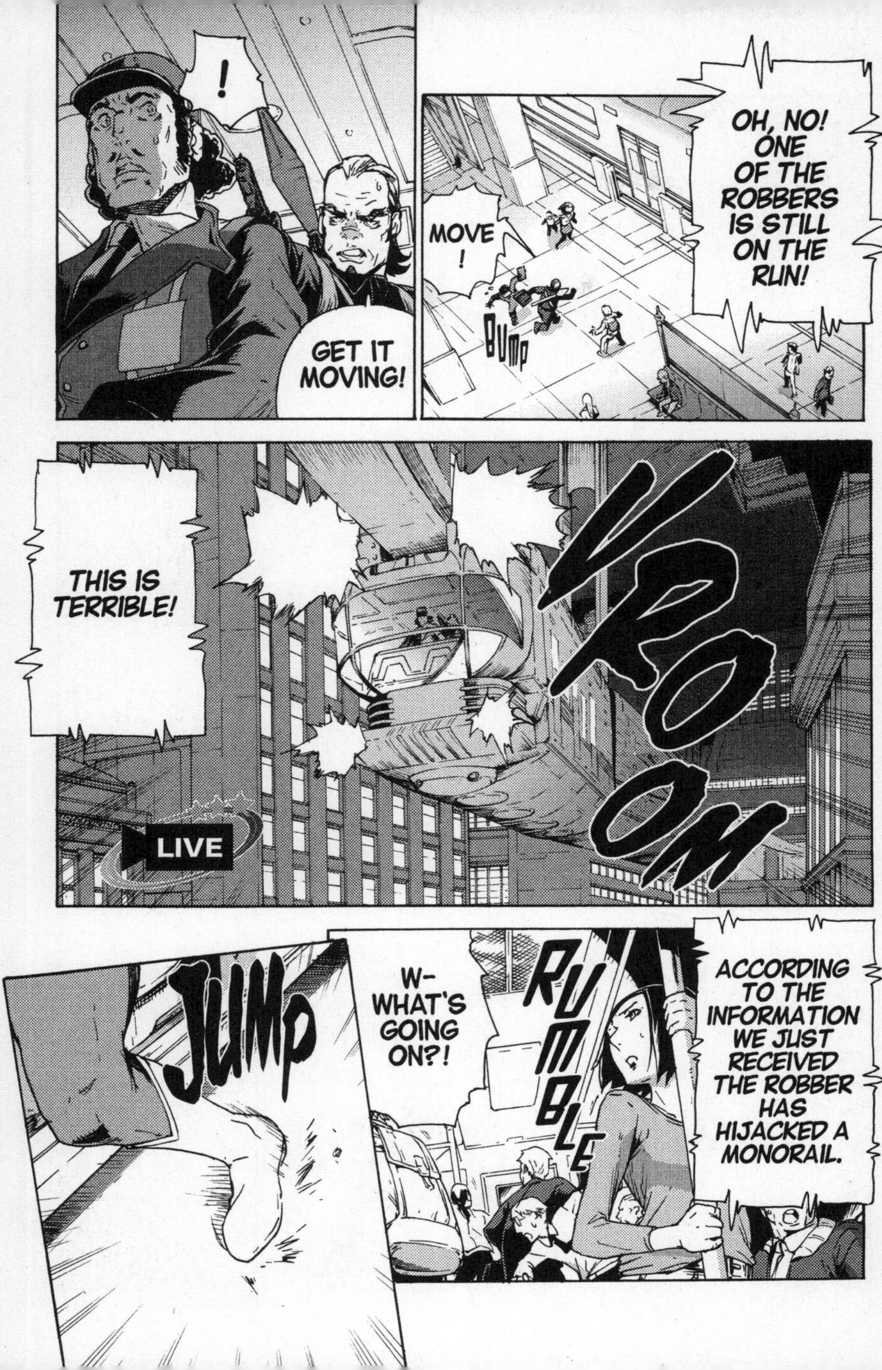

OH, NO! ONE OF THE ROBBERS IS STILL ON THE RUN!
MOVE !
BUMP
!
GET IT MOVING!
VROOM
THIS IS TERRIBLE!
LIVE
ACCORDING TO THE INFORMATION WE JUST RECEIVED THE ROBBER HAS HIJACKED A MONORAIL.
RUMBLE
W- WHAT'S GOING ON?!
JUMP

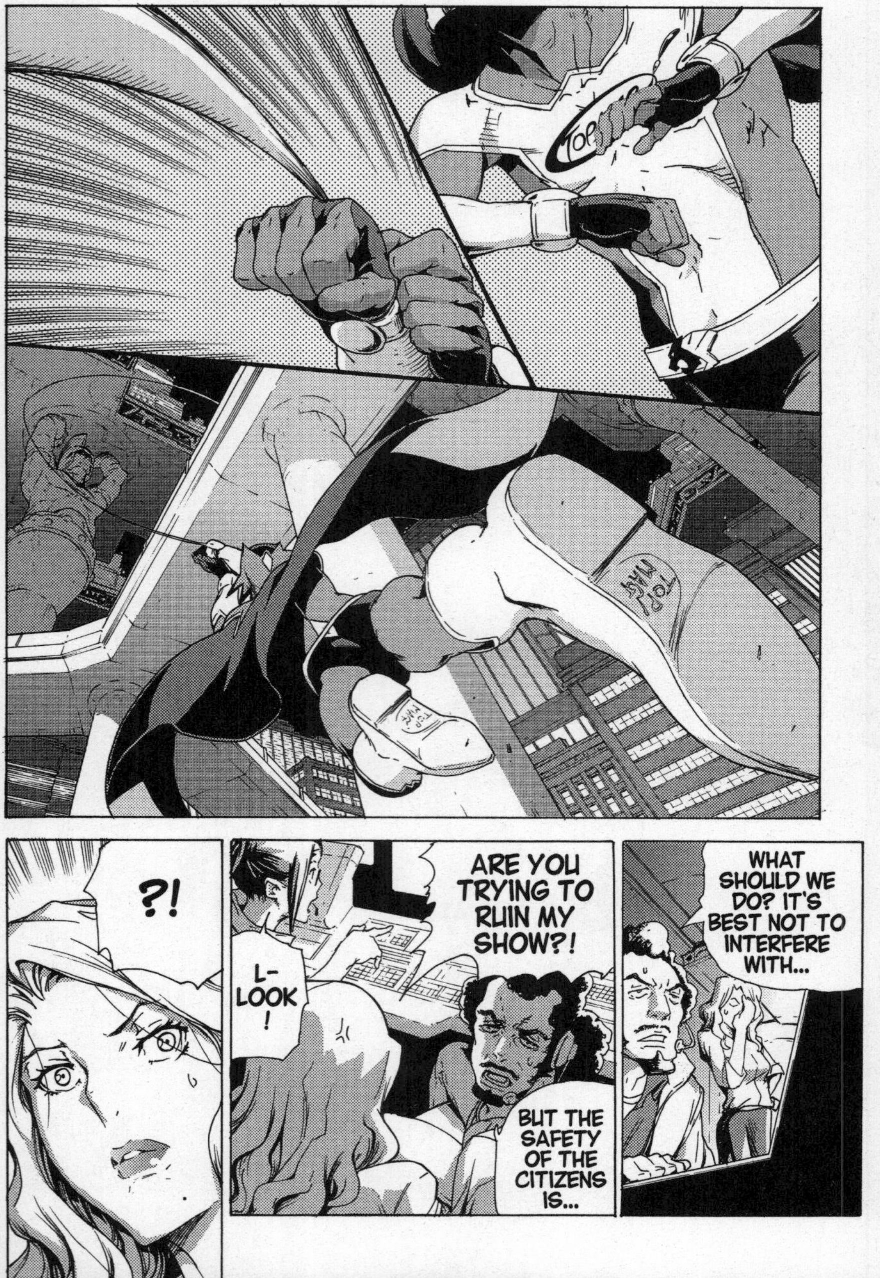
WHAT SHOULD WE DO? IT'S BEST NOT TO INTERFERE WITH...
ARE YOU TRYING TO RUIN MY SHOW?!
L- LOOK!
BUT THE SAFETY OF THE CITIZENS IS...
?!

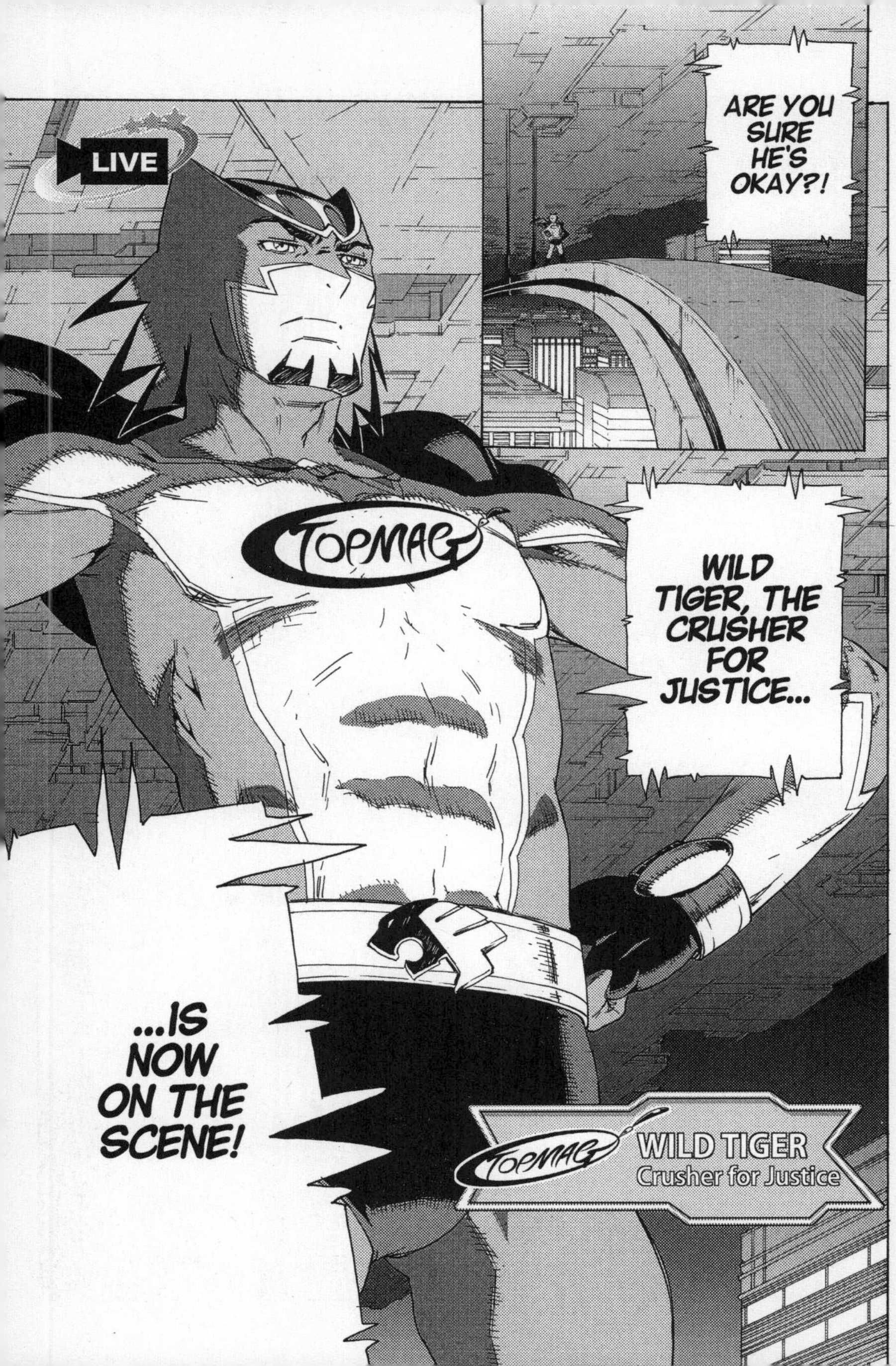
ARE YOU SURE HE'S OKAY?!
LIVE
TOPMAG
WILD TIGER, THE CRUSHER FOR JUSTICE...
...IS NOW ON THE SCENE!
TOPMAG
WILD TIGER
Crusher for Justice

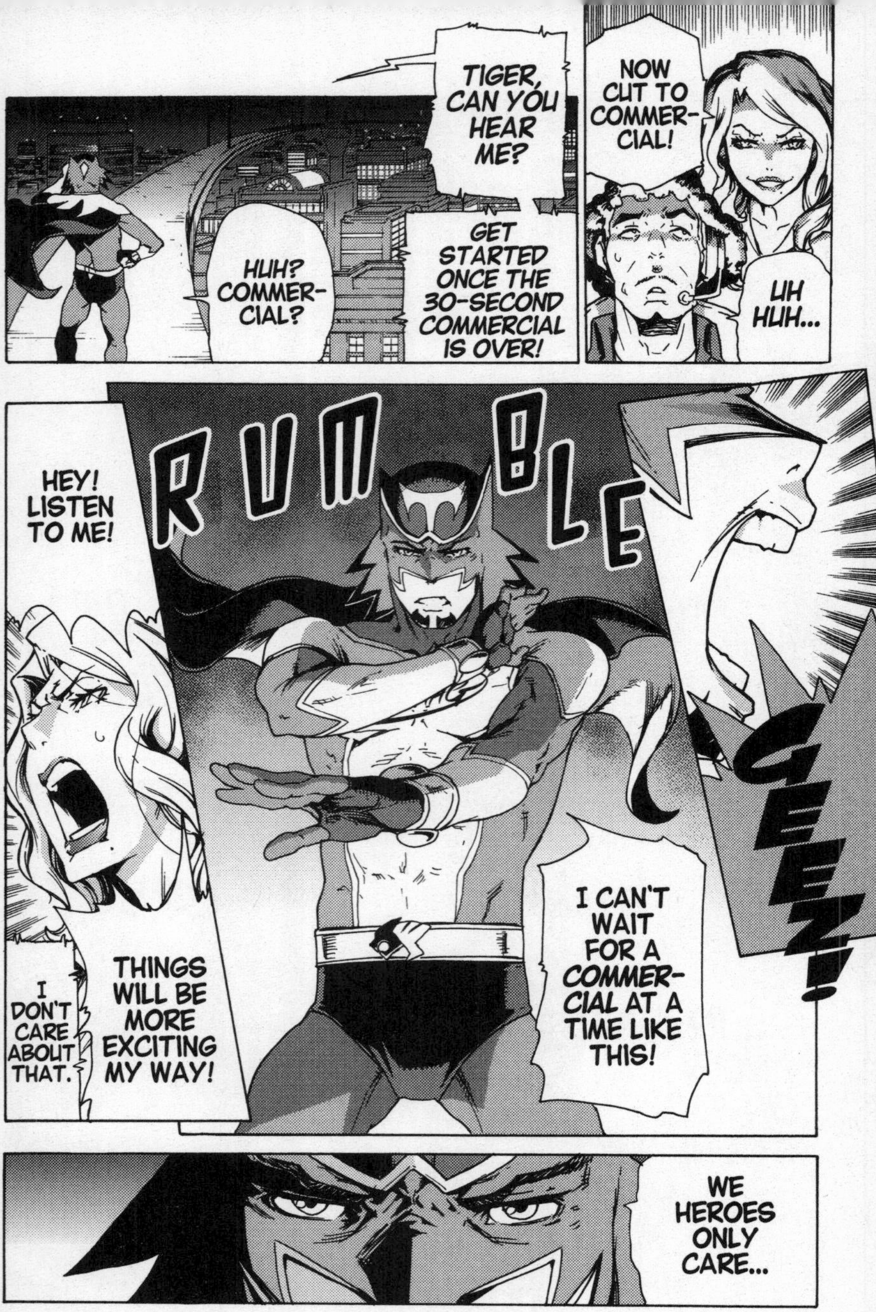
NOW CUT TO COMMERCIAL!
UH HUH...
TIGER, CAN YOU HEAR ME?
GET STARTED ONCE THE 30-SECOND COMMERCIAL IS OVER!
HUH? COMMERCIAL?
GEEZ!
RUMBLE
I CAN'T WAIT FOR A COMMERCIAL AT A TIME LIKE THIS!
HEY! LISTEN TO ME!
THINGS WILL BE MORE EXCITING MY WAY!
I DON'T CARE ABOUT THAT.
WE HEROES ONLY CARE...

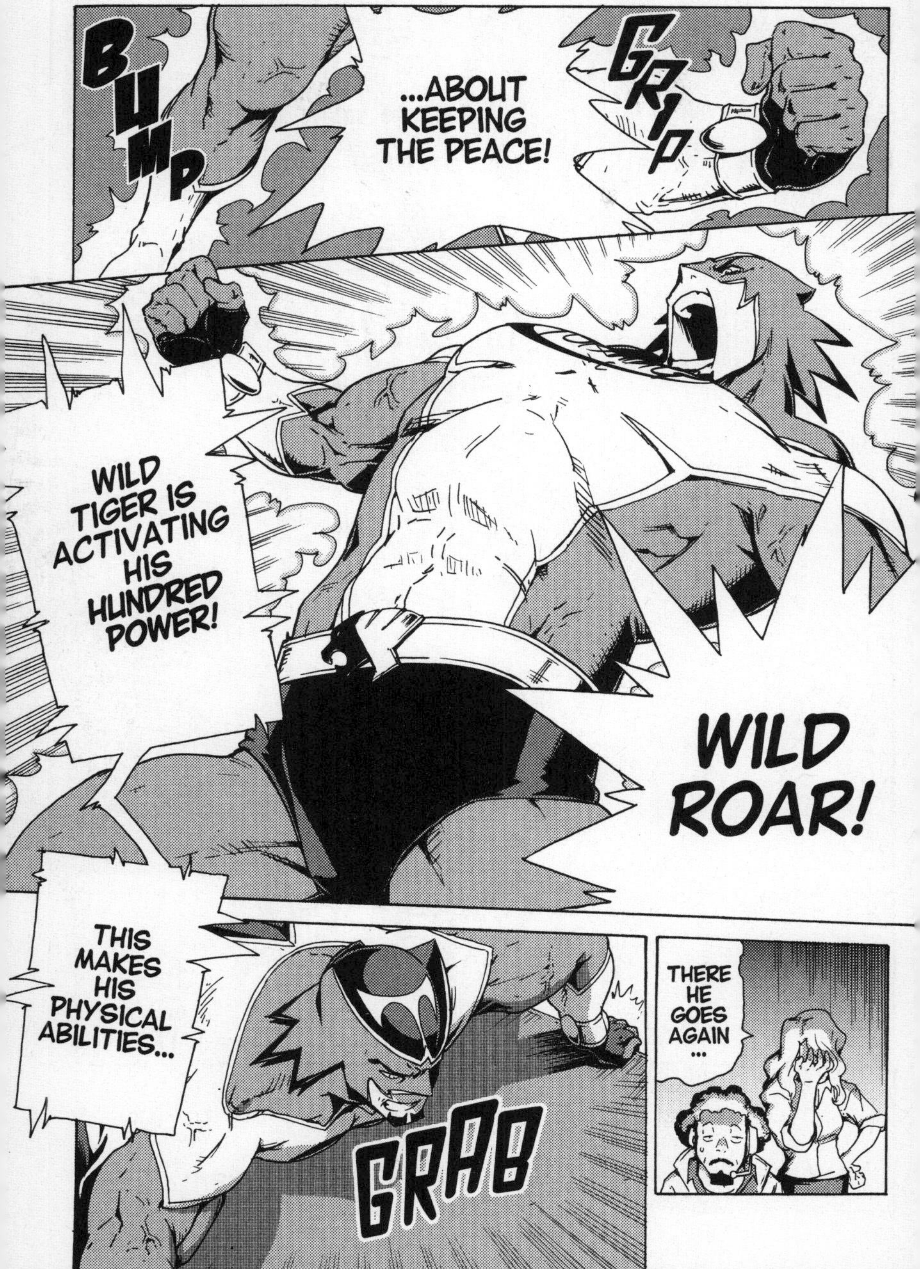
GRIP
...ABOUT KEEPING THE PEACE!
BUMP
WILD ROAR!
WILD TIGER IS ACTIVATING HIS HUNDRED POWER!
THERE HE GOES AGAIN ...
THIS MAKES HIS PHYSICAL ABILITIES...
GRAB

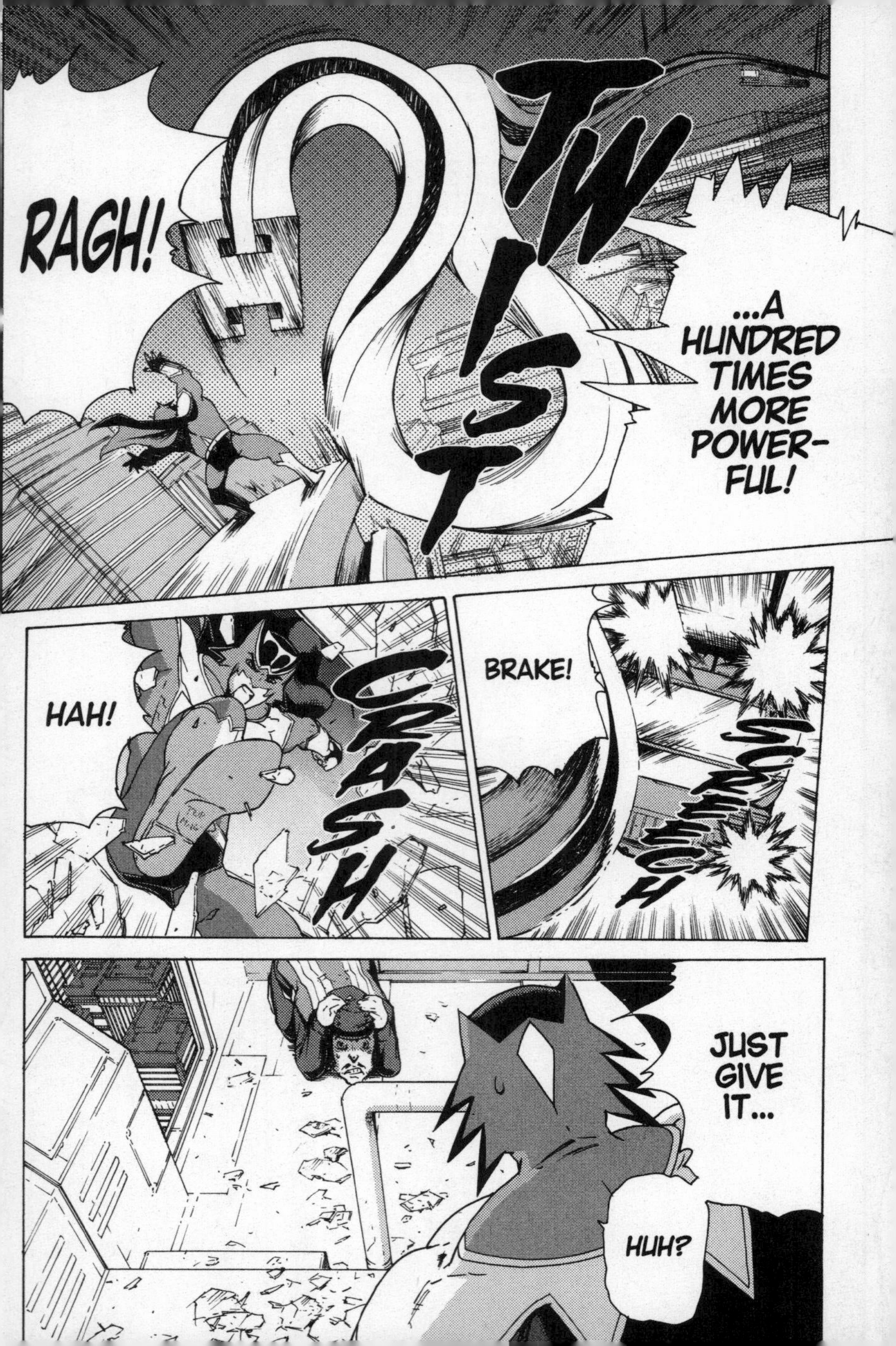
...A HUNDRED TIMES MORE POWER-FUL!
TWIST
RAGH!
BRAKE!
SCREECH
HAH!
CRASH
JUST GIVE IT...
HUH?

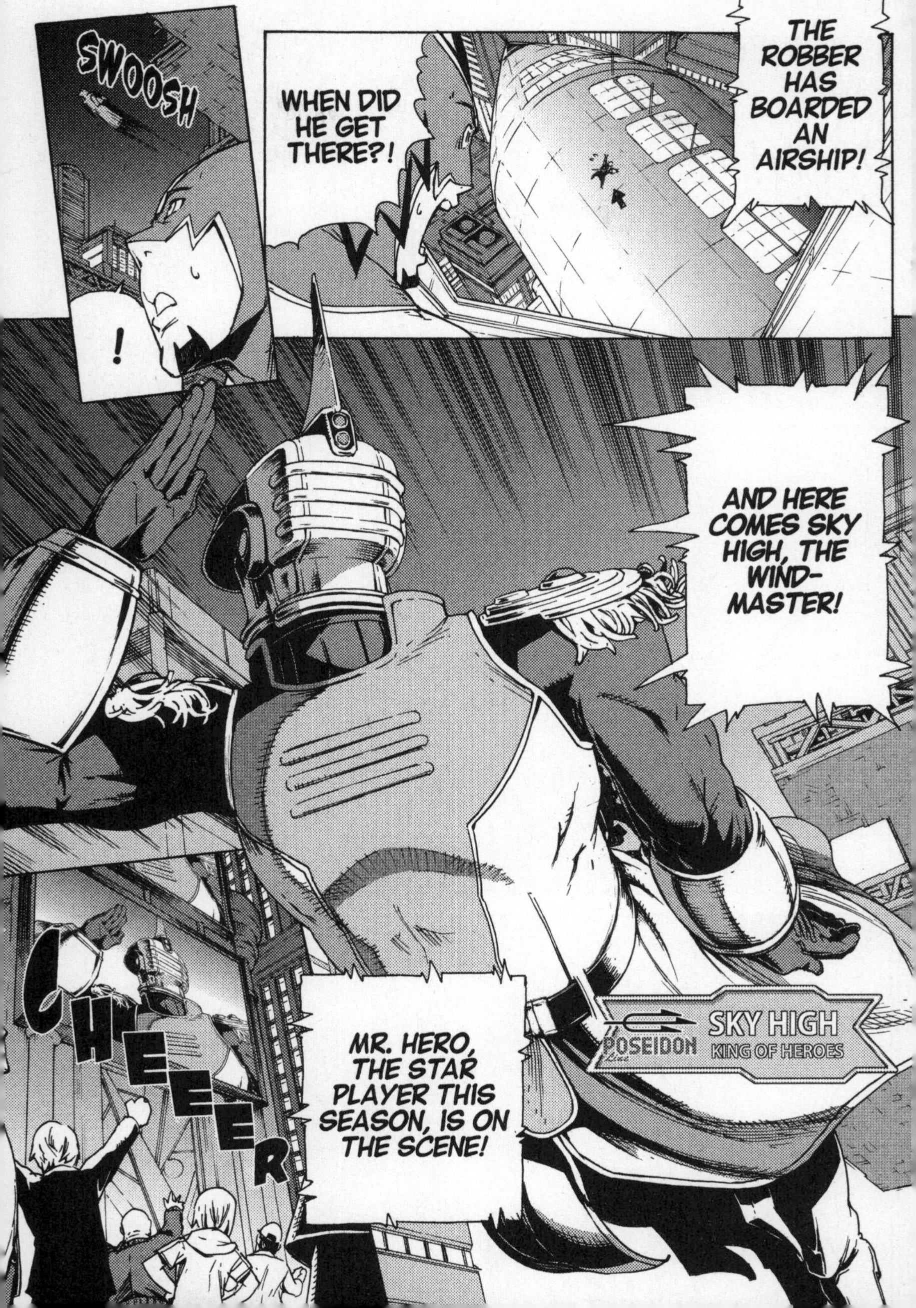
THE ROBBER HAS BOARDED AN AIRSHIP!
WHEN DID HE GET THERE?!
SWOOSH
!
AND HERE COMES SKY HIGH, THE WIND-MASTER!
POSEIDON Line
SKY HIGH
KING OF HEROES
MR. HERO, THE STAR PLAYER THIS SEASON, IS ON THE SCENE!
CHEEEER

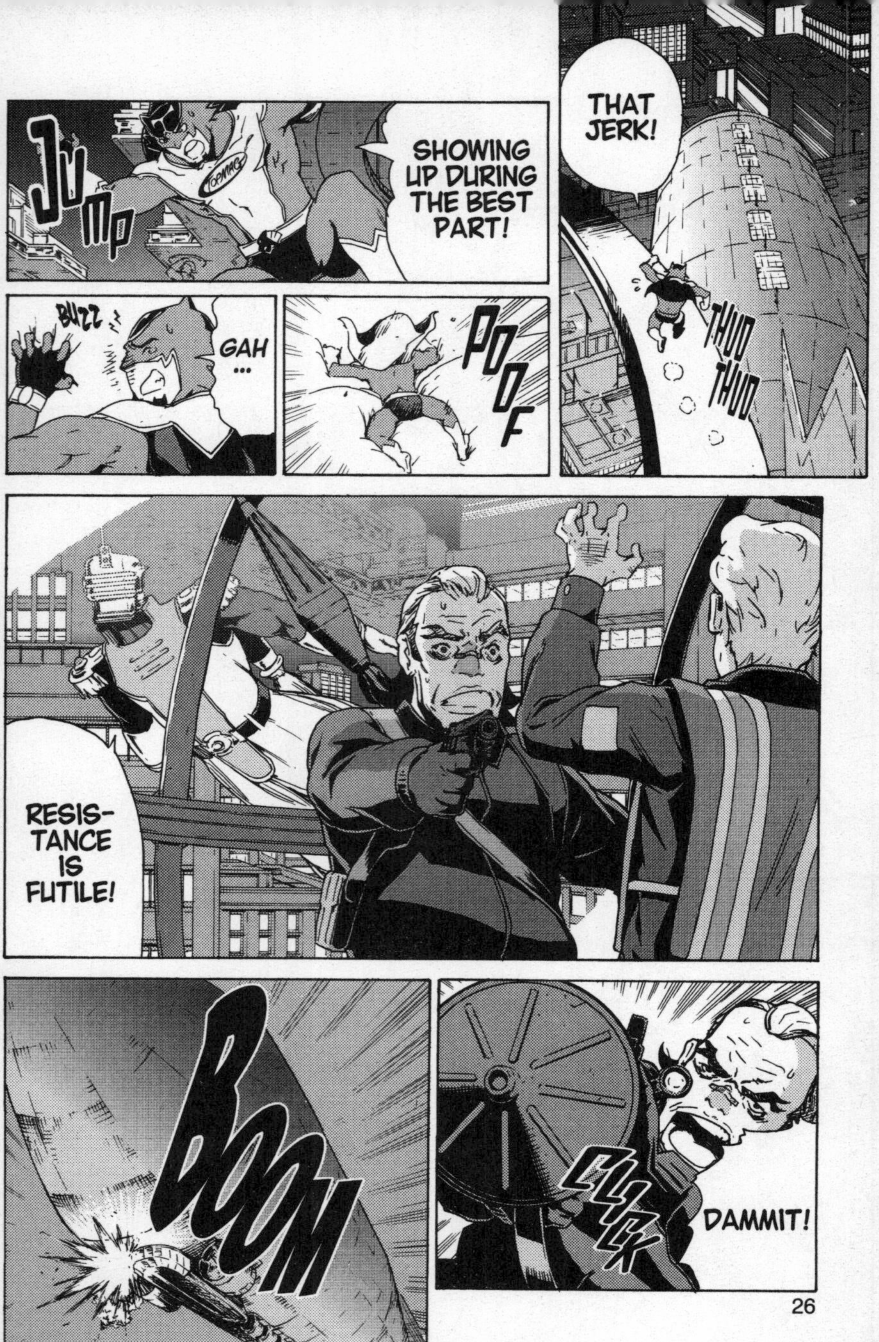
THAT JERK!
THUD THUD
SHOWING UP DURING THE BEST PART!
JUMP
POOF
BUZZ
GAH ...
RESIS-TANCE IS FUTILE!
DAMMIT!
CLICK
BOOM

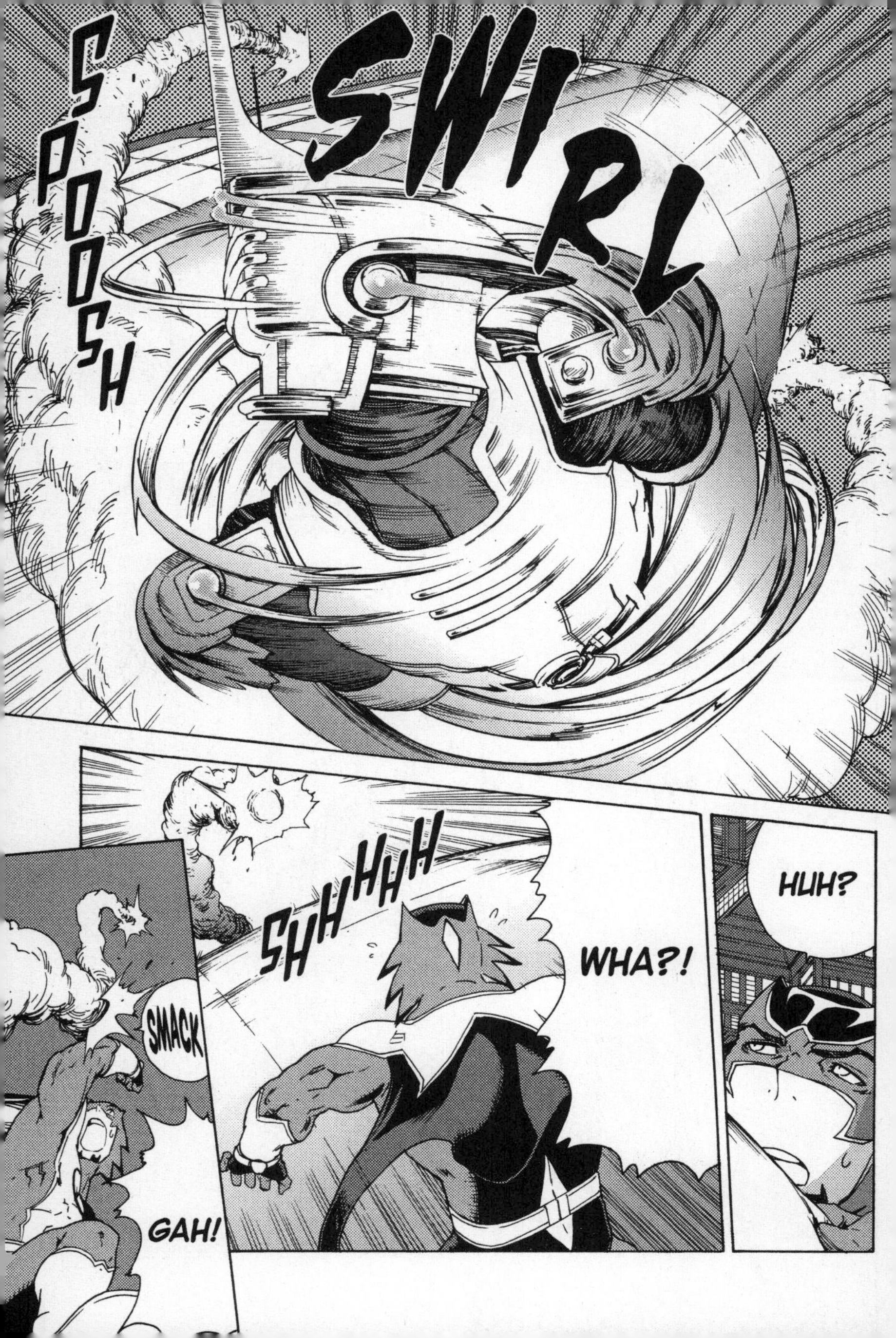
SWIRL
SPOOSH
HUH?
SHHHHHH
WHA?!
SMACK
GAH!

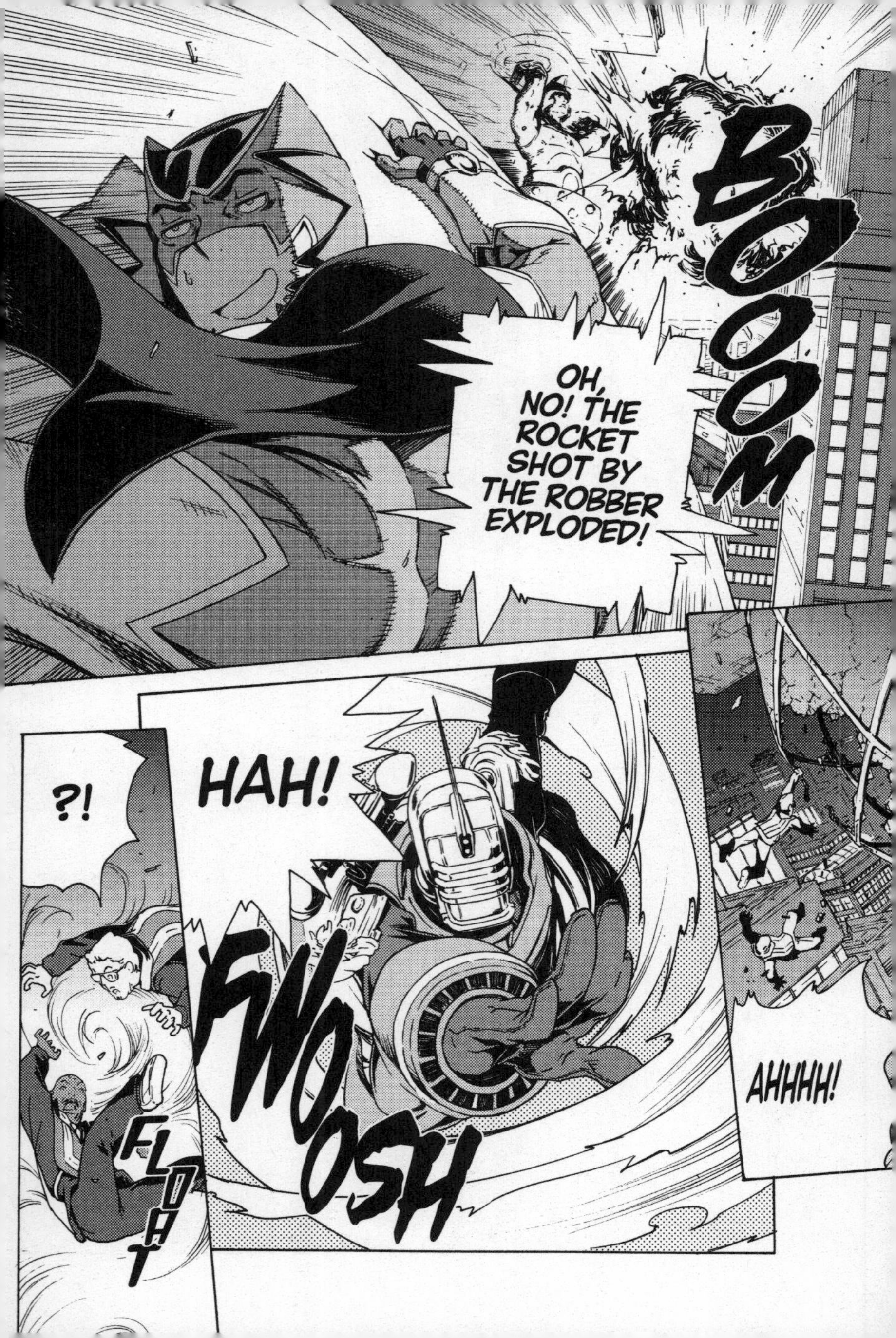
BOOOM
OH, NO! THE ROCKET SHOT BY THE ROBBER EXPLODED!
AHHHH!
HAH!
FWOOSH
?!
FLOAT

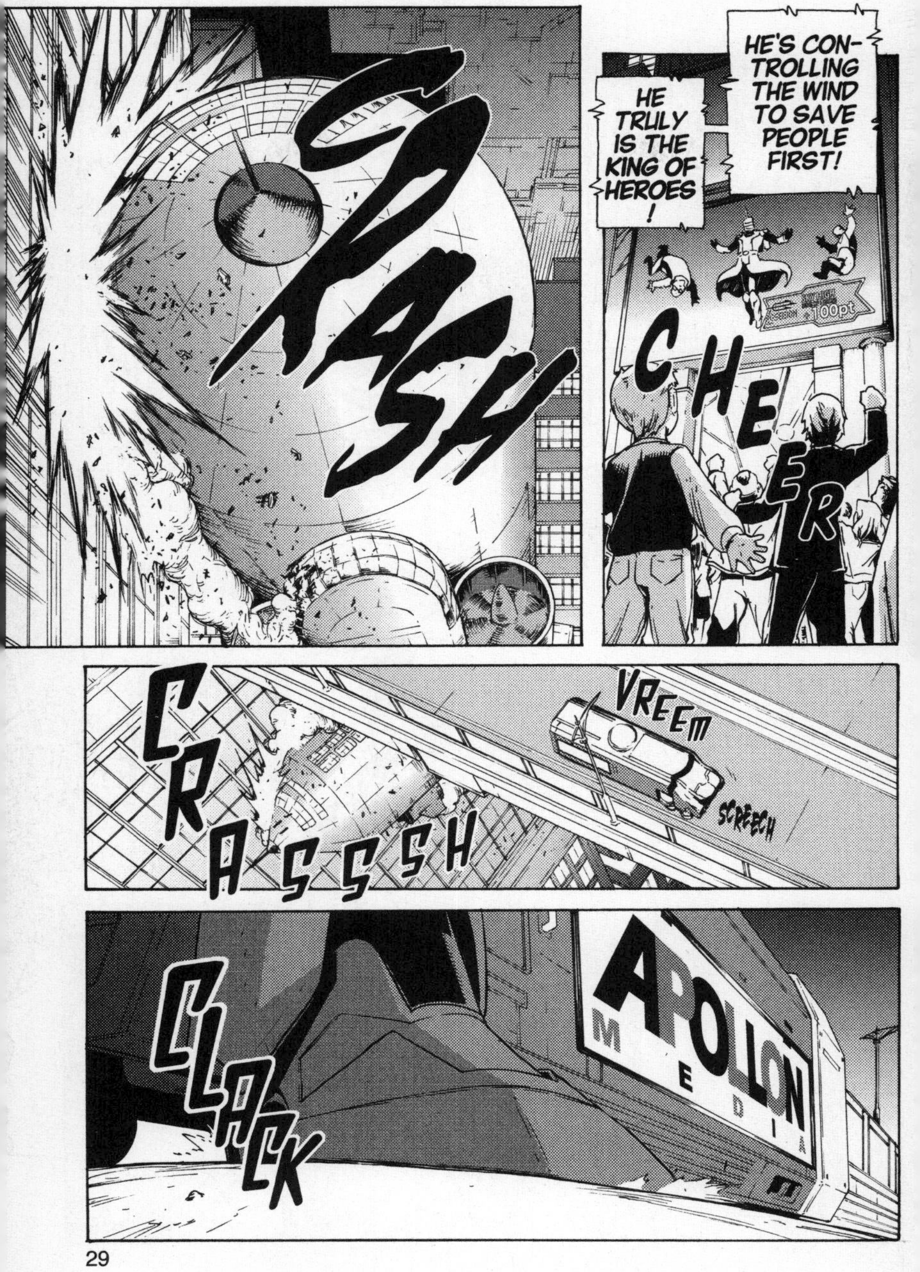
HE'S CONTROLLING THE WIND TO SAVE PEOPLE FIRST!
HE TRULY IS THE KING OF HEROES!
100pt
CHEER
CRASH
VREEM
SCREECH
CRASSSH
APOLLON MEDIA
CLACK

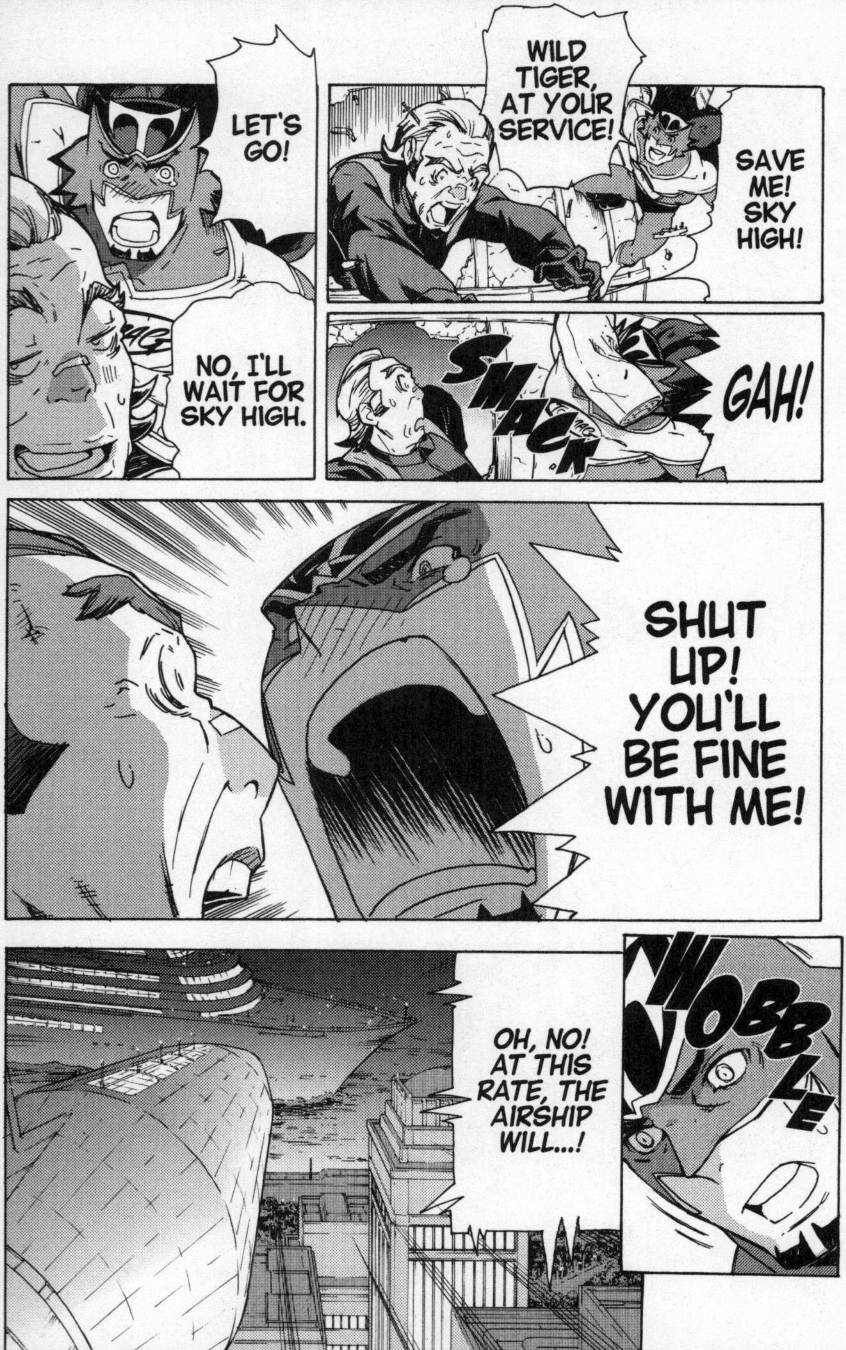
WILD TIGER, AT YOUR SERVICE!
SAVE ME! SKY HIGH!
GAH!
SMACK
LET'S GO!
NO, I'LL WAIT FOR SKY HIGH.
SHUT UP! YOU'LL BE FINE WITH ME!
WOBBLE
OH, NO! AT THIS RATE, THE AIRSHIP WILL...!

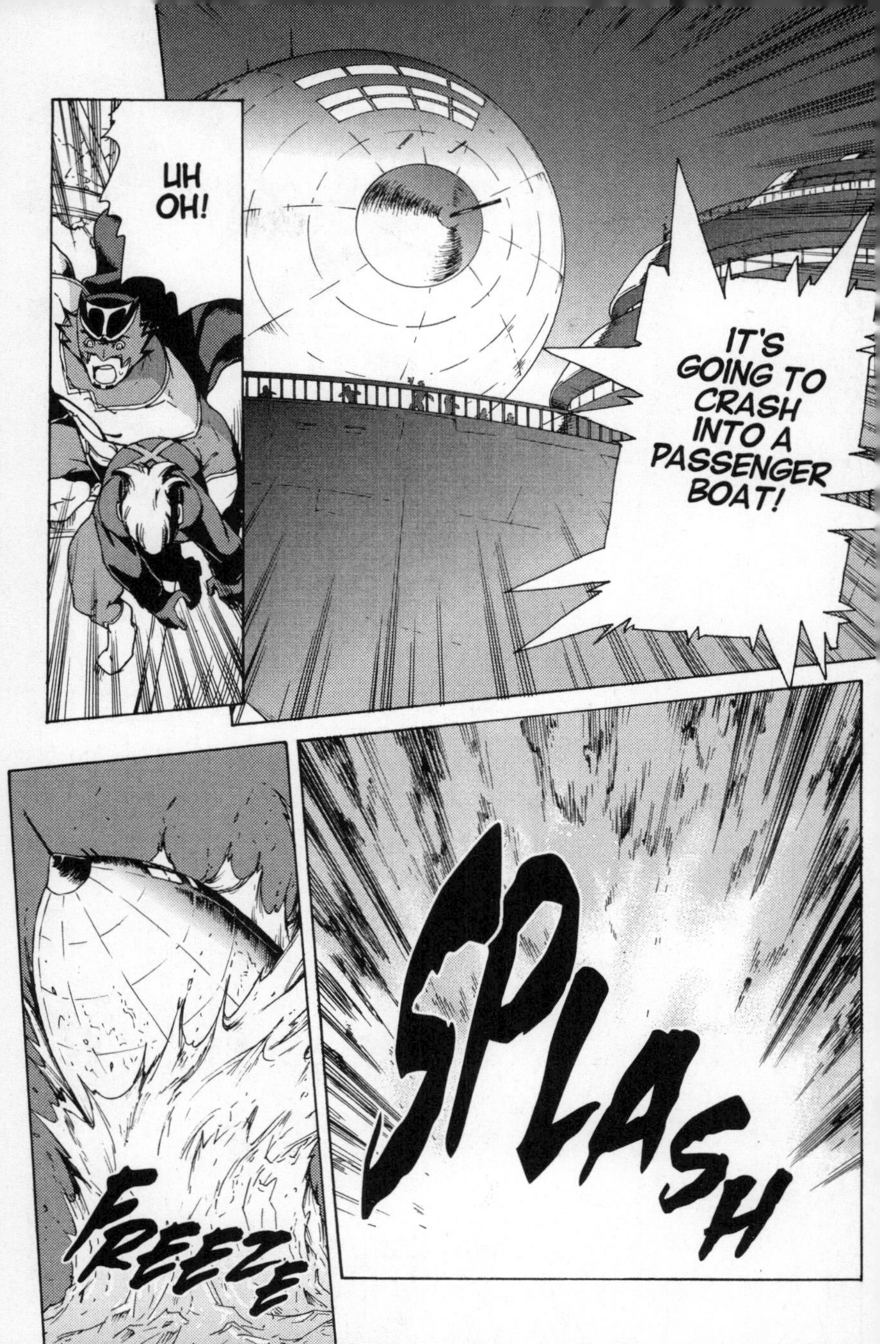
IT'S GOING TO CRASH INTO A PASSENGER BOAT!
UH OH!
SPLASH
FREEZE

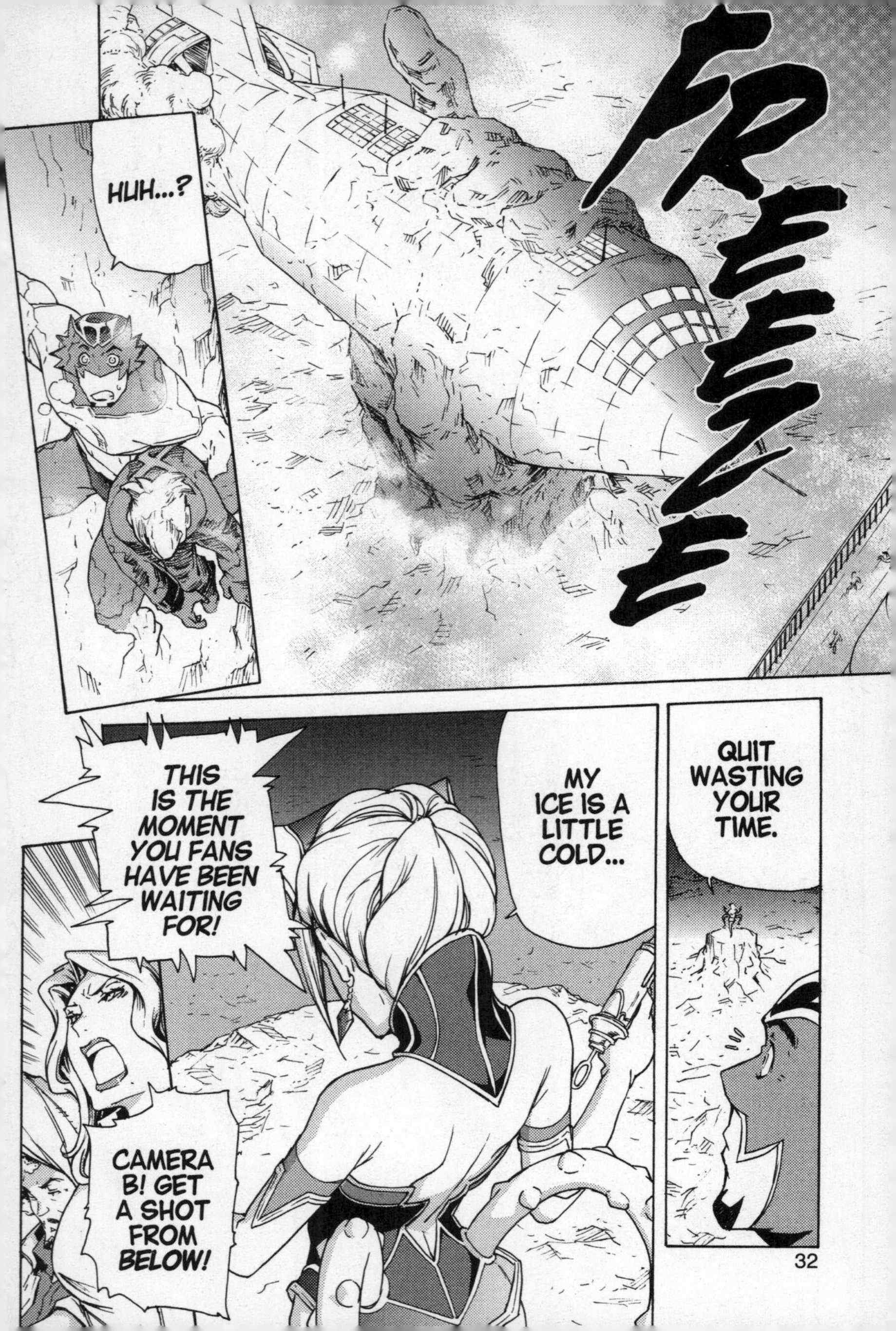
FREEZE
HUH...?
QUIT WASTING YOUR TIME.
MY ICE IS A LITTLE COLD...
THIS IS THE MOMENT YOU FANS HAVE BEEN WAITING FOR!
CAMERA B! GET A SHOT FROM BELOW!

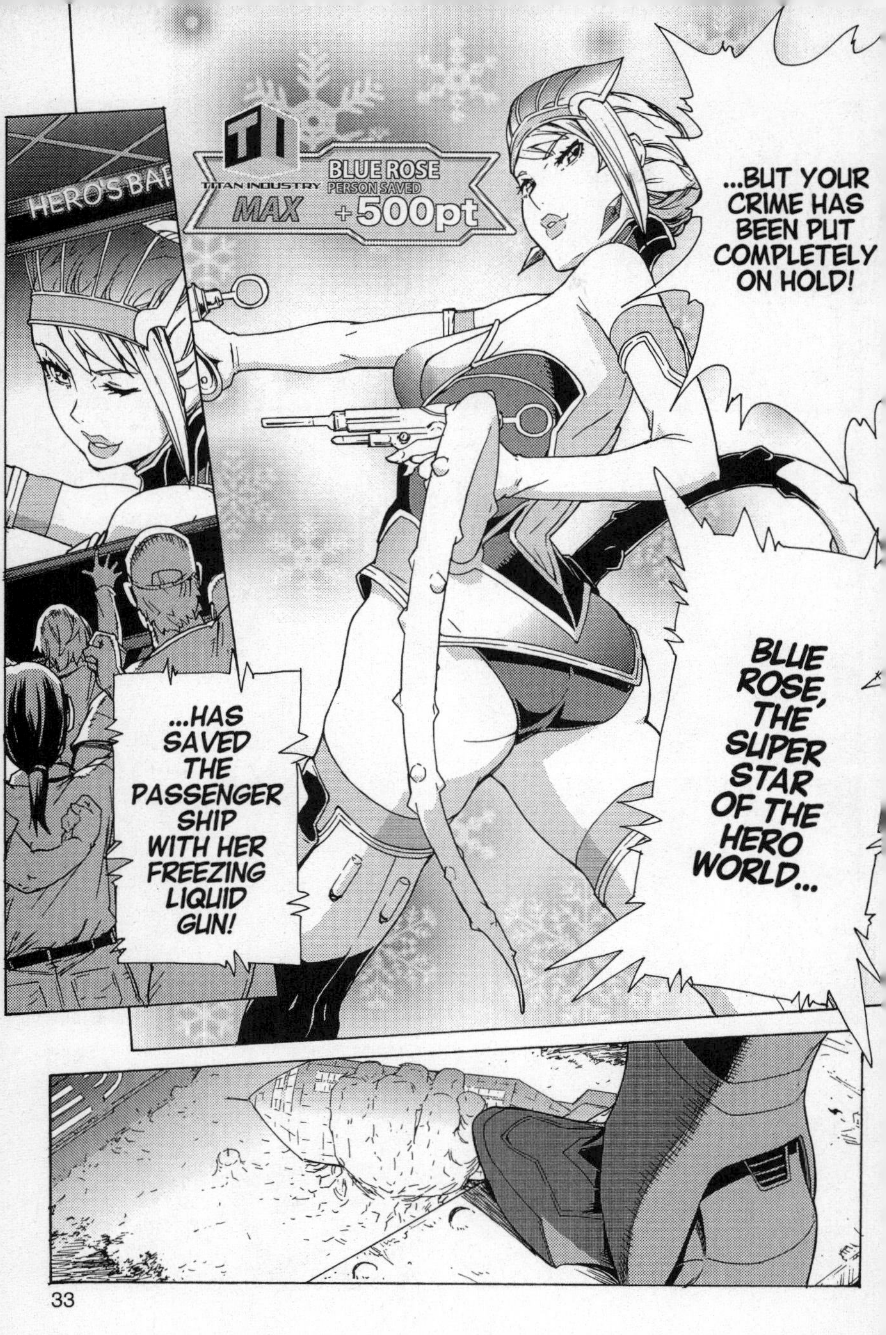

...BUT YOUR CRIME HAS BEEN PUT COMPLETELY ON HOLD!
TI TITAN INDUSTRY MAX
BLUE ROSE PERSON SAVED +500pt
BLUE ROSE, THE SUPER STAR OF THE HERO WORLD...
HERO'S BA
...HAS SAVED THE PASSENGER SHIP WITH HER FREEZING LIQUID GUN!

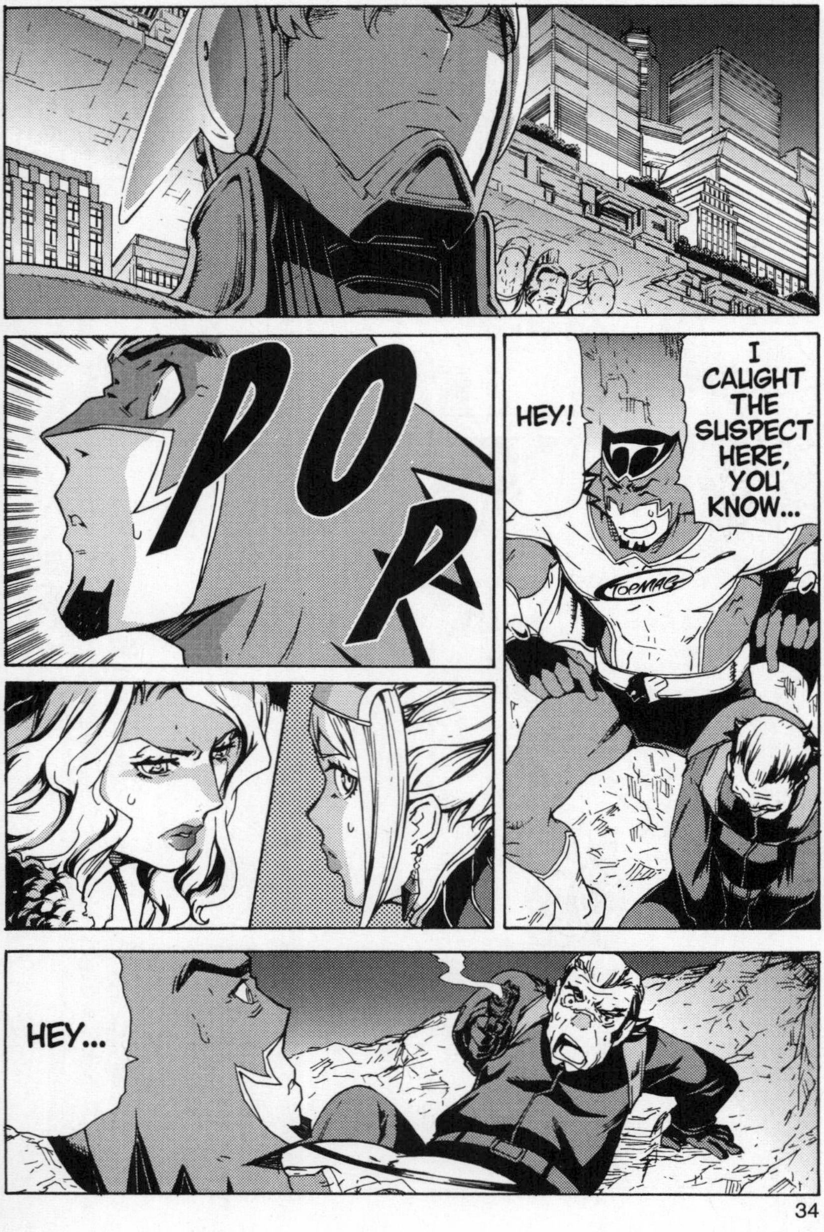
I CAUGHT THE SUSPECT HERE, YOU KNOW...
HEY!
POP
HEY...

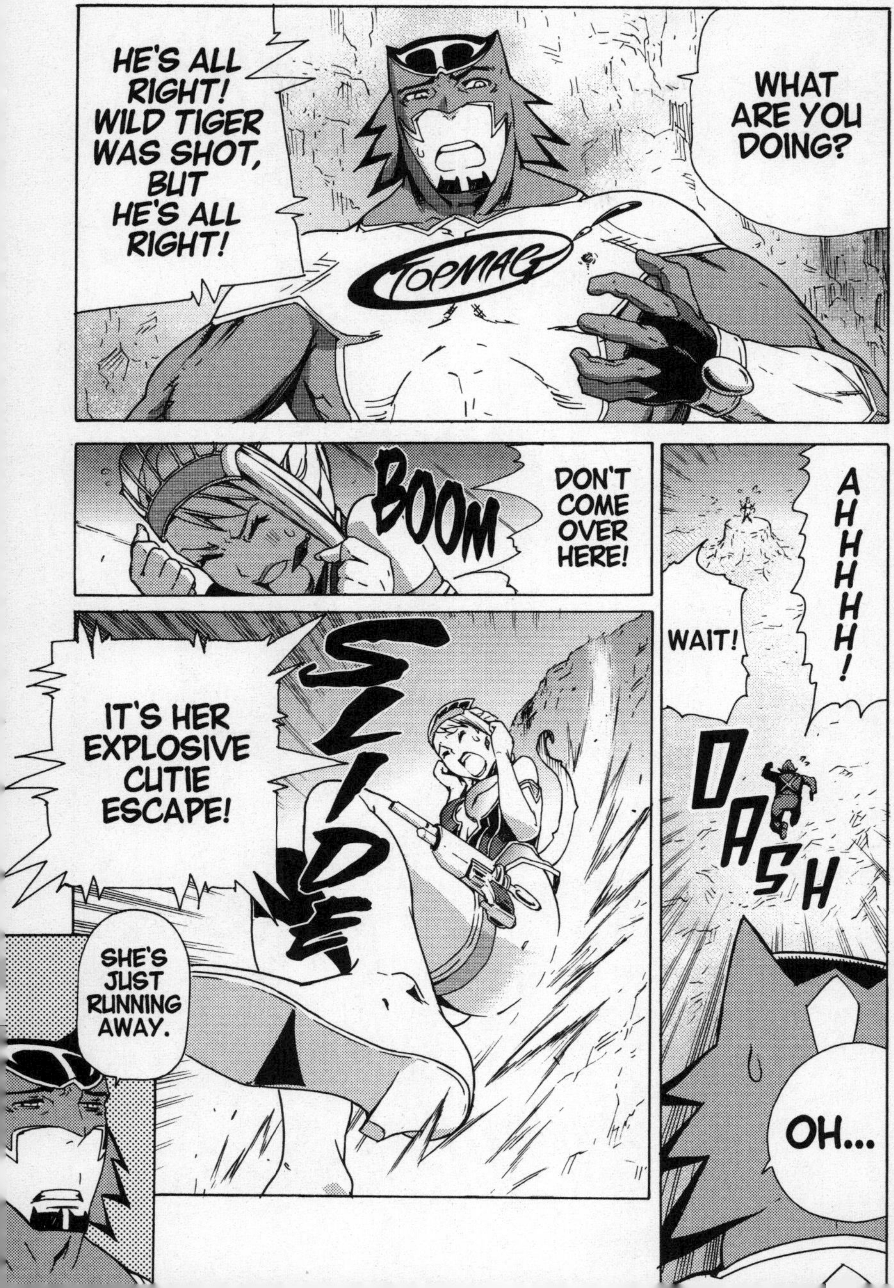
WHAT ARE YOU DOING?
HE'S ALL RIGHT! WILD TIGER WAS SHOT, BUT HE'S ALL RIGHT!
TOPMAG
AHHHHH!
WAIT!
DASH
BOOM
DON'T COME OVER HERE!
SLIDE
IT'S HER EXPLOSIVE CUTIE ESCAPE!
OH...
SHE'S JUST RUNNING AWAY.

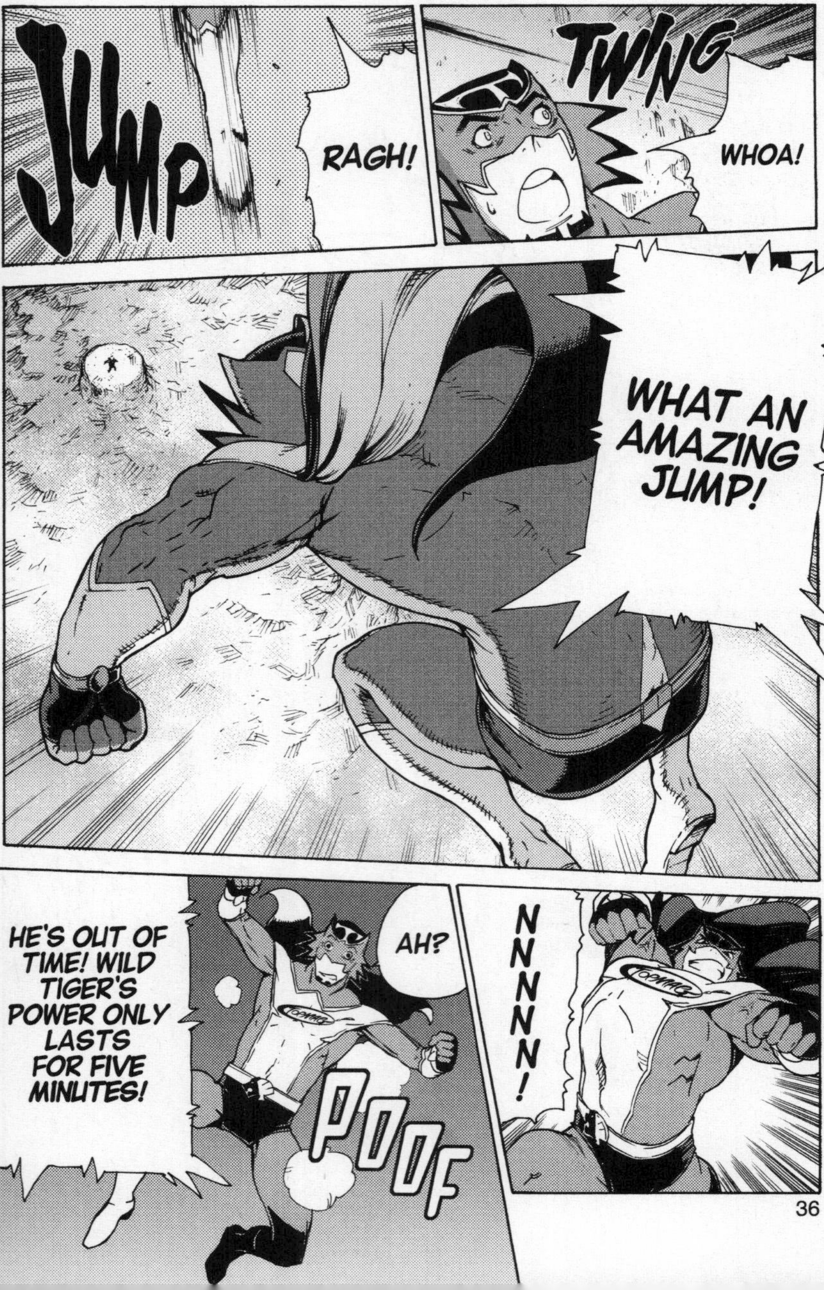
TWING
WHOA!
RAGH!
JUMP
WHAT AN AMAZING JUMP!
NNNNNN!
AH?
HE'S OUT OF TIME! WILD TIGER'S POWER ONLY LASTS FOR FIVE MINUTES!
POOF

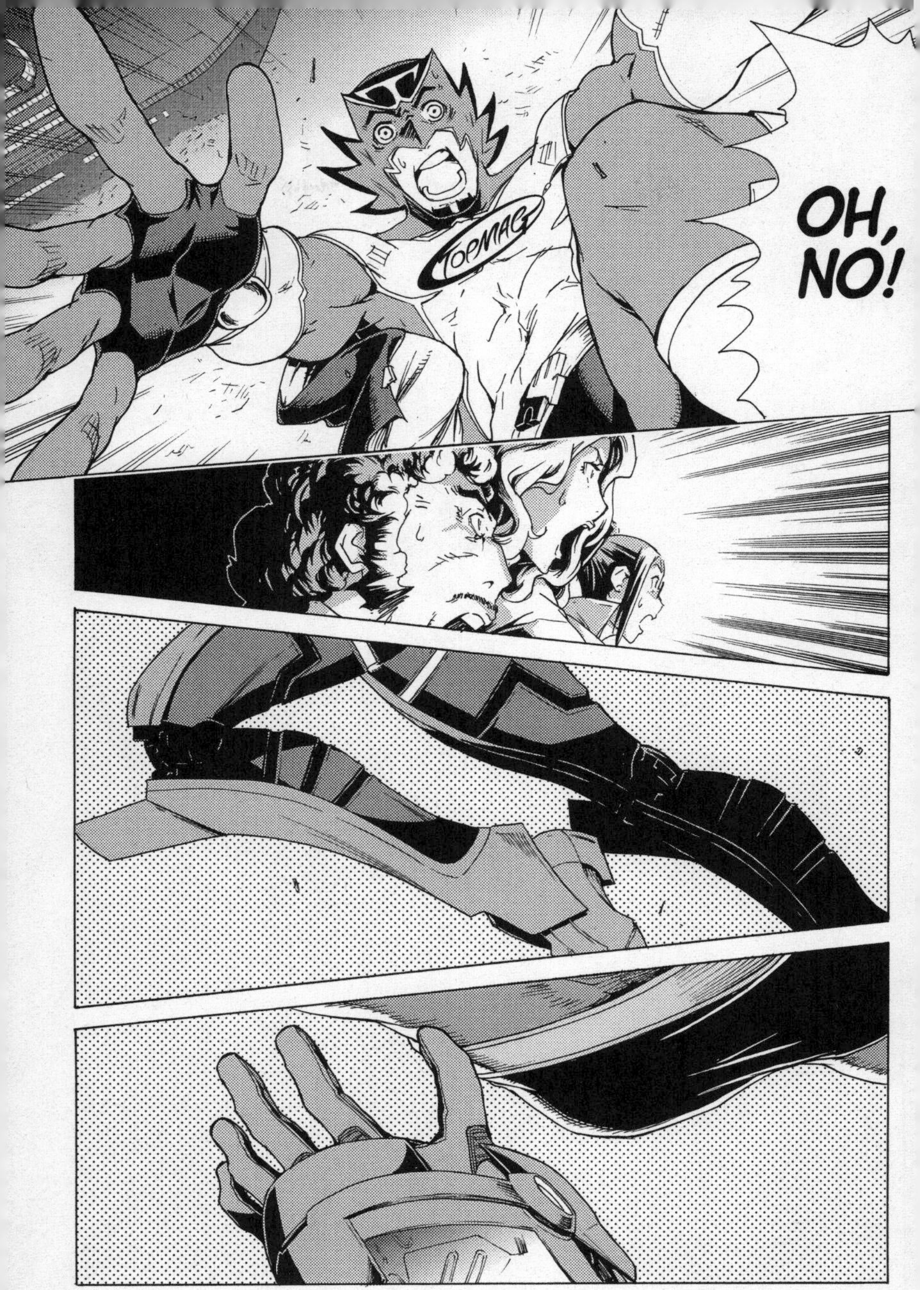
OH, NO!
TOPMAG

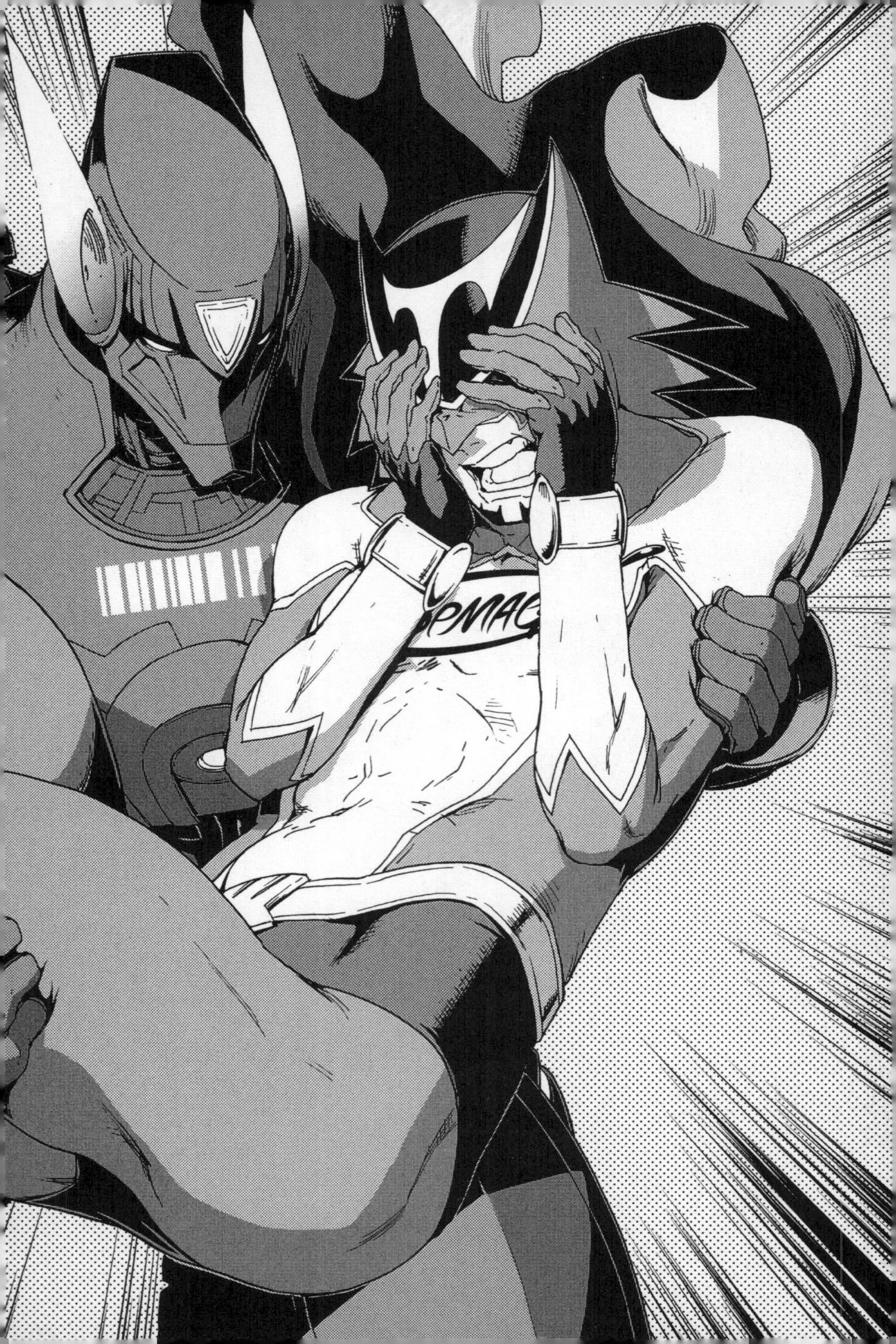
PMAG

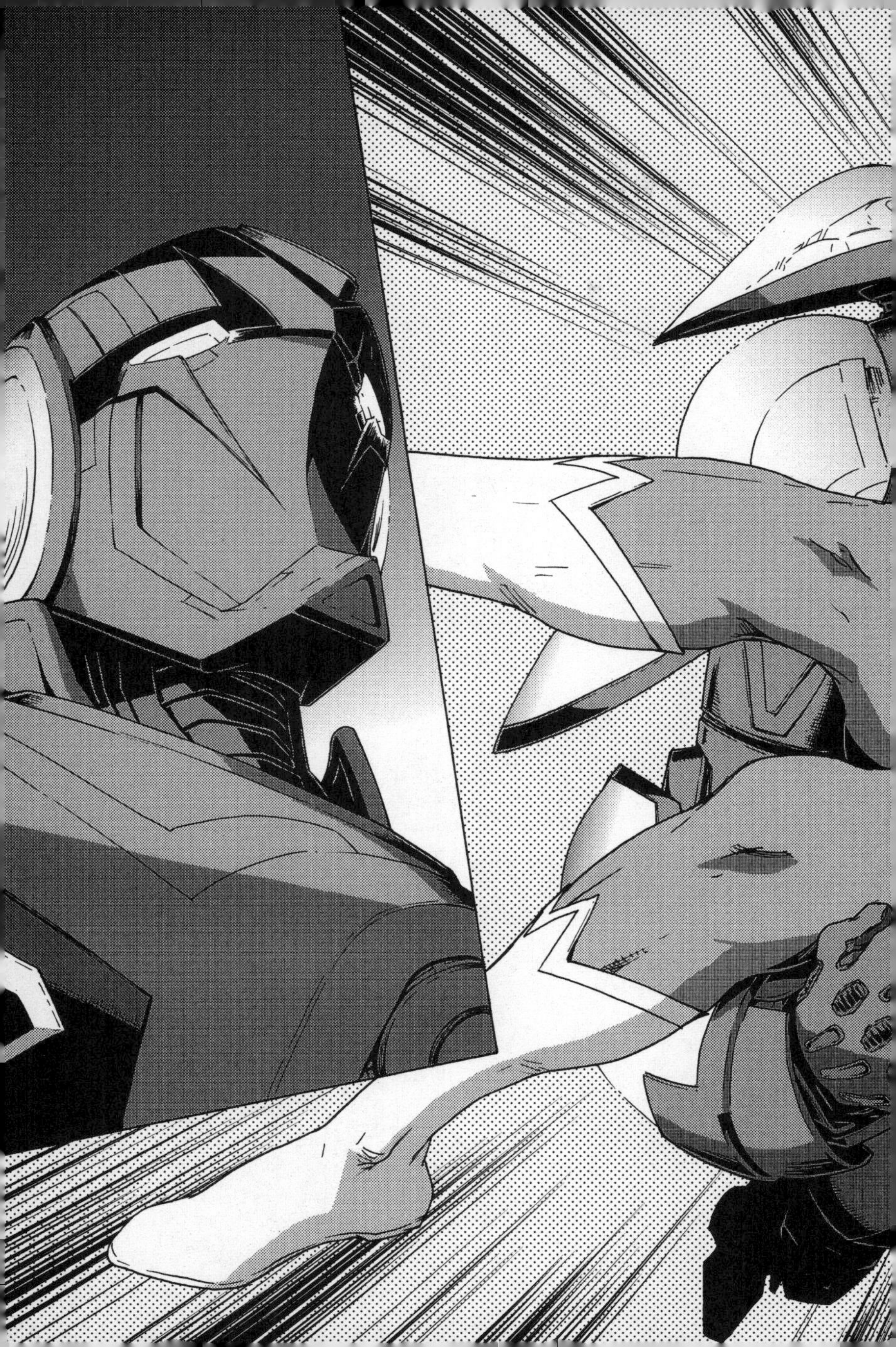

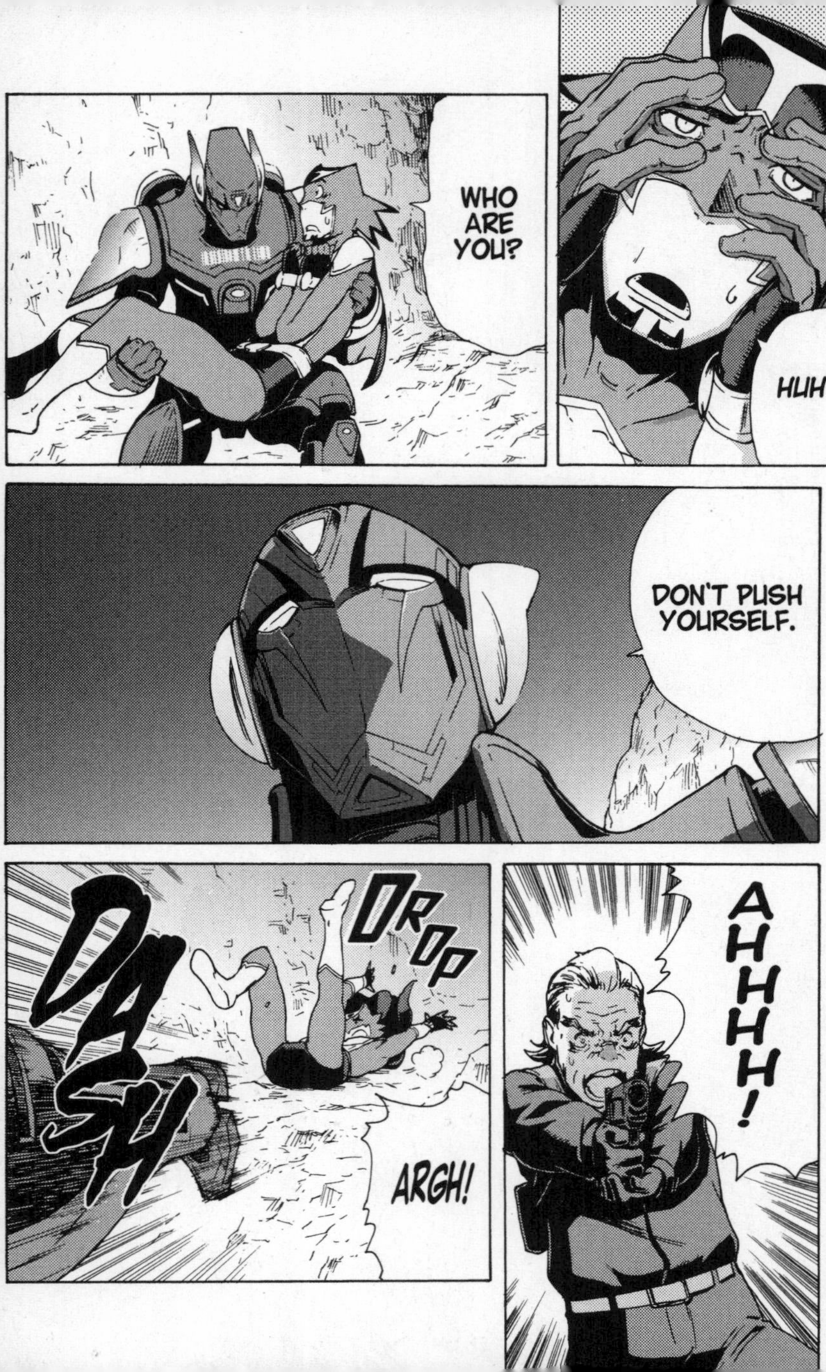
HUH?
WHO ARE YOU?
DON'T PUSH YOURSELF.
AHHHH!
DROP
DASH
ARGH!

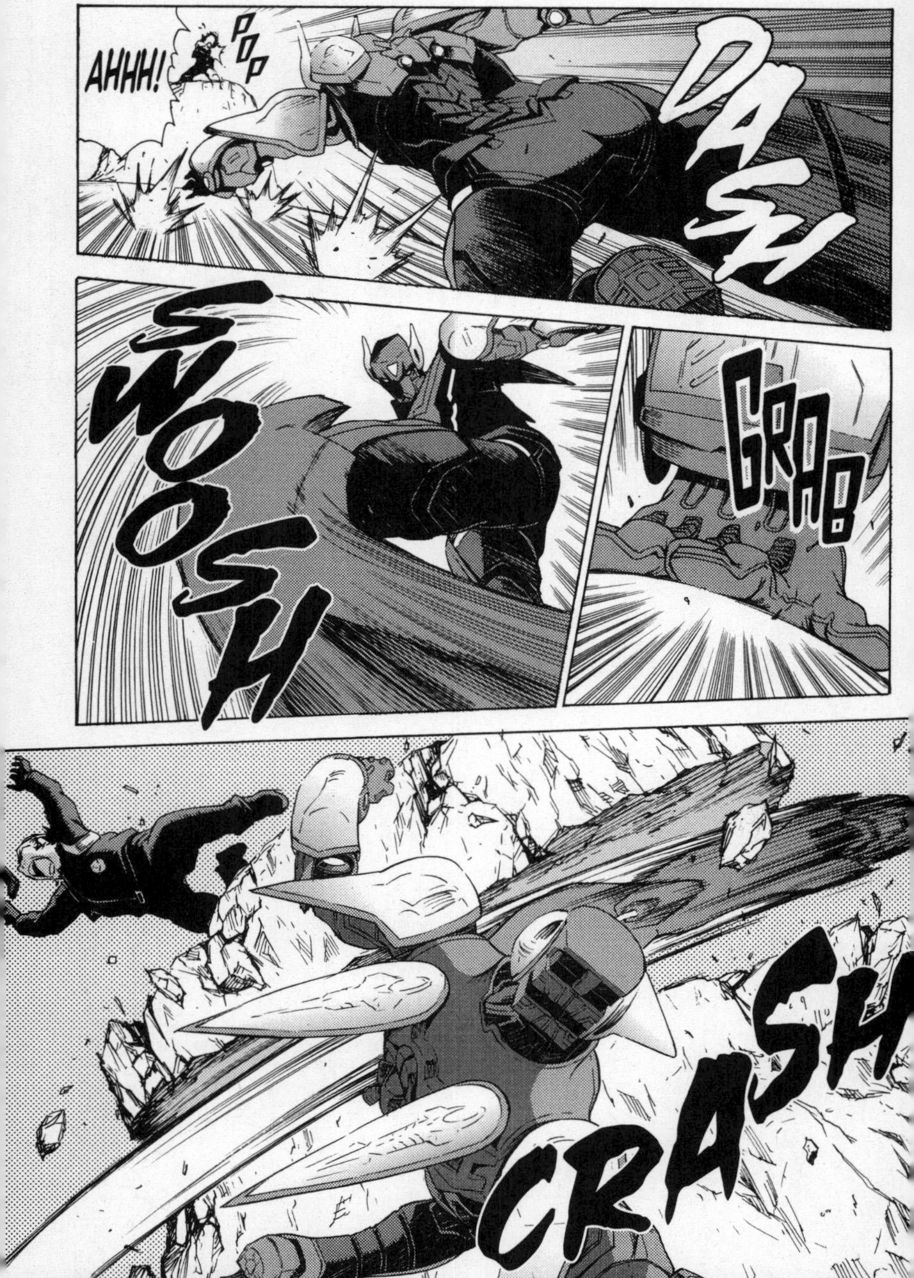
DASH
POP
AHHH!
GRAB
SWOOSH
CRASH

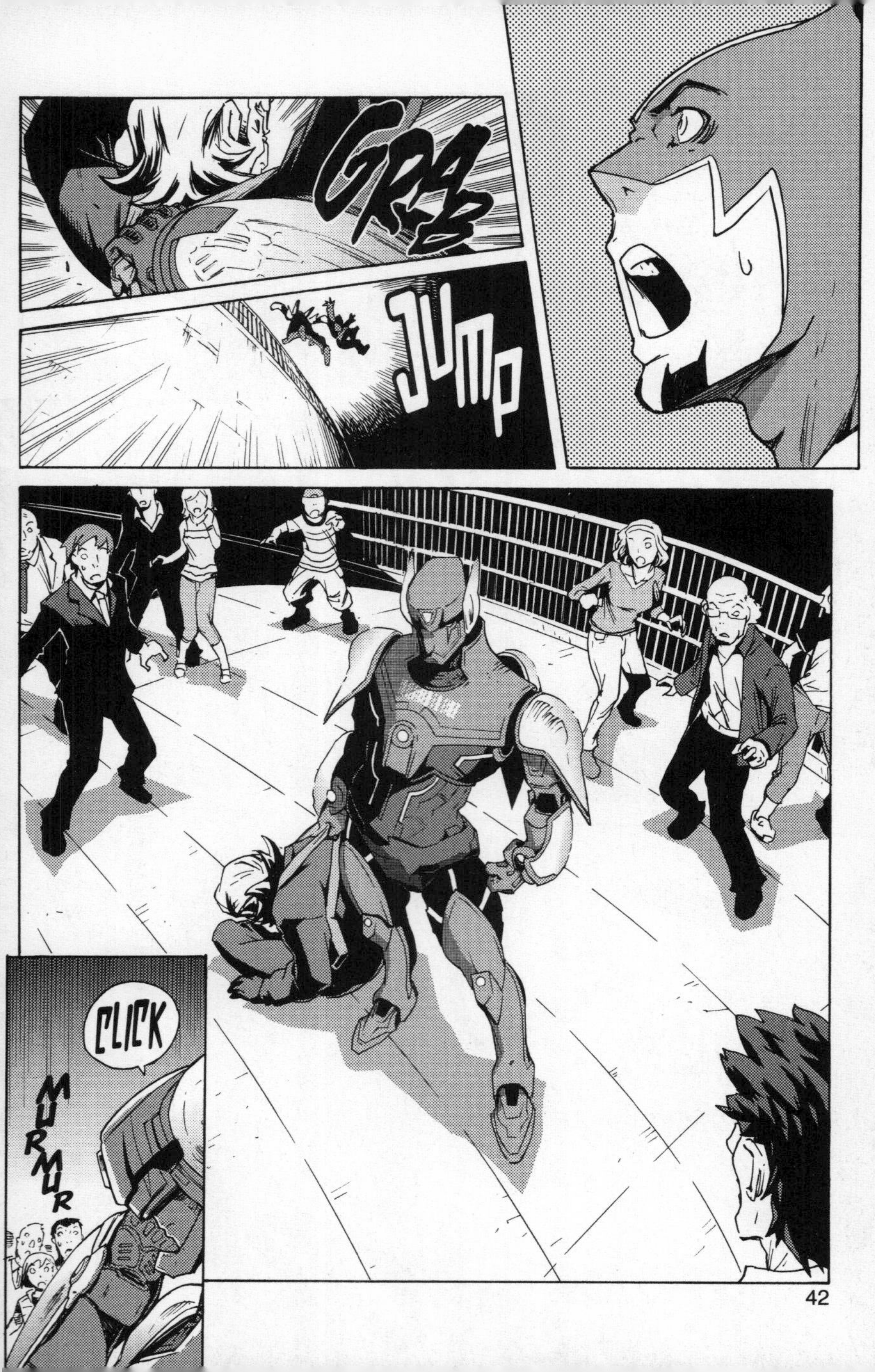
GRAB
JUMP
CLICK
MURMUR

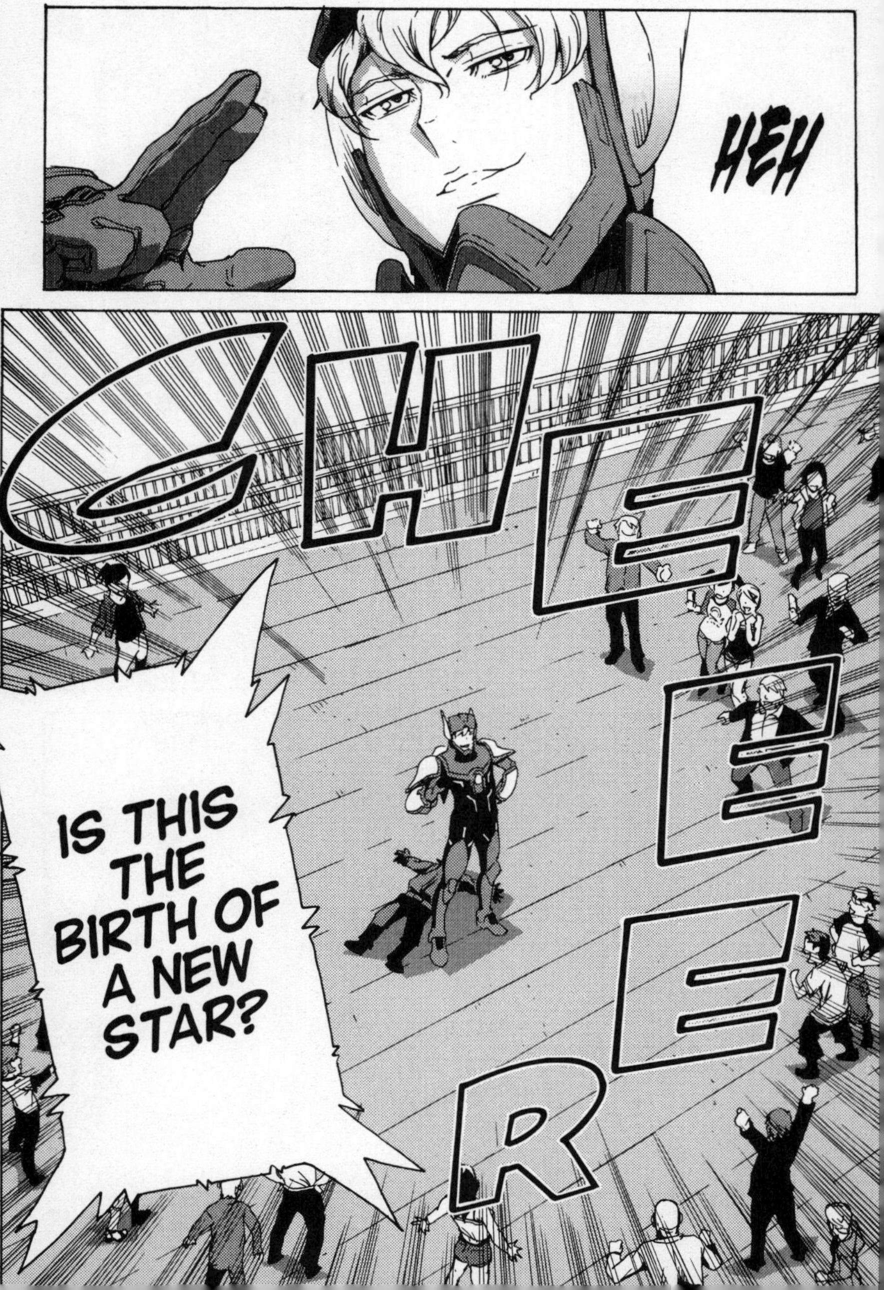
HEH
CHEEEER
IS THIS THE BIRTH OF A NEW STAR?

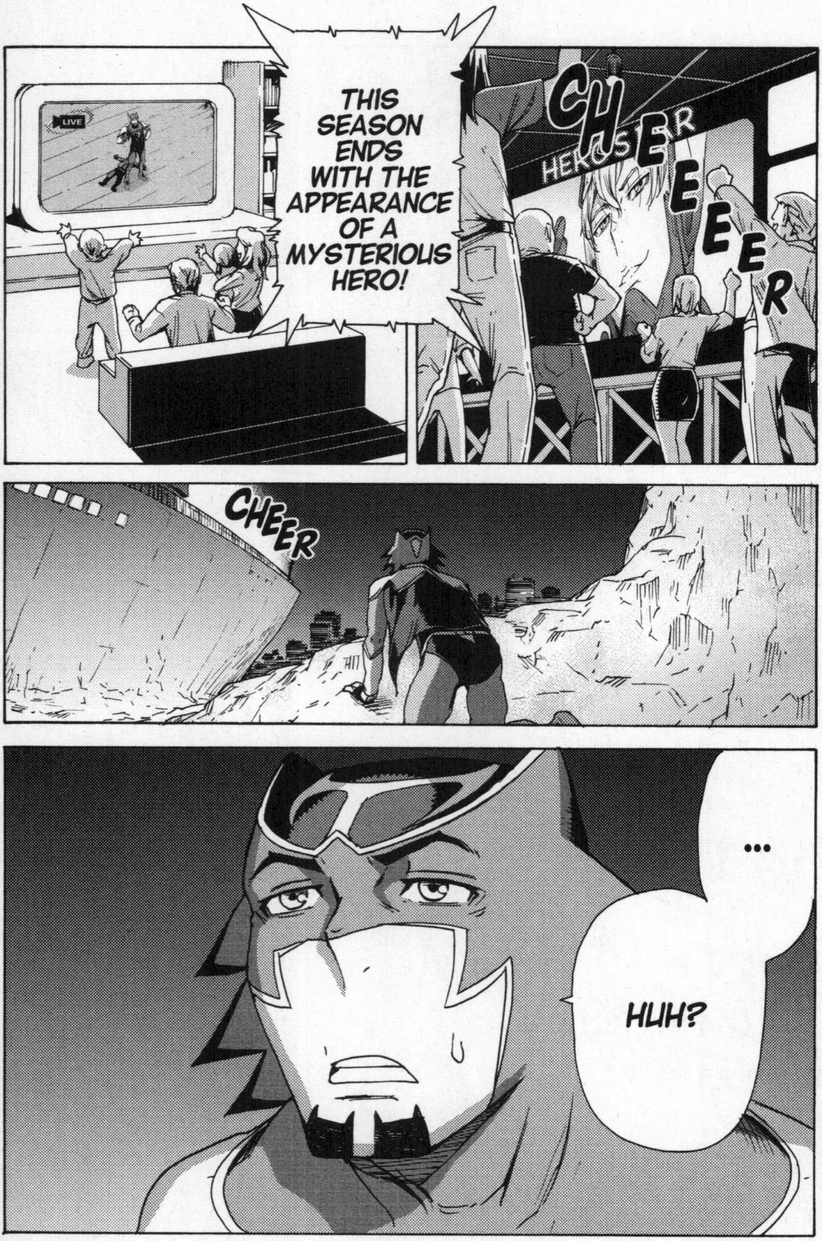
CHEEEEER
THIS SEASON ENDS WITH THE APPEARANCE OF A MYSTERIOUS HERO!
CHEER
...
HUH?

TIGER & BUNNY THE MOVIE
The Beginning

TIGER & BUNNY THE MOVIE
The Beginning

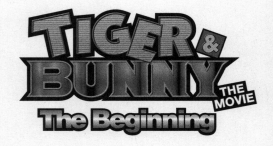

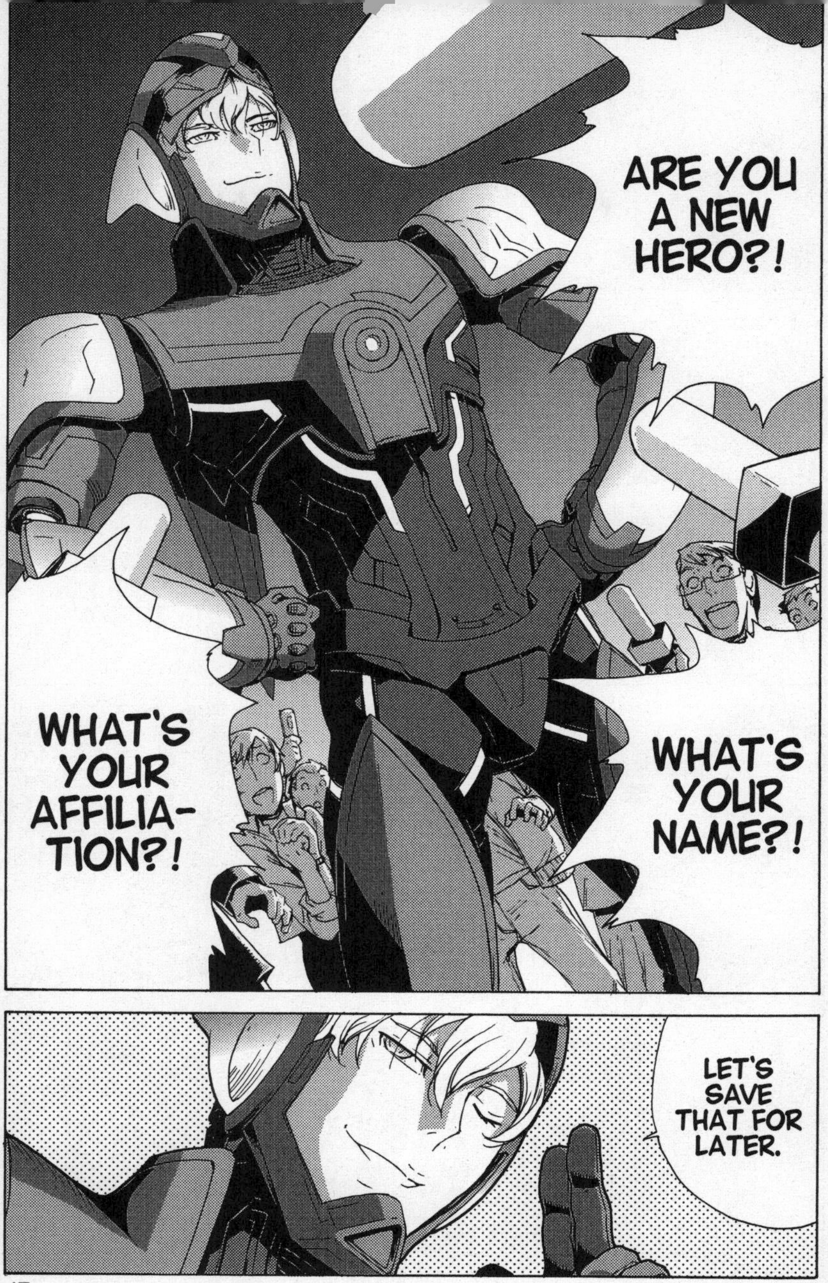
ARE YOU A NEW HERO?!
WHAT'S YOUR NAME?!
WHAT'S YOUR AFFILIATION?!
LET'S SAVE THAT FOR LATER.

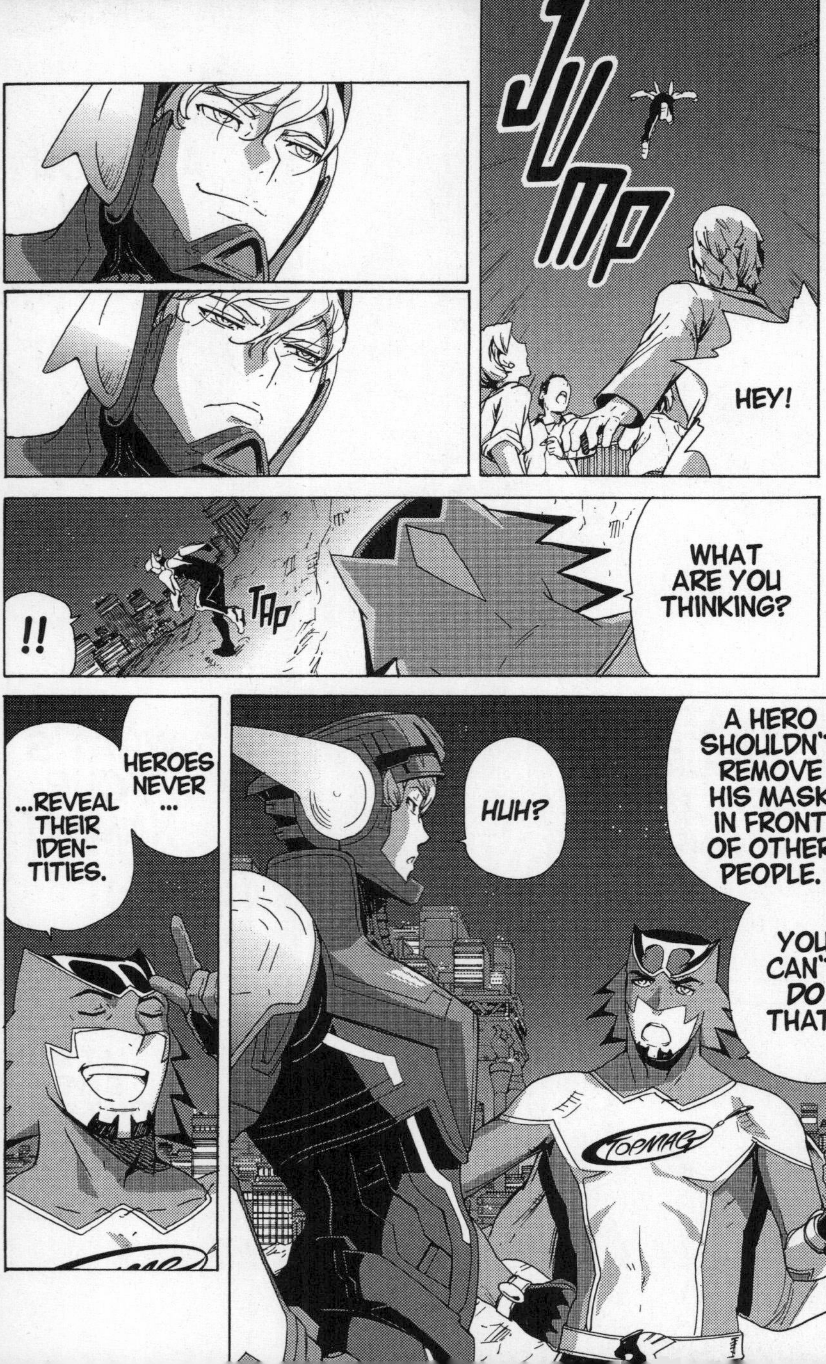
JUMP
HEY!
WHAT ARE YOU THINKING?
TAP
!!
A HERO SHOULDN'T REMOVE HIS MASK IN FRONT OF OTHER PEOPLE.
YOU CAN'T DO THAT!
TOPMAG
HUH?
HEROES NEVER...
...REVEAL THEIR IDEN-TITIES.

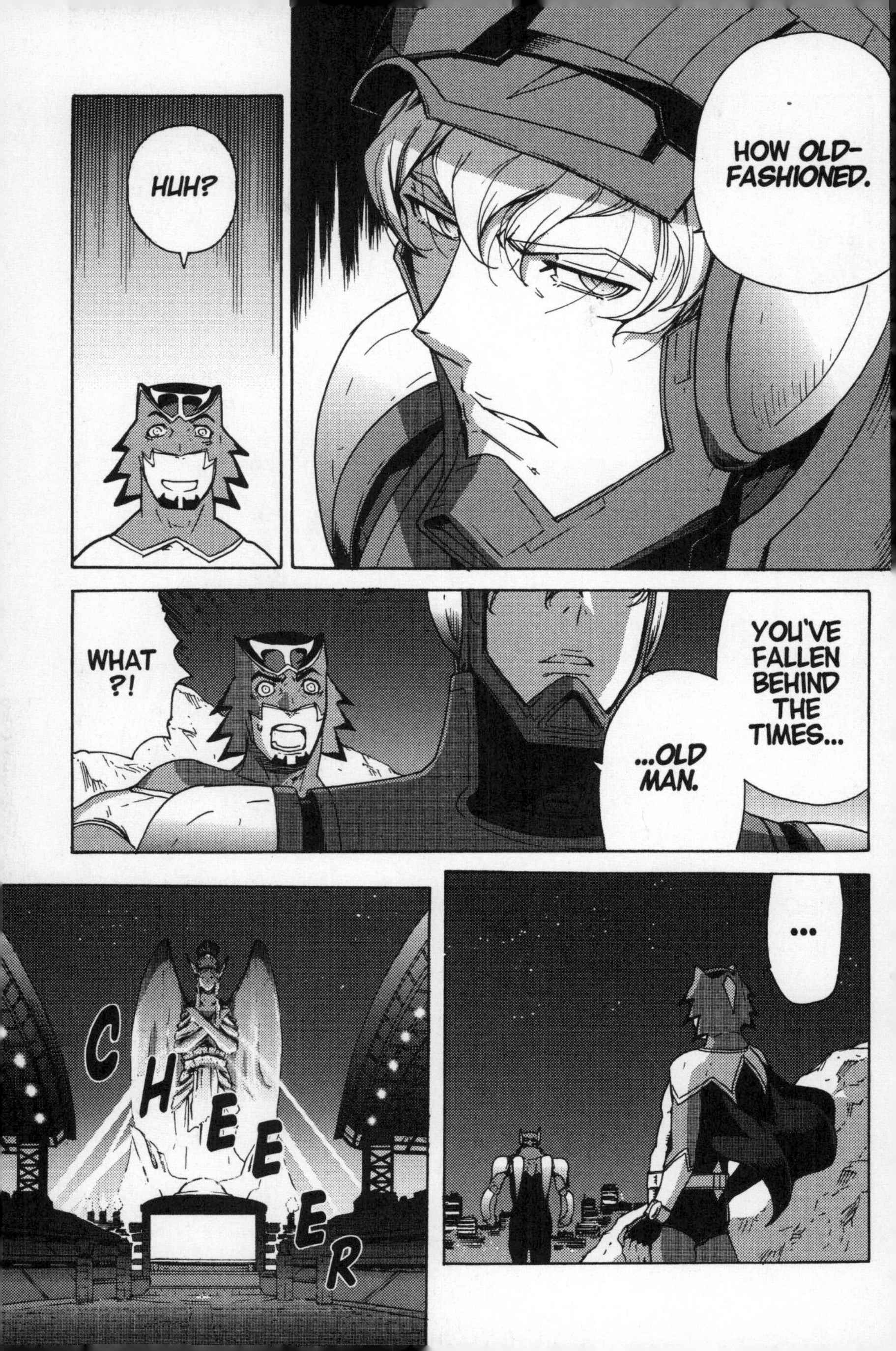
HOW OLD-FASHIONED.
HUH?
YOU'VE FALLEN BEHIND THE TIMES...
...OLD MAN.
WHAT?!
...
CHEEER

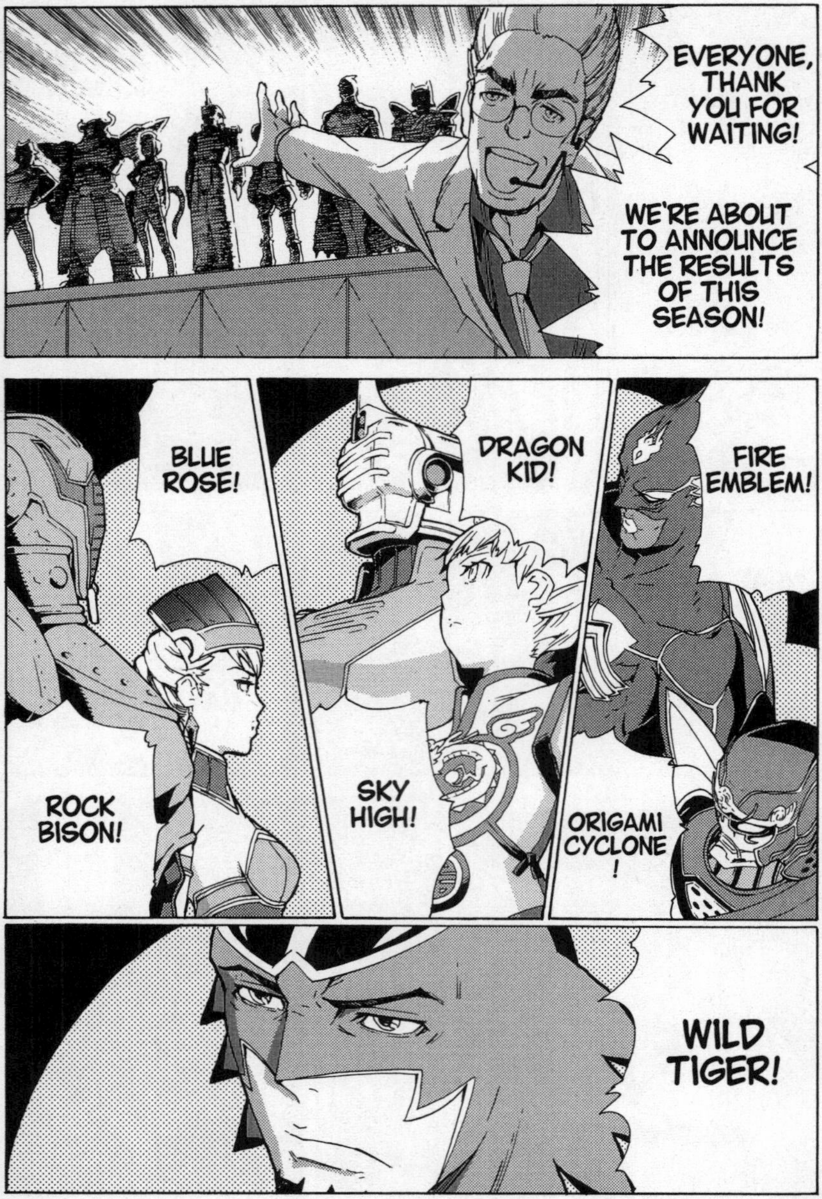
EVERYONE, THANK YOU FOR WAITING!
WE'RE ABOUT TO ANNOUNCE THE RESULTS OF THIS SEASON!
FIRE EMBLEM!
ORIGAMI CYCLONE!
DRAGON KID!
SKY HIGH!
BLUE ROSE!
ROCK BISON!
WILD TIGER!

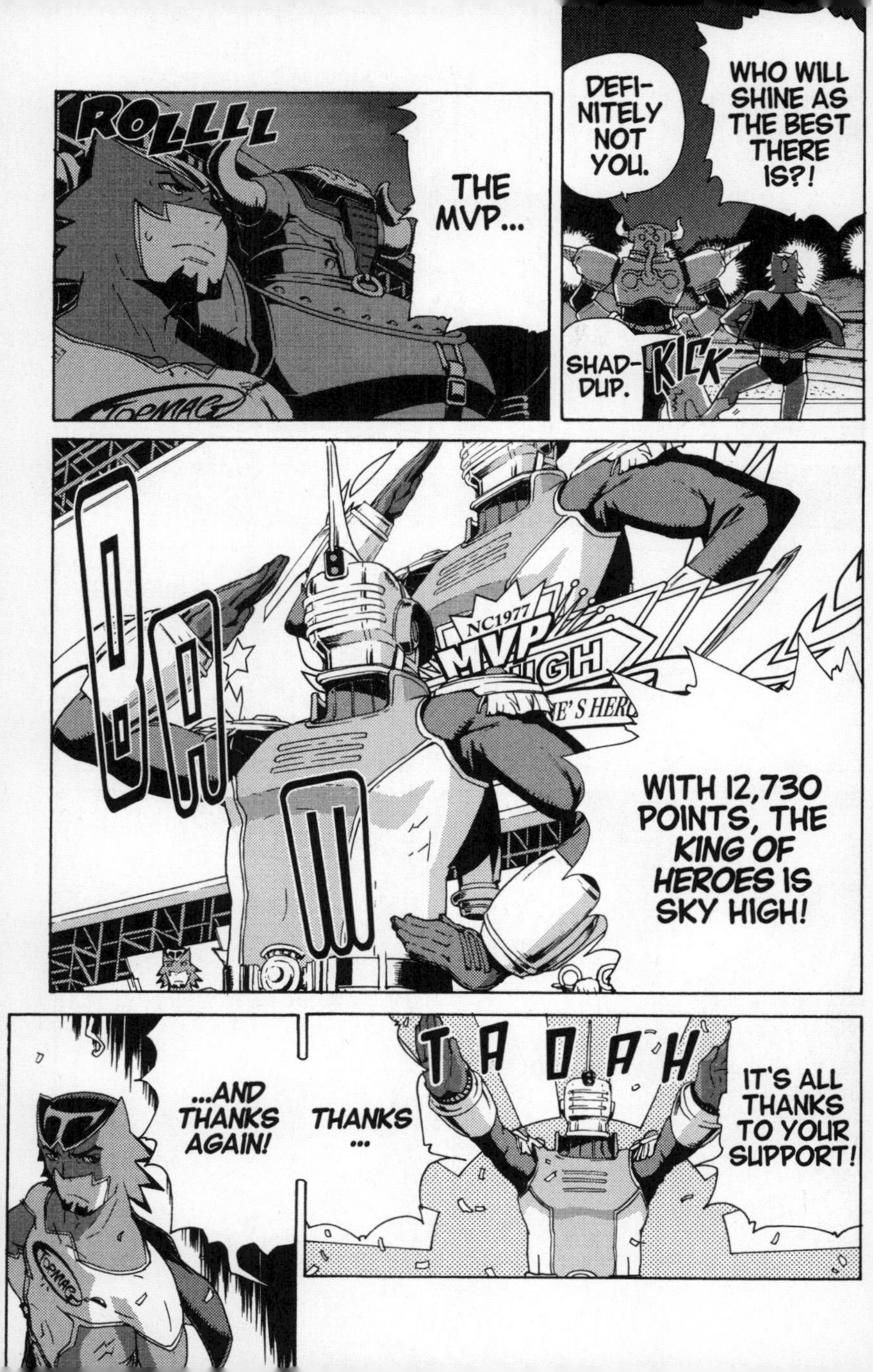
WHO WILL SHINE AS THE BEST THERE IS?!
DEFI-NITELY NOT YOU.
SHAD-DUP.
KICK
ROLLLL
THE MVP...
BAM
NC1977 MVP
WITH 12,730 POINTS, THE KING OF HEROES IS SKY HIGH!
TADAH
IT'S ALL THANKS TO YOUR SUPPORT!
THANKS ...
...AND THANKS AGAIN!

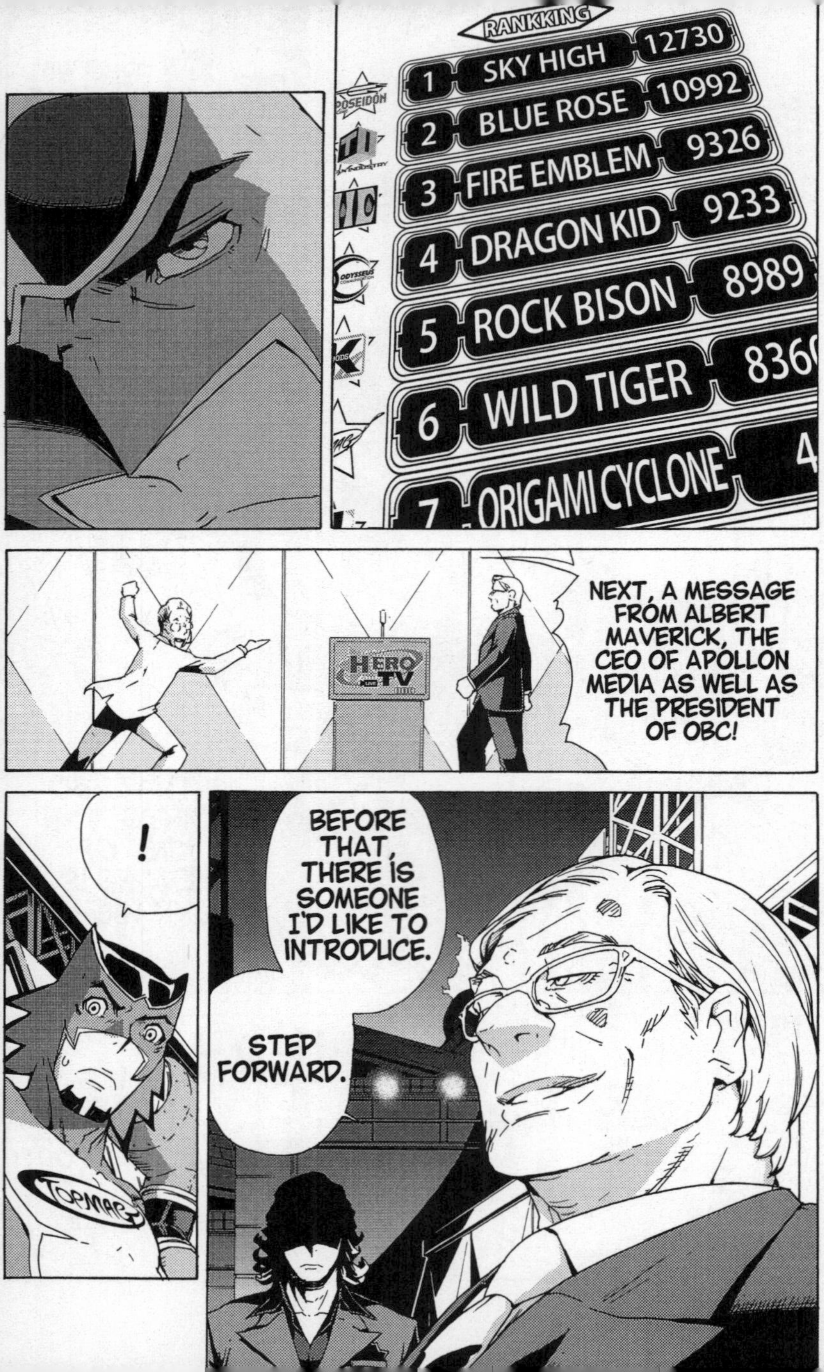
RANKKING
1 SKY HIGH 12730
2 BLUE ROSE 10992
3 FIRE EMBLEM 9326
4 DRAGON KID 9233
5 ROCK BISON 8989
6 WILD TIGER 836
7 ORIGAMI CYCLONE 4
NEXT, A MESSAGE FROM ALBERT MAVERICK, THE CEO OF APOLLON MEDIA AS WELL AS THE PRESIDENT OF OBC!
HERO TV
BEFORE THAT, THERE IS SOMEONE I'D LIKE TO INTRODUCE.
STEP FORWARD.
!
TOPMAG

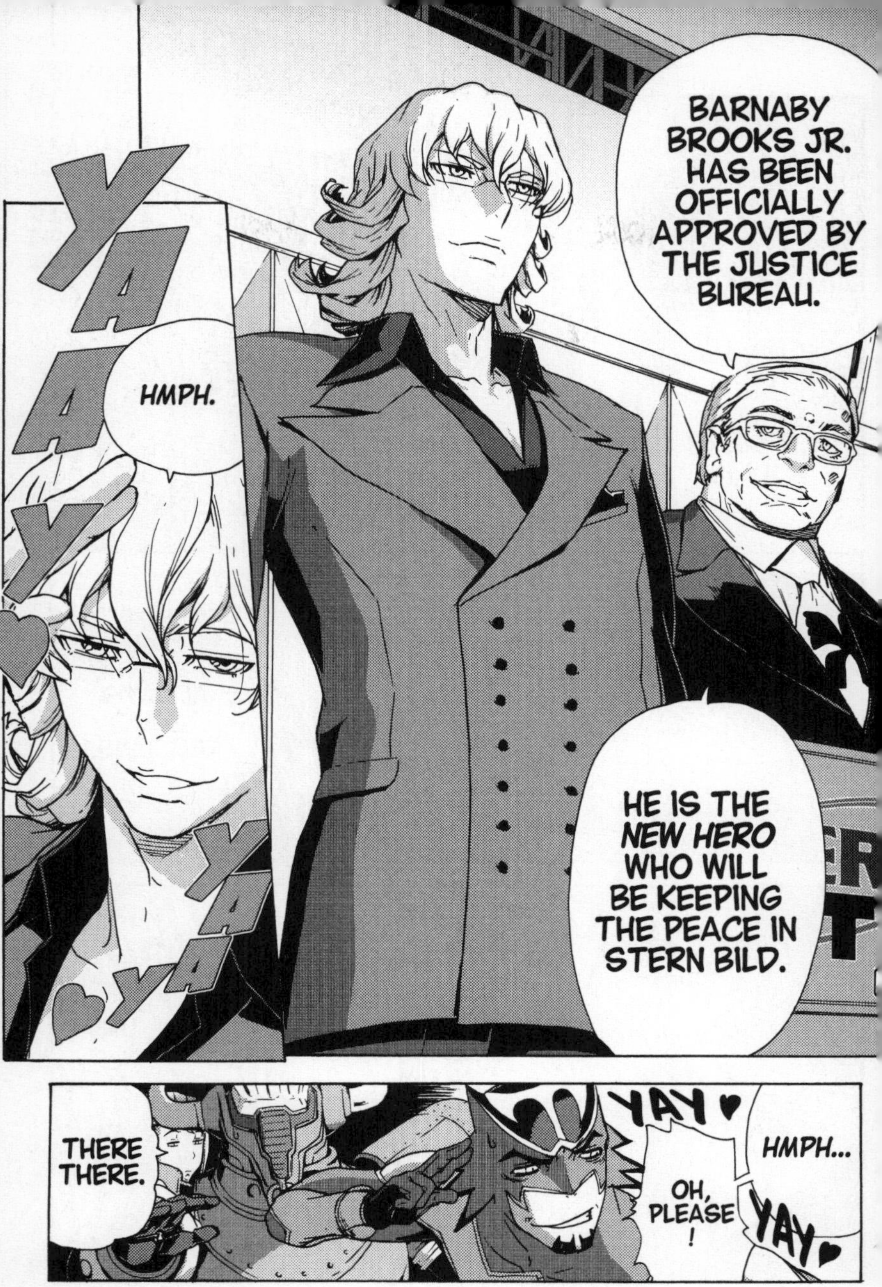

BARNABY BROOKS JR. HAS BEEN OFFICIALLY APPROVED BY THE JUSTICE BUREAU.
HE IS THE *NEW HERO* WHO WILL BE KEEPING THE PEACE IN STERN BILD.
YAAY♥
HMPH.
YAAY♥
YAY♥
HMPH...
OH, PLEASE!
YAY♥
THERE THERE.

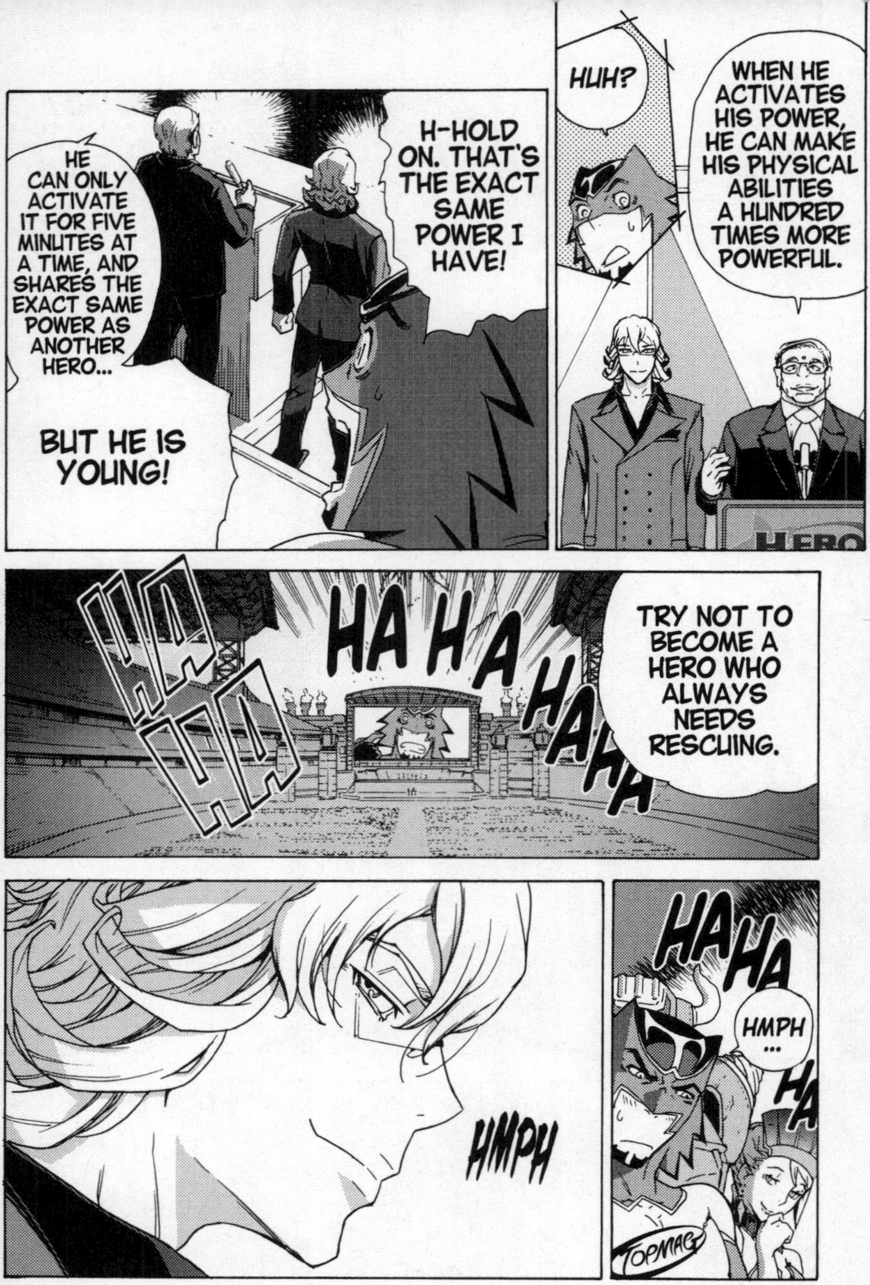
WHEN HE ACTIVATES HIS POWER, HE CAN MAKE HIS PHYSICAL ABILITIES A HUNDRED TIMES MORE POWERFUL.
HUH?
H-HOLD ON. THAT'S THE EXACT SAME POWER I HAVE!
HE CAN ONLY ACTIVATE IT FOR FIVE MINUTES AT A TIME, AND SHARES THE EXACT SAME POWER AS ANOTHER HERO...
BUT HE IS YOUNG!
HERO
TRY NOT TO BECOME A HERO WHO ALWAYS NEEDS RESCUING.
HA HA HA HA HA
HA HA HA
HAHA HA
HMPH...
HA HA
TOPMAG
HMPH

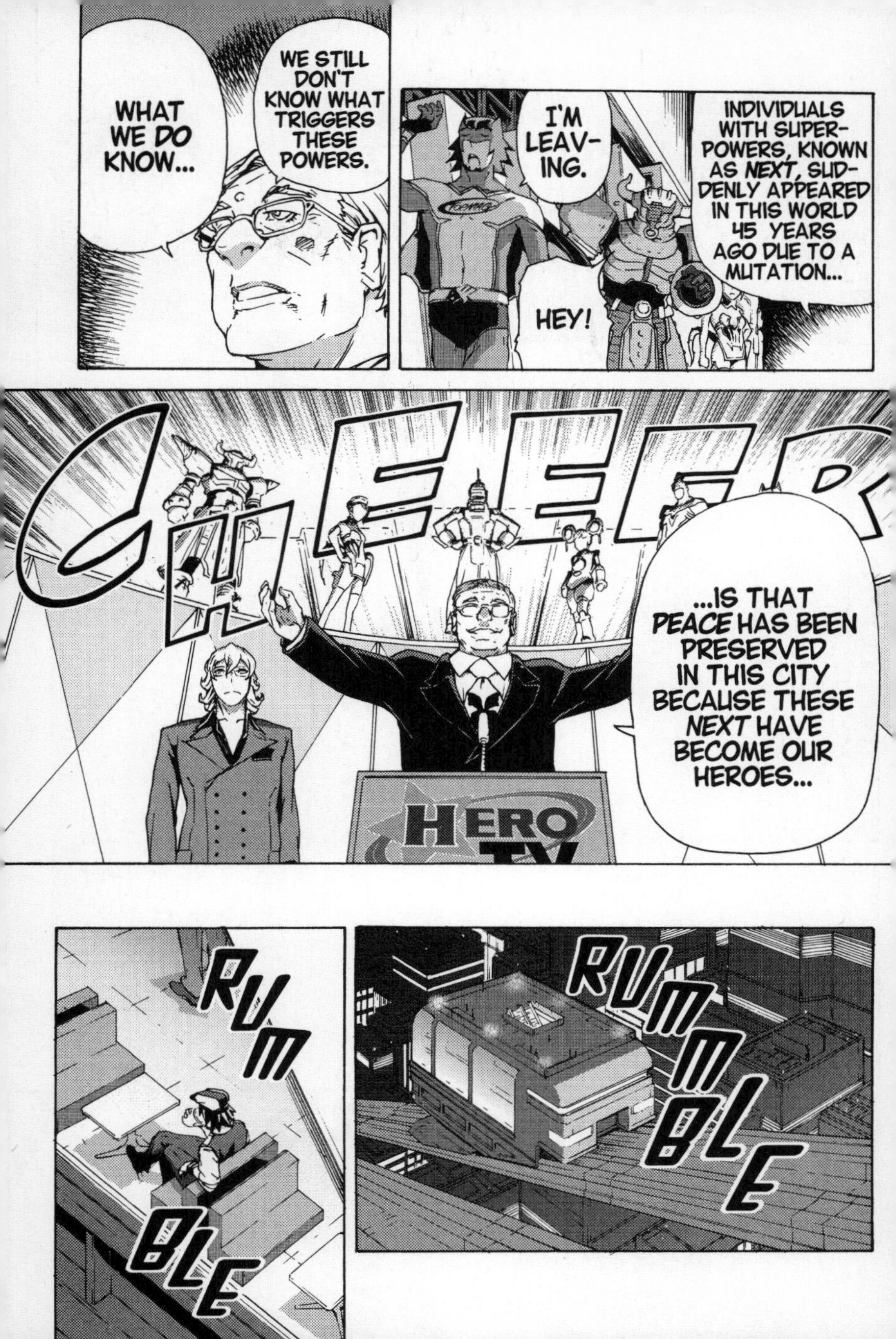
INDIVIDUALS WITH SUPER-POWERS, KNOWN AS NEXT, SUD-DENLY APPEARED IN THIS WORLD 45 YEARS AGO DUE TO A MUTATION...
I'M LEAV-ING.
HEY!
WE STILL DON'T KNOW WHAT TRIGGERS THESE POWERS.
WHAT WE DO KNOW...
CHEEER
...IS THAT PEACE HAS BEEN PRESERVED IN THIS CITY BECAUSE THESE NEXT HAVE BECOME OUR HEROES...
HERO TV
RUMMBLE
RUMBLE

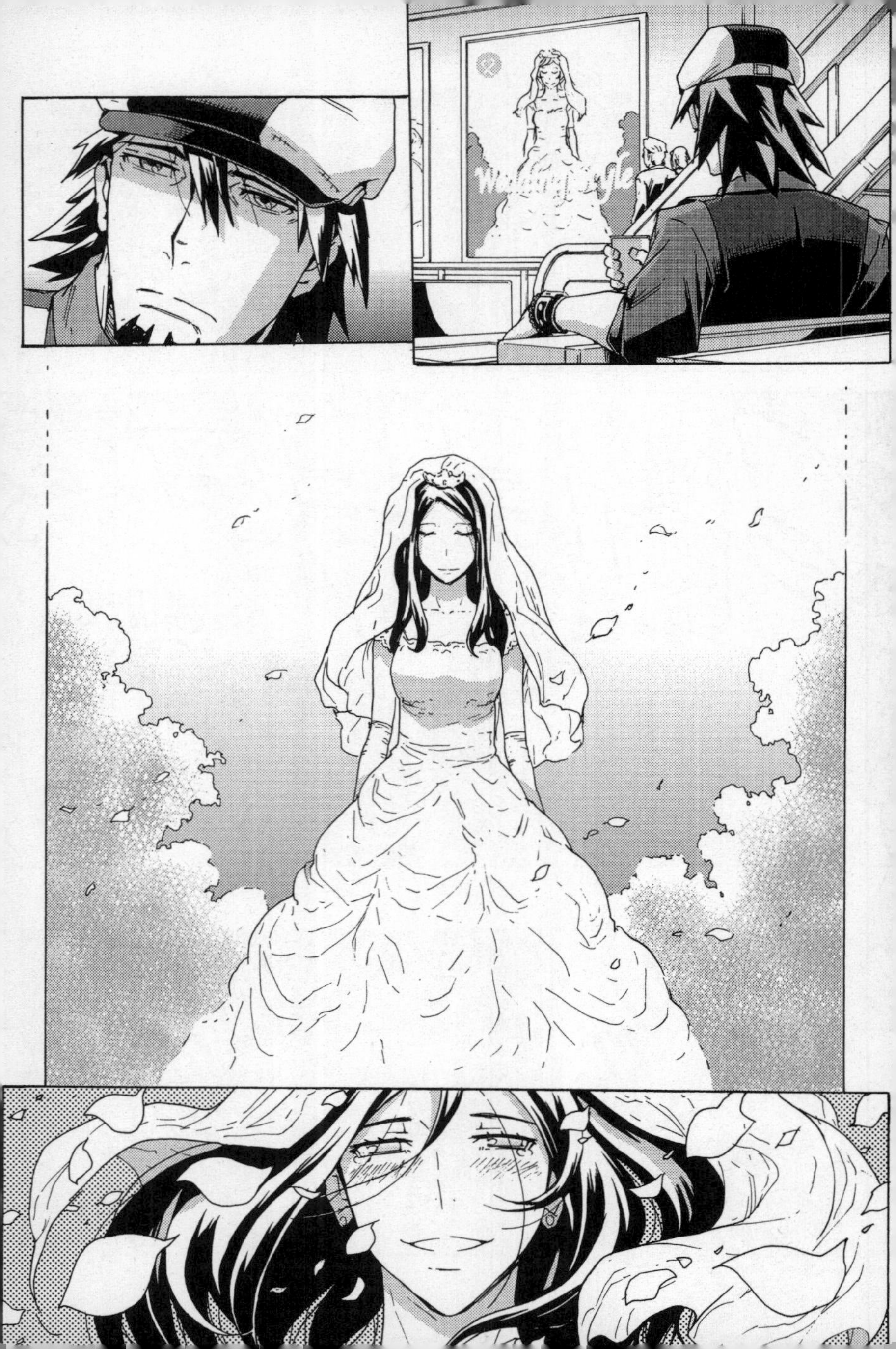

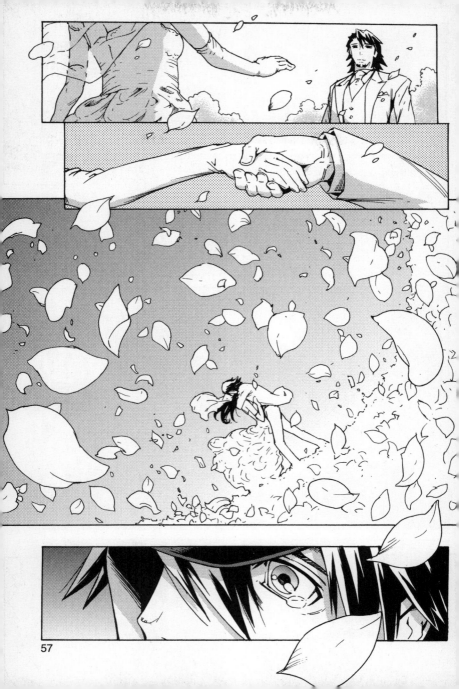

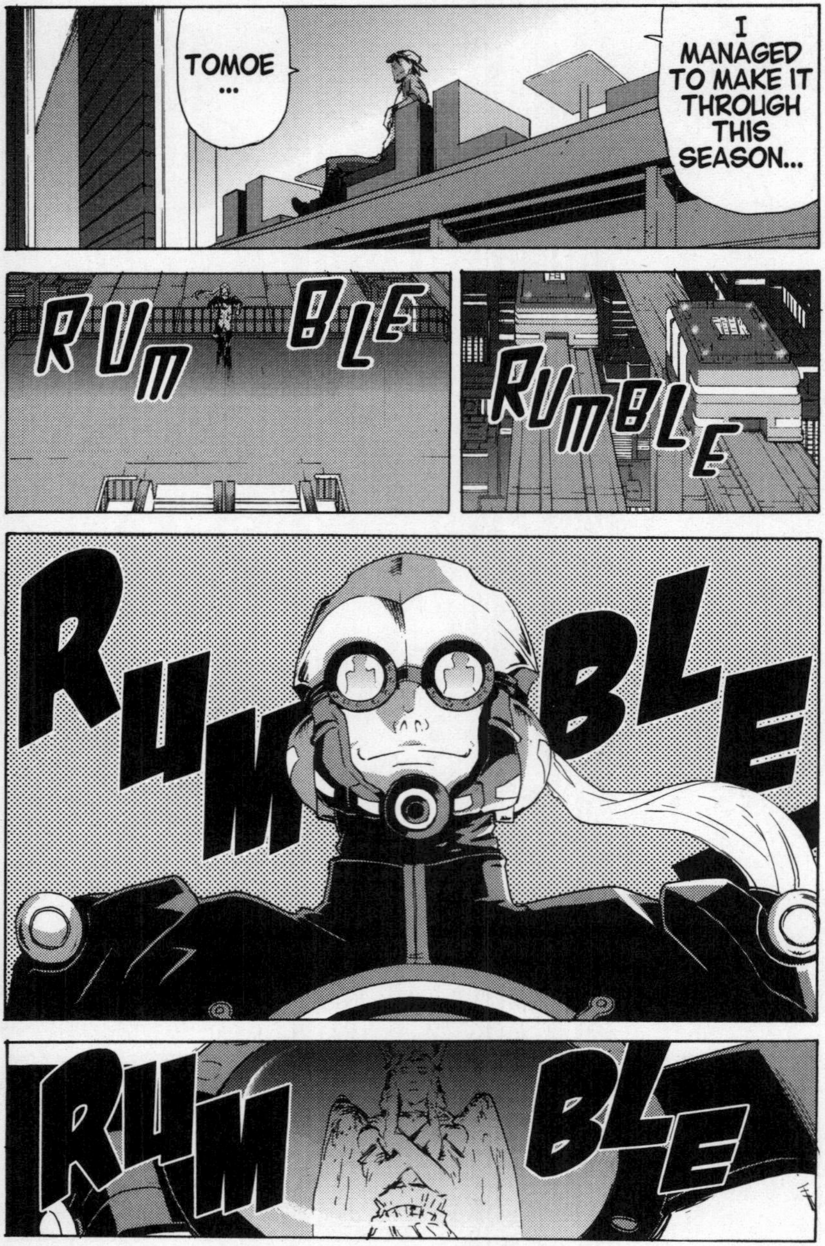
I MANAGED TO MAKE IT THROUGH THIS SEASON...
TOMOE ...
RUMBLE
RUMBLE
RUMBLE
RUMBLE

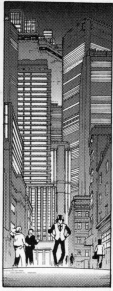

SOLD OUT

BOOM

•••

HEY, LADY, I'LL TAKE TEN OF THESE!

VVV

AREN'T YOU GOING TO COME TO THE PARTY?

YOU SHOULD GREET THE BIGWIGS...

WHAT'S UP?

!

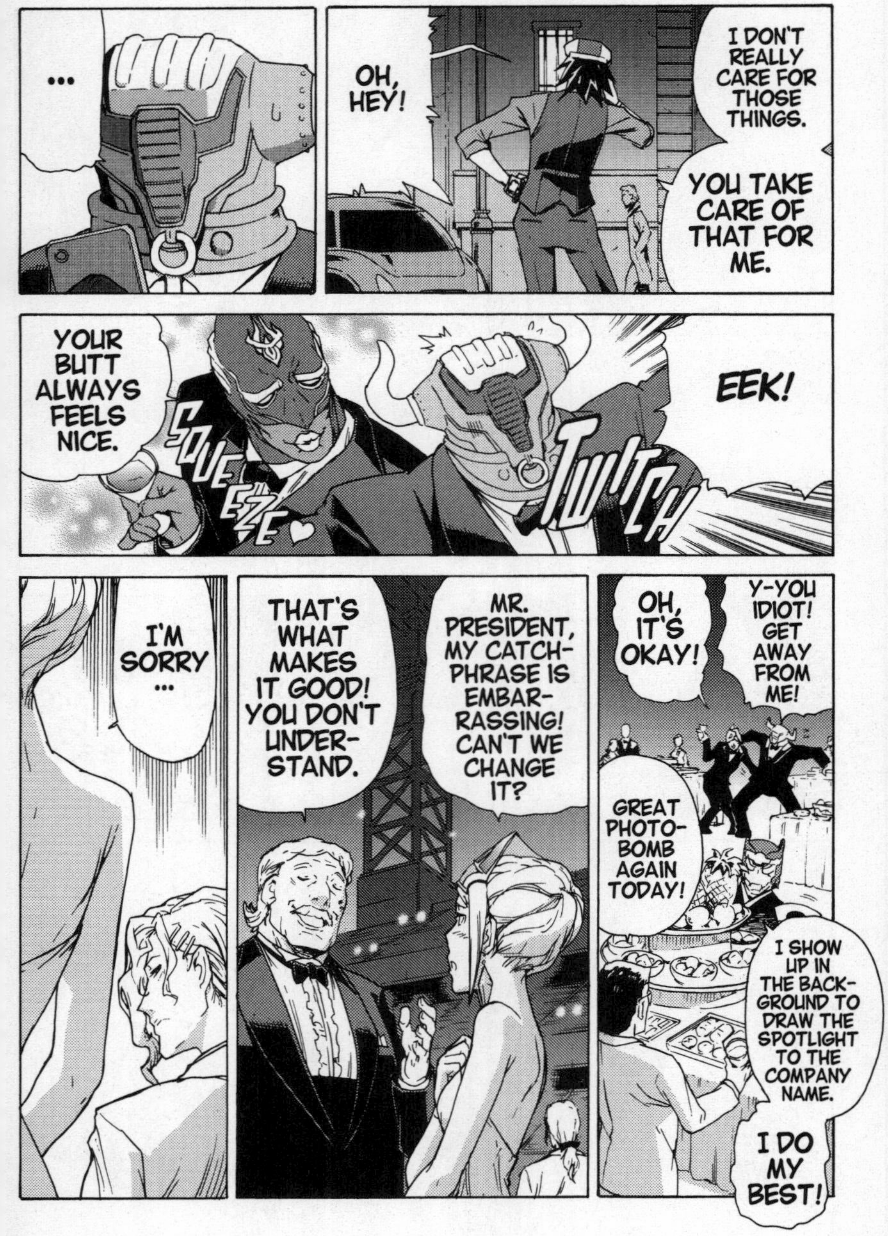
I DON'T REALLY CARE FOR THOSE THINGS.
YOU TAKE CARE OF THAT FOR ME.
OH, HEY!
...
EEK!
TWITCH
SQUEEZE ♥
YOUR BUTT ALWAYS FEELS NICE.
Y-YOU IDIOT! GET AWAY FROM ME!
OH, IT'S OKAY!
GREAT PHOTO-BOMB AGAIN TODAY!
I SHOW UP IN THE BACK-GROUND TO DRAW THE SPOTLIGHT TO THE COMPANY NAME.
I DO MY BEST!
MR. PRESIDENT, MY CATCH-PHRASE IS EMBAR-RASSING! CAN'T WE CHANGE IT?
THAT'S WHAT MAKES IT GOOD! YOU DON'T UNDER-STAND.
I'M SORRY ...

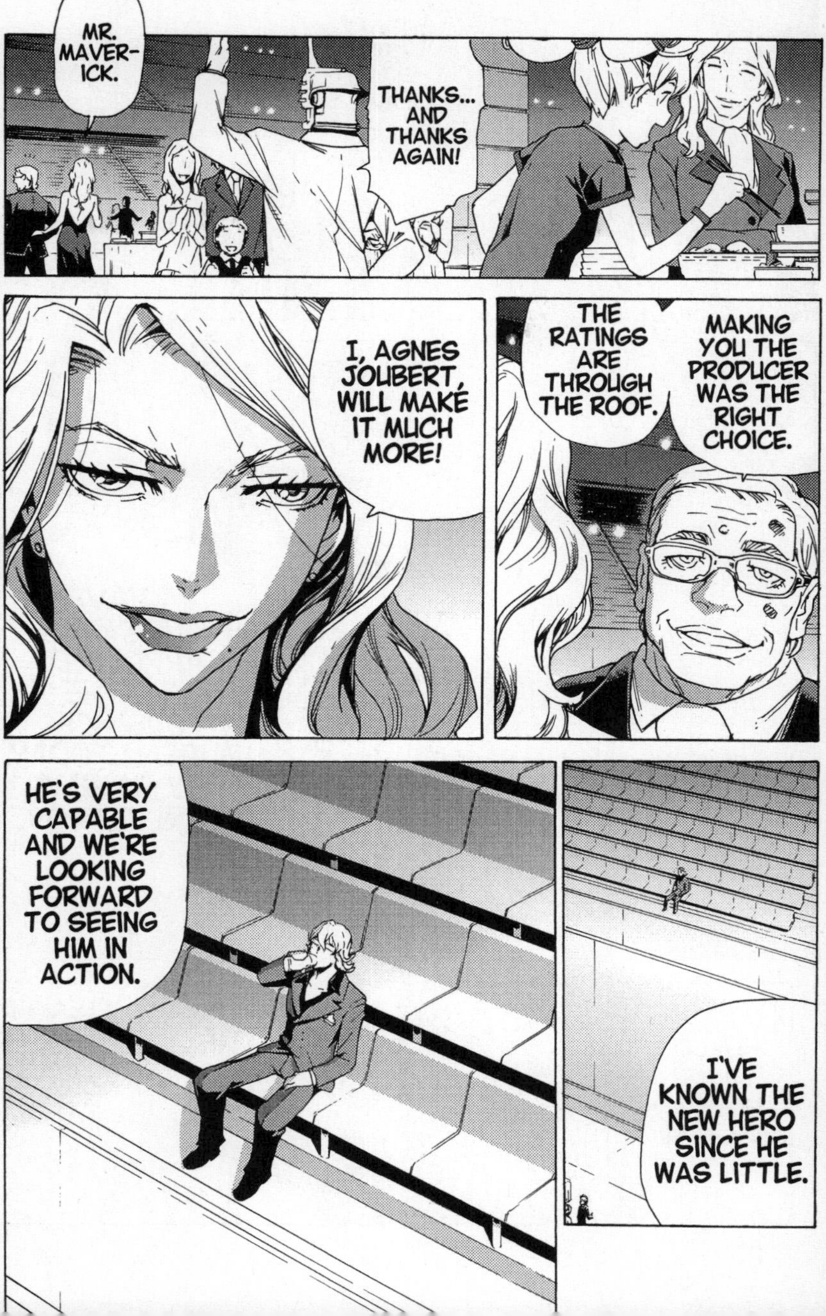
MR. MAVERICK.
THANKS... AND THANKS AGAIN!
THE RATINGS ARE THROUGH THE ROOF.
MAKING YOU THE PRODUCER WAS THE RIGHT CHOICE.
I, AGNES JOUBERT, WILL MAKE IT MUCH MORE!
I'VE KNOWN THE NEW HERO SINCE HE WAS LITTLE.
HE'S VERY CAPABLE AND WE'RE LOOKING FORWARD TO SEEING HIM IN ACTION.

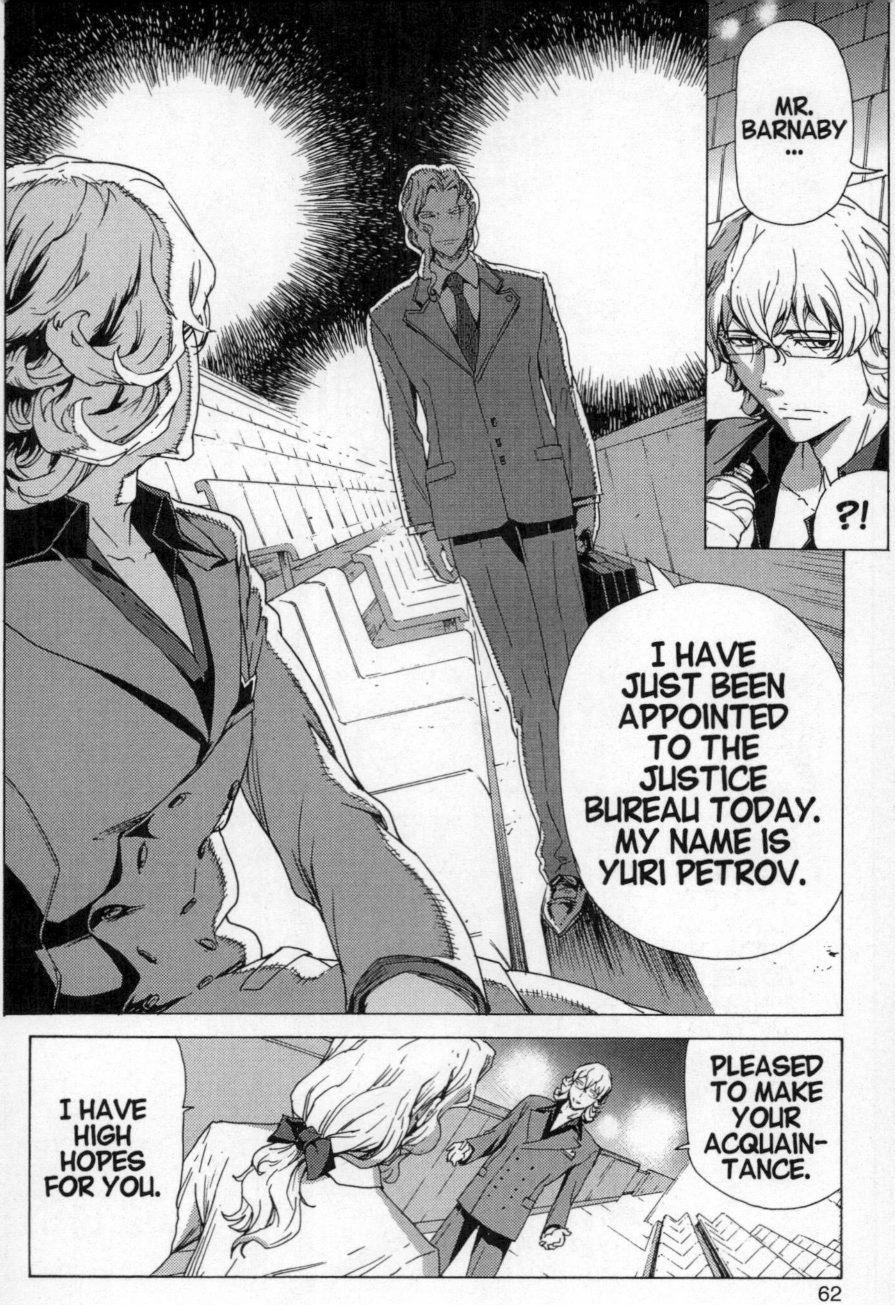
MR. BARNABY ...
?!
I HAVE JUST BEEN APPOINTED TO THE JUSTICE BUREAU TODAY. MY NAME IS YURI PETROV.
PLEASED TO MAKE YOUR ACQUAIN-TANCE.
I HAVE HIGH HOPES FOR YOU.

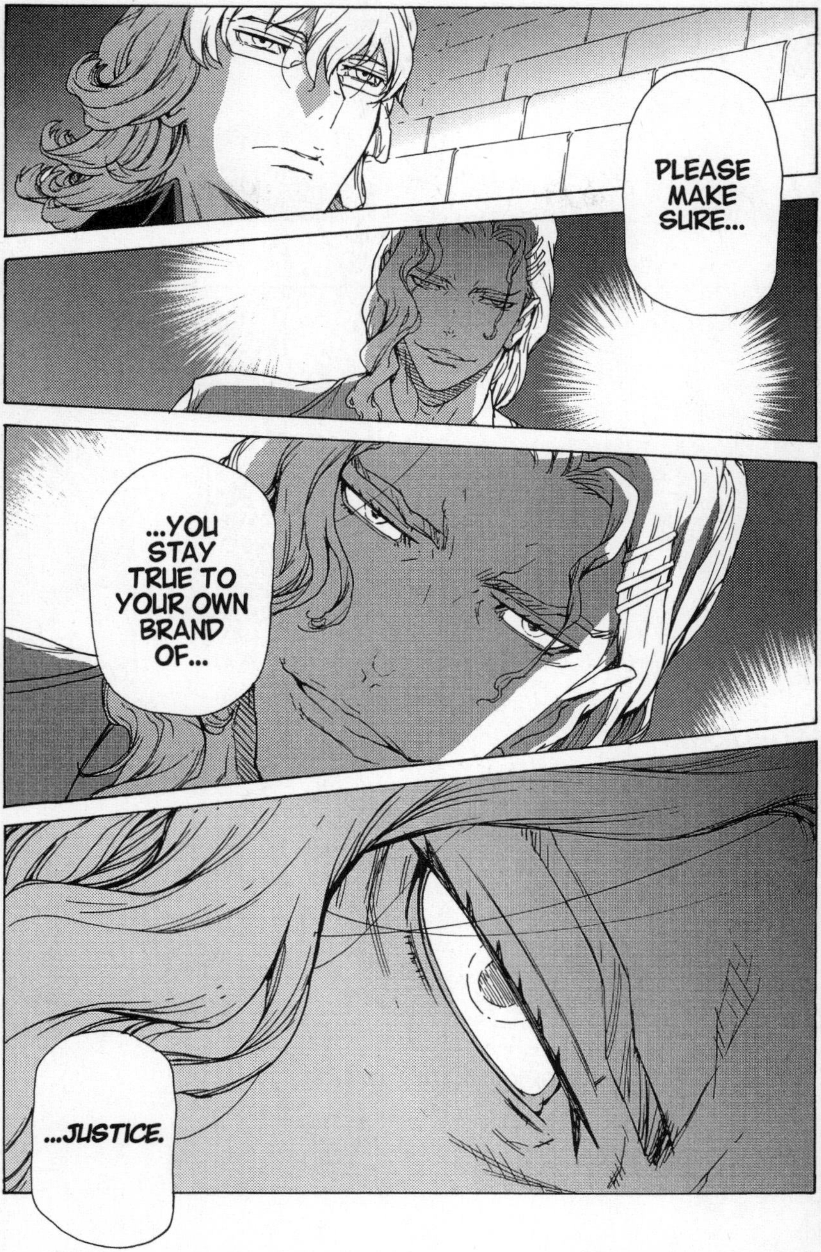
PLEASE MAKE SURE...
...YOU STAY TRUE TO YOUR OWN BRAND OF...
...JUSTICE.

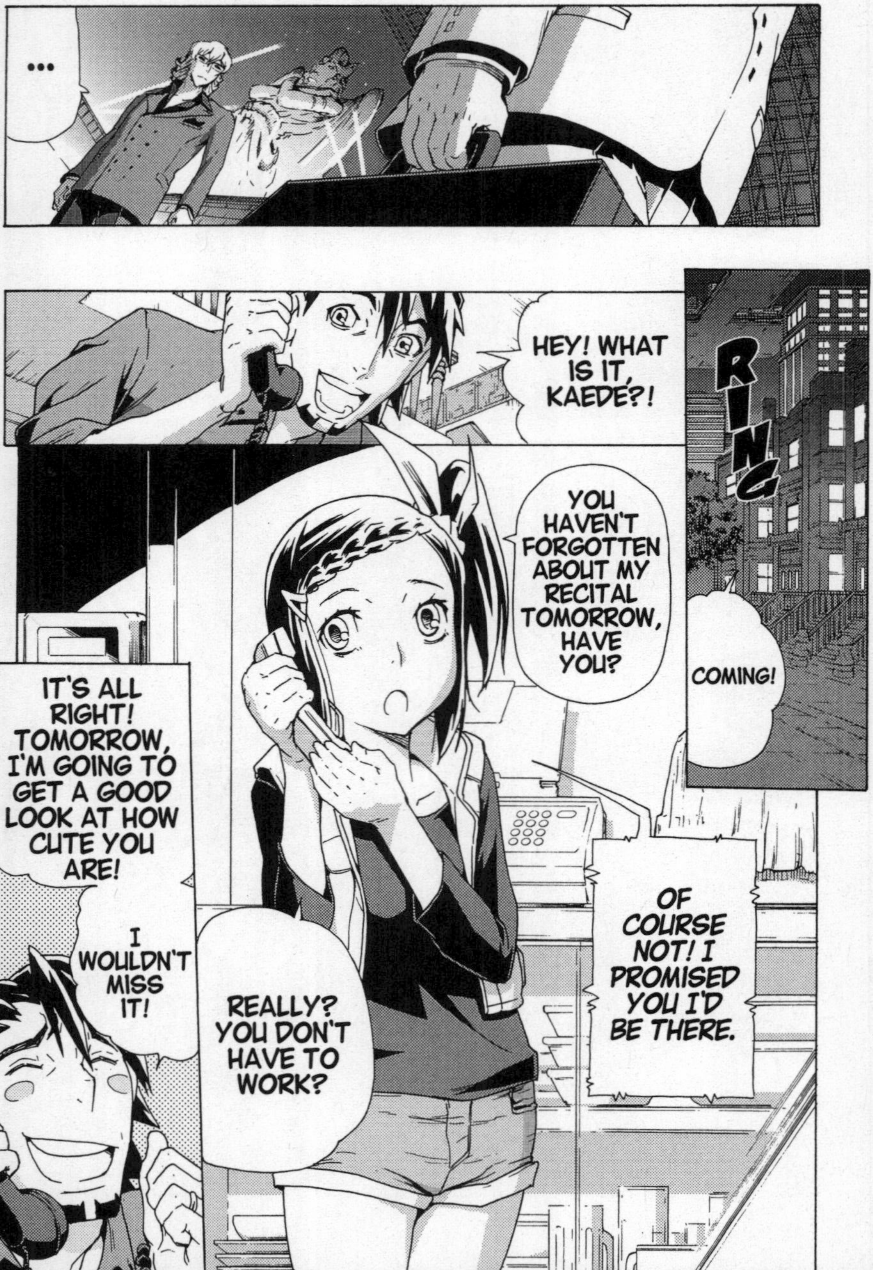

...
RING
COMING!
HEY! WHAT IS IT, KAEDE?!
YOU HAVEN'T FORGOTTEN ABOUT MY RECITAL TOMORROW, HAVE YOU?
OF COURSE NOT! I PROMISED YOU I'D BE THERE.
REALLY? YOU DON'T HAVE TO WORK?
IT'S ALL RIGHT! TOMORROW, I'M GOING TO GET A GOOD LOOK AT HOW CUTE YOU ARE!
I WOULDN'T MISS IT!

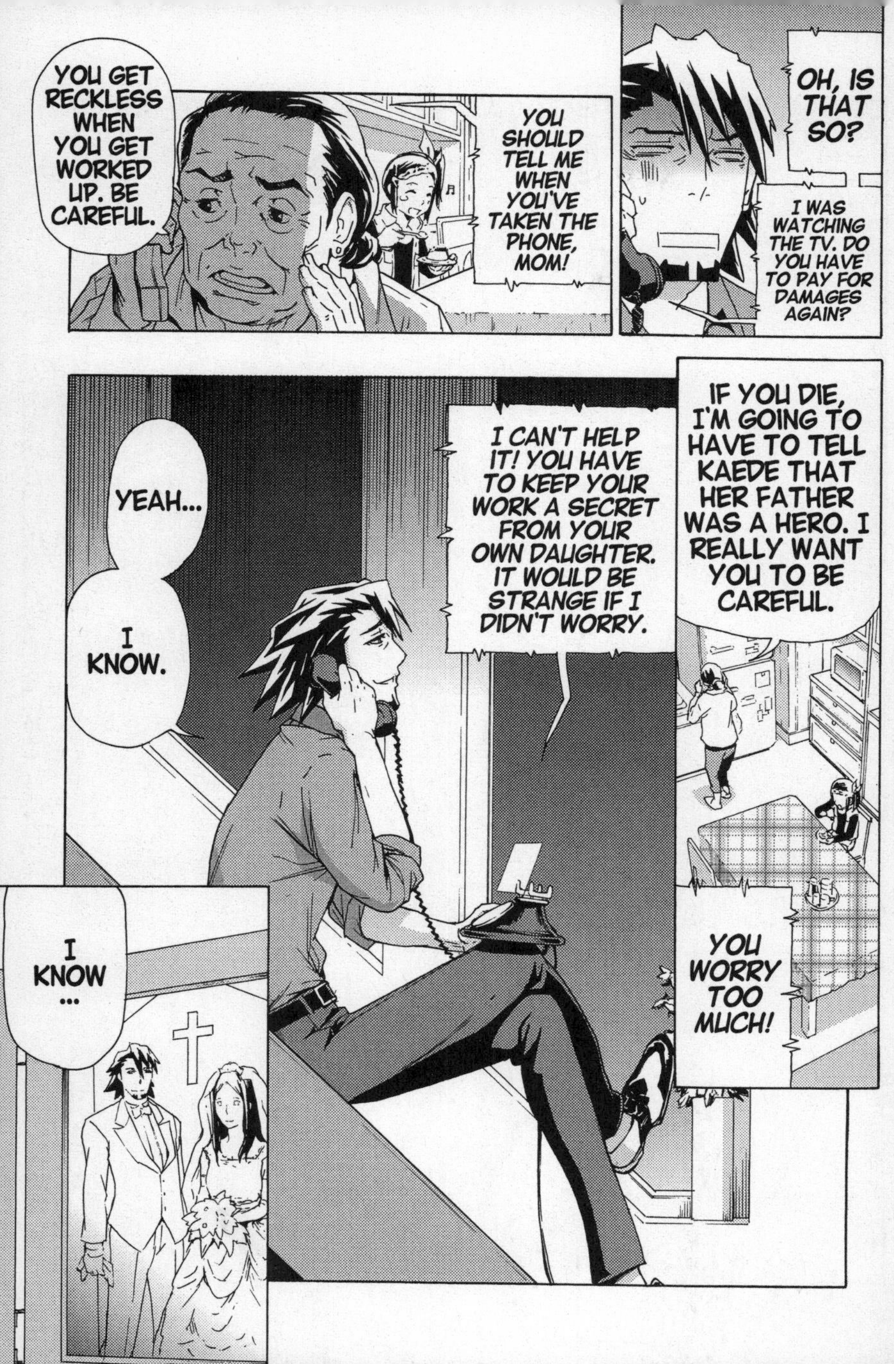
OH, IS THAT SO?
I WAS WATCHING THE TV. DO YOU HAVE TO PAY FOR DAMAGES AGAIN?
YOU SHOULD TELL ME WHEN YOU'VE TAKEN THE PHONE, MOM!
YOU GET RECKLESS WHEN YOU GET WORKED UP. BE CAREFUL.
IF YOU DIE, I'M GOING TO HAVE TO TELL KAEDE THAT HER FATHER WAS A HERO. I REALLY WANT YOU TO BE CAREFUL.
YOU WORRY TOO MUCH!
I CAN'T HELP IT! YOU HAVE TO KEEP YOUR WORK A SECRET FROM YOUR OWN DAUGHTER. IT WOULD BE STRANGE IF I DIDN'T WORRY.
YEAH...
I KNOW.
I KNOW...

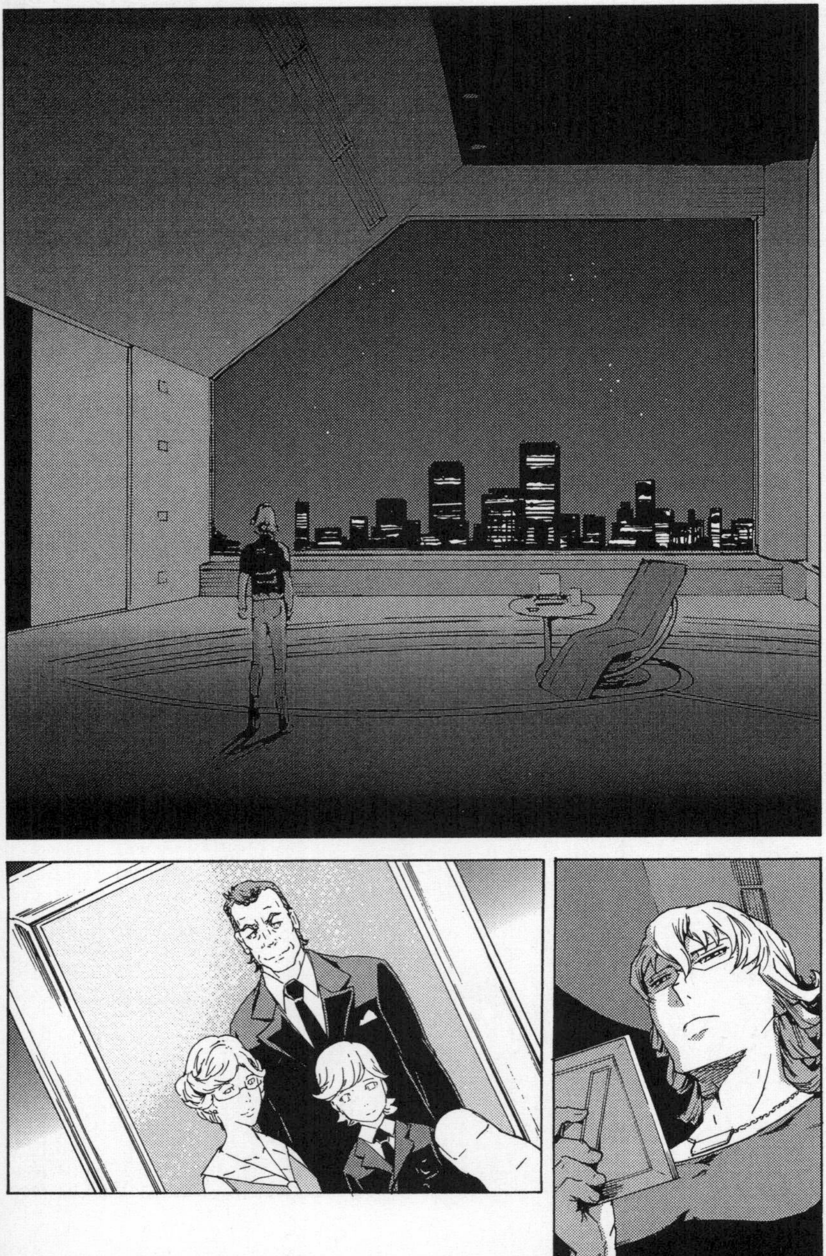

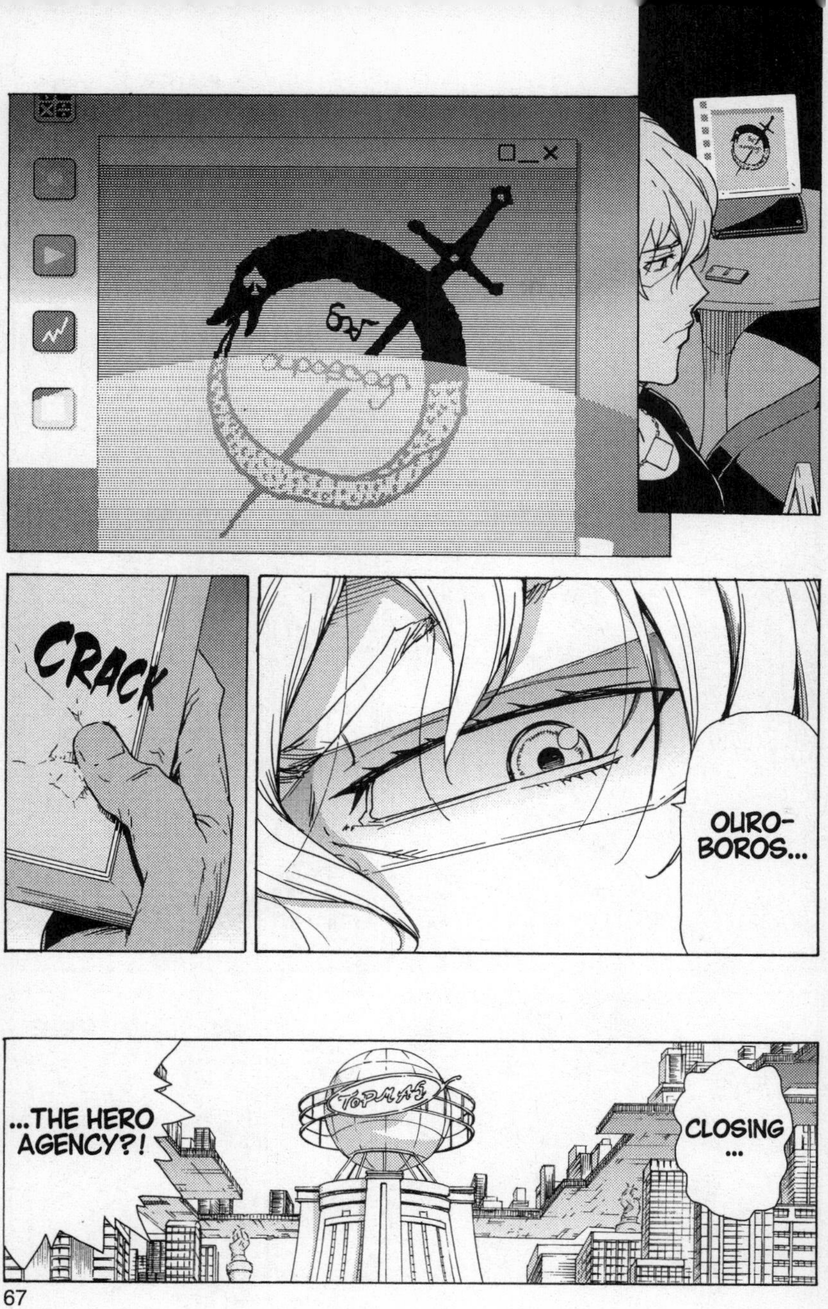
CRACK
OURO-BOROS...
CLOSING...
...THE HERO AGENCY?!
TOPMAG

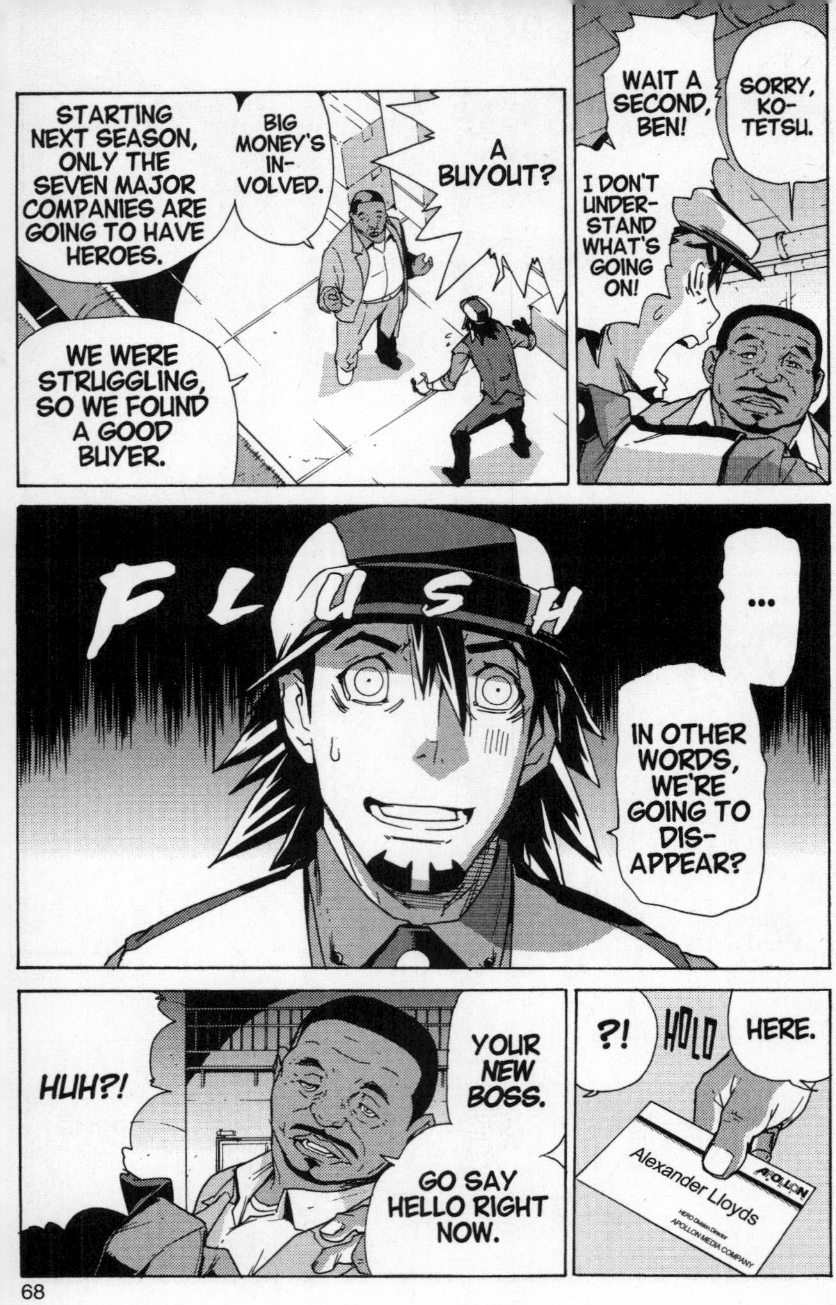
SORRY, KO-TETSU.
WAIT A SECOND, BEN!
I DON'T UNDER-STAND WHAT'S GOING ON!
A BUYOUT?
BIG MONEY'S IN-VOLVED.
STARTING NEXT SEASON, ONLY THE SEVEN MAJOR COMPANIES ARE GOING TO HAVE HEROES.
WE WERE STRUGGLING, SO WE FOUND A GOOD BUYER.
...
FLUSH
IN OTHER WORDS, WE'RE GOING TO DIS-APPEAR?
HERE.
HOLD
?!
Alexander Lloyds
HERO Division Director
APOLLON MEDIA COMPANY
APOLLON
YOUR NEW BOSS.
HUH?!
GO SAY HELLO RIGHT NOW.

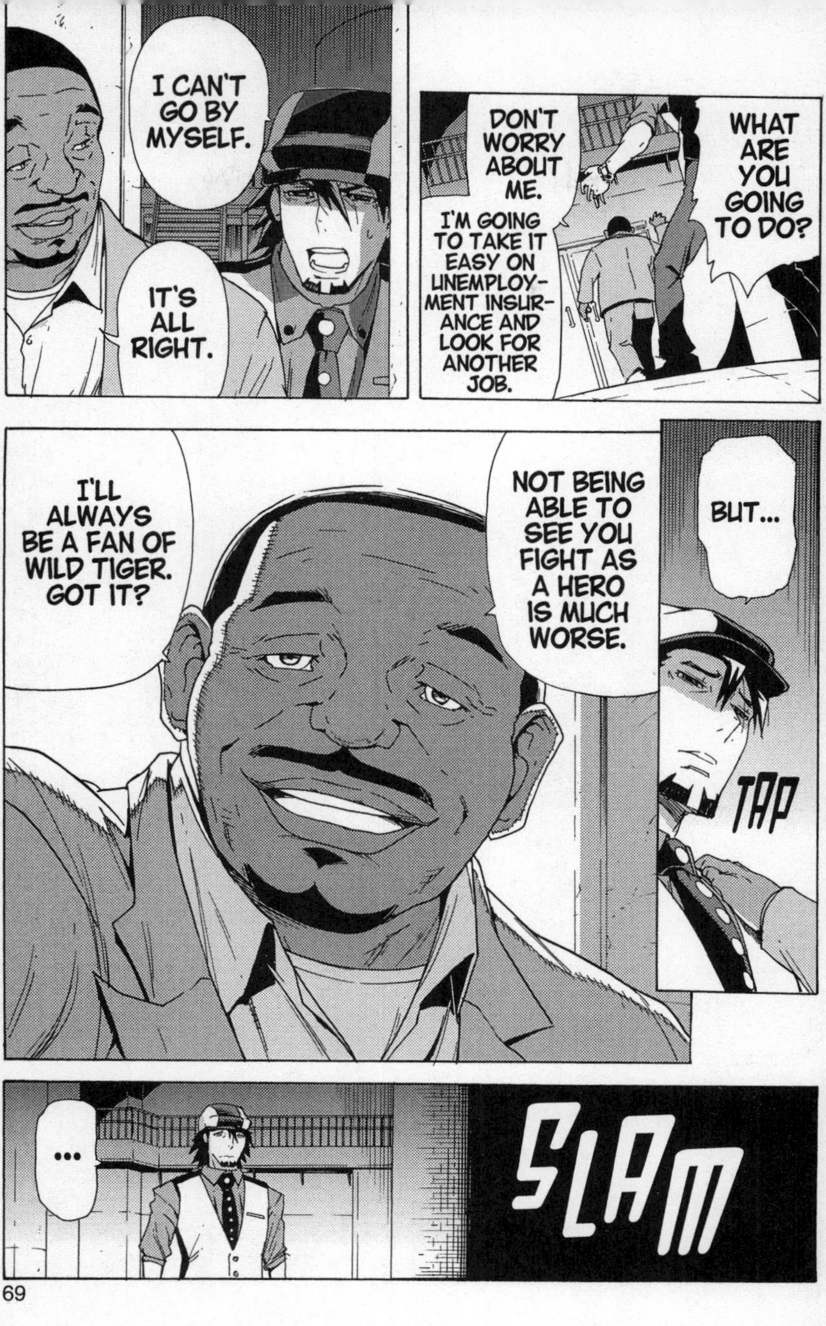
WHAT ARE YOU GOING TO DO?
DON'T WORRY ABOUT ME.
I'M GOING TO TAKE IT EASY ON UNEMPLOY-MENT INSUR-ANCE AND LOOK FOR ANOTHER JOB.
I CAN'T GO BY MYSELF.
IT'S ALL RIGHT.
BUT...
TAP
NOT BEING ABLE TO SEE YOU FIGHT AS A HERO IS MUCH WORSE.
I'LL ALWAYS BE A FAN OF WILD TIGER. GOT IT?
SLAM
...

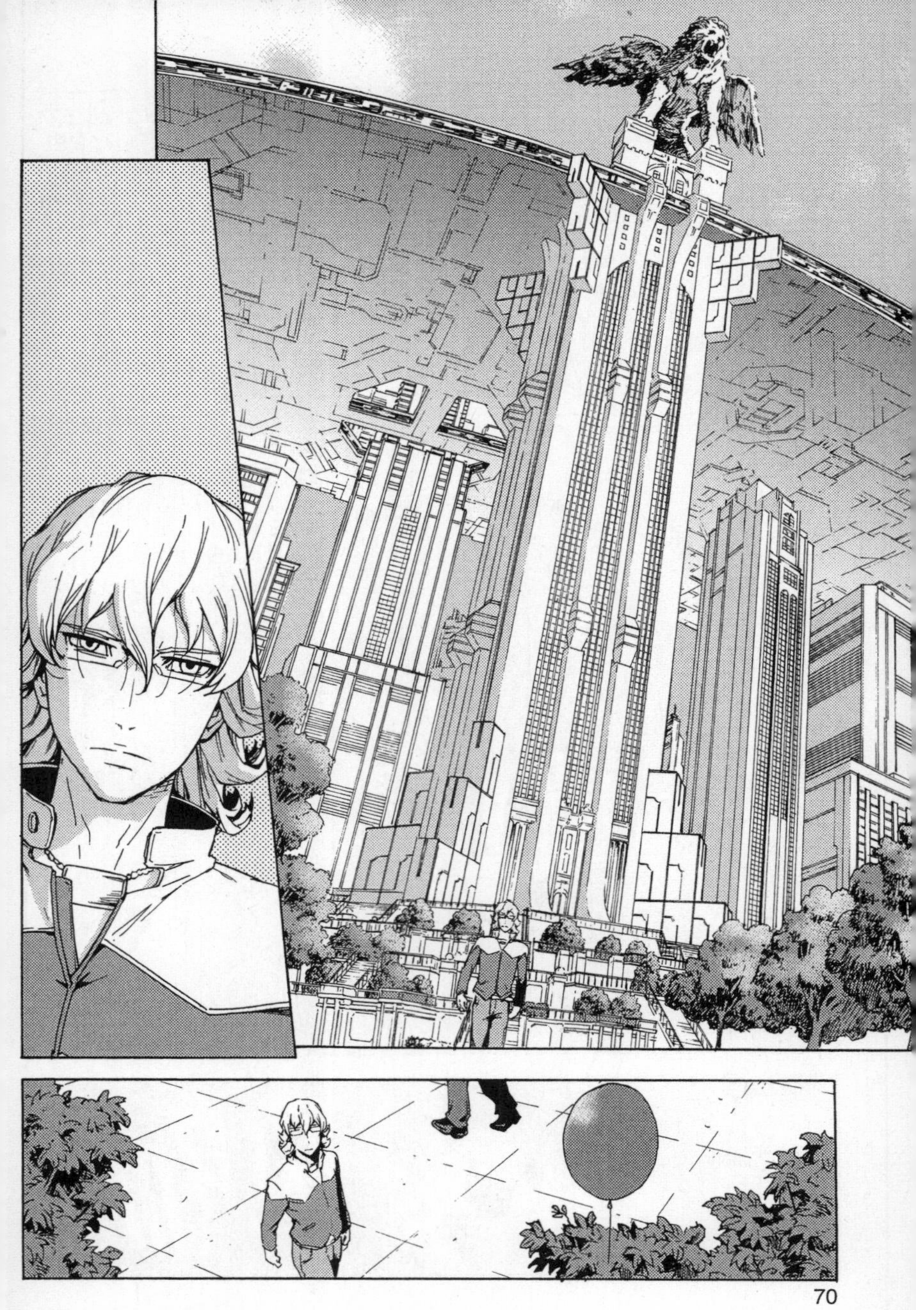

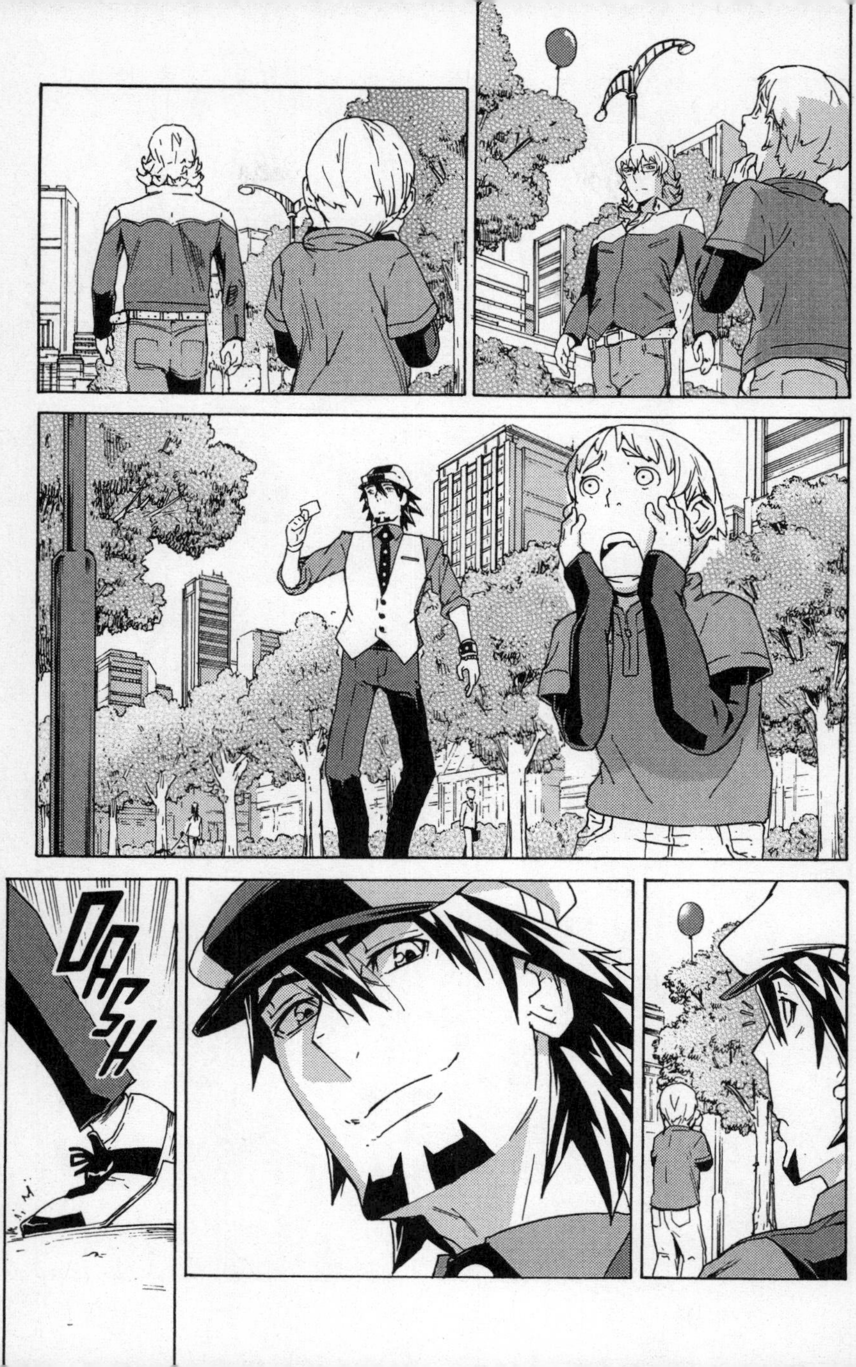
DASH

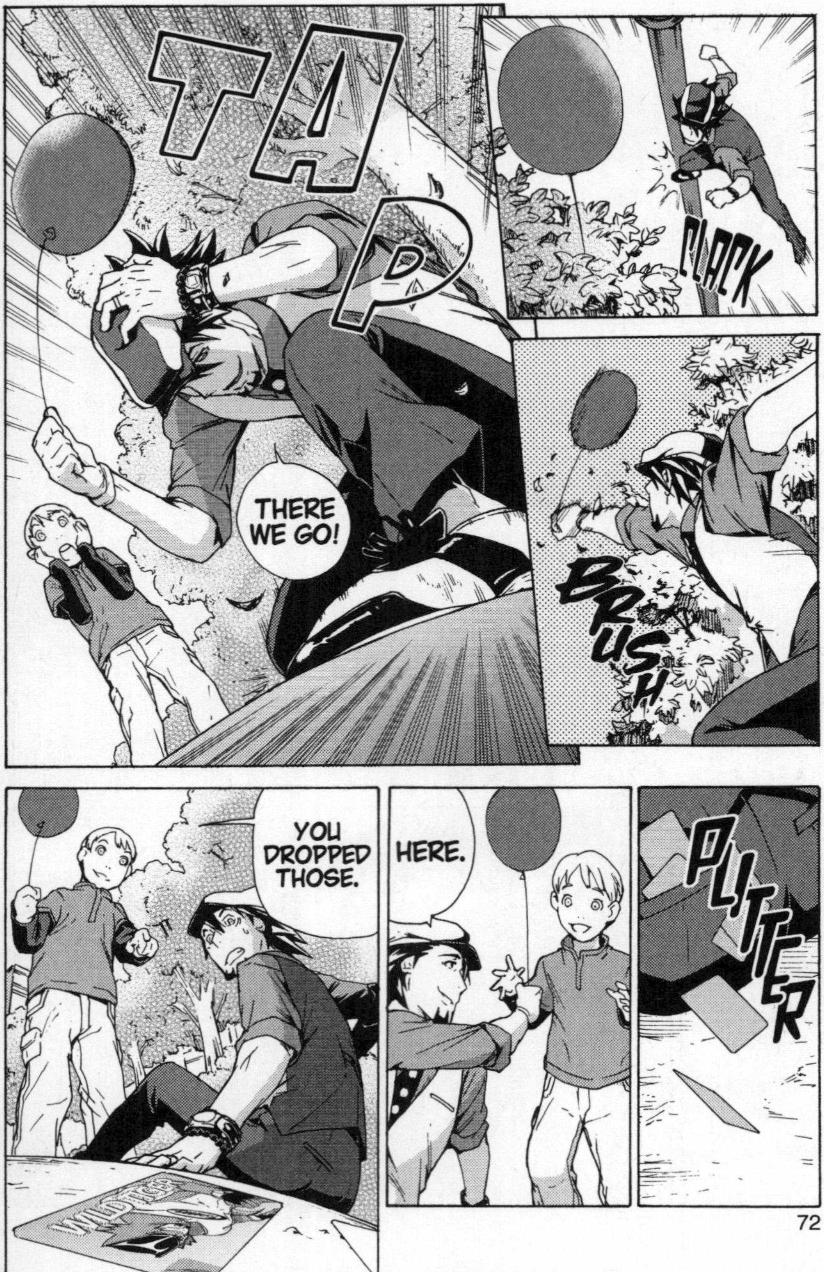
CLACK
BRUSH
TAP
THERE WE GO!
PLITTER
HERE.
YOU DROPPED THOSE.

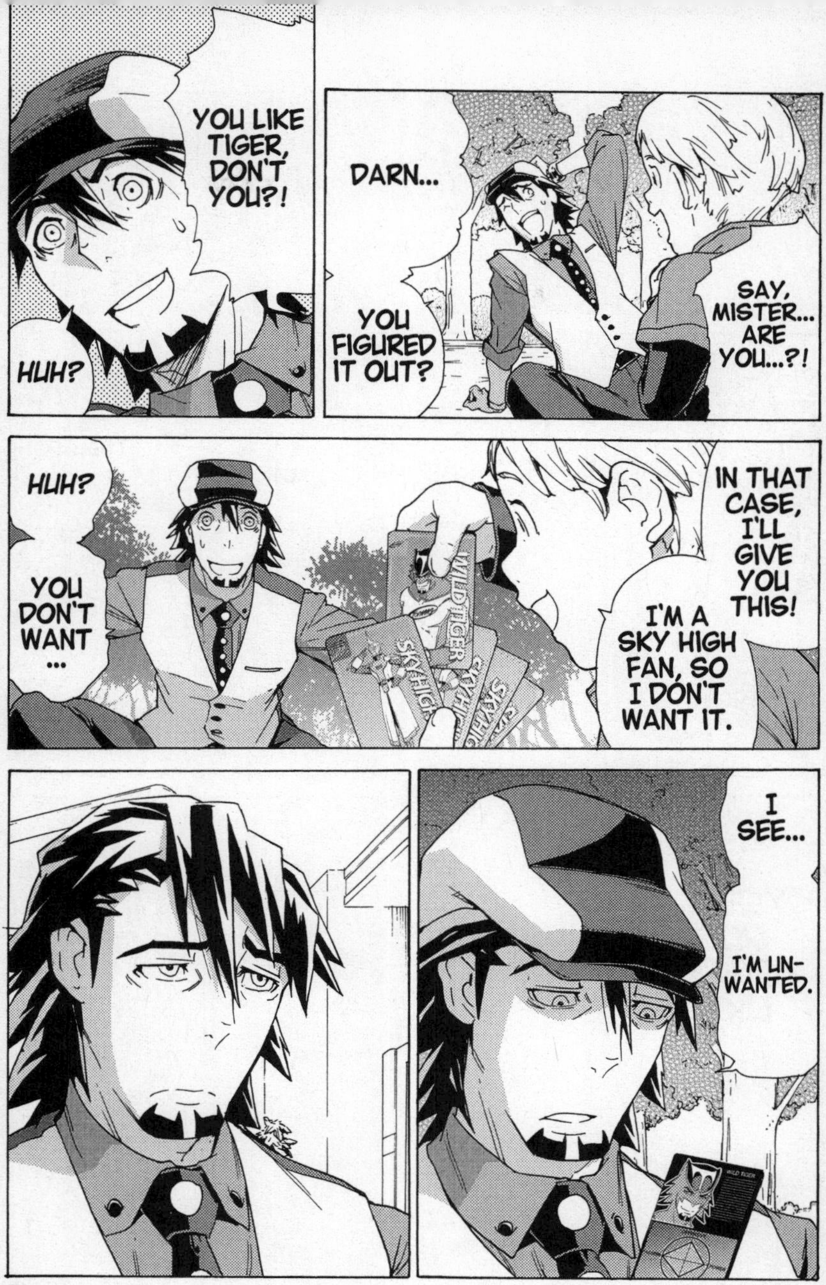
SAY, MISTER... ARE YOU...?!
DARN...
YOU FIGURED IT OUT?
YOU LIKE TIGER, DON'T YOU?!
HUH?
IN THAT CASE, I'LL GIVE YOU THIS!
I'M A SKY HIGH FAN, SO I DON'T WANT IT.
HUH?
YOU DON'T WANT ...
I SEE...
I'M UN-WANTED.

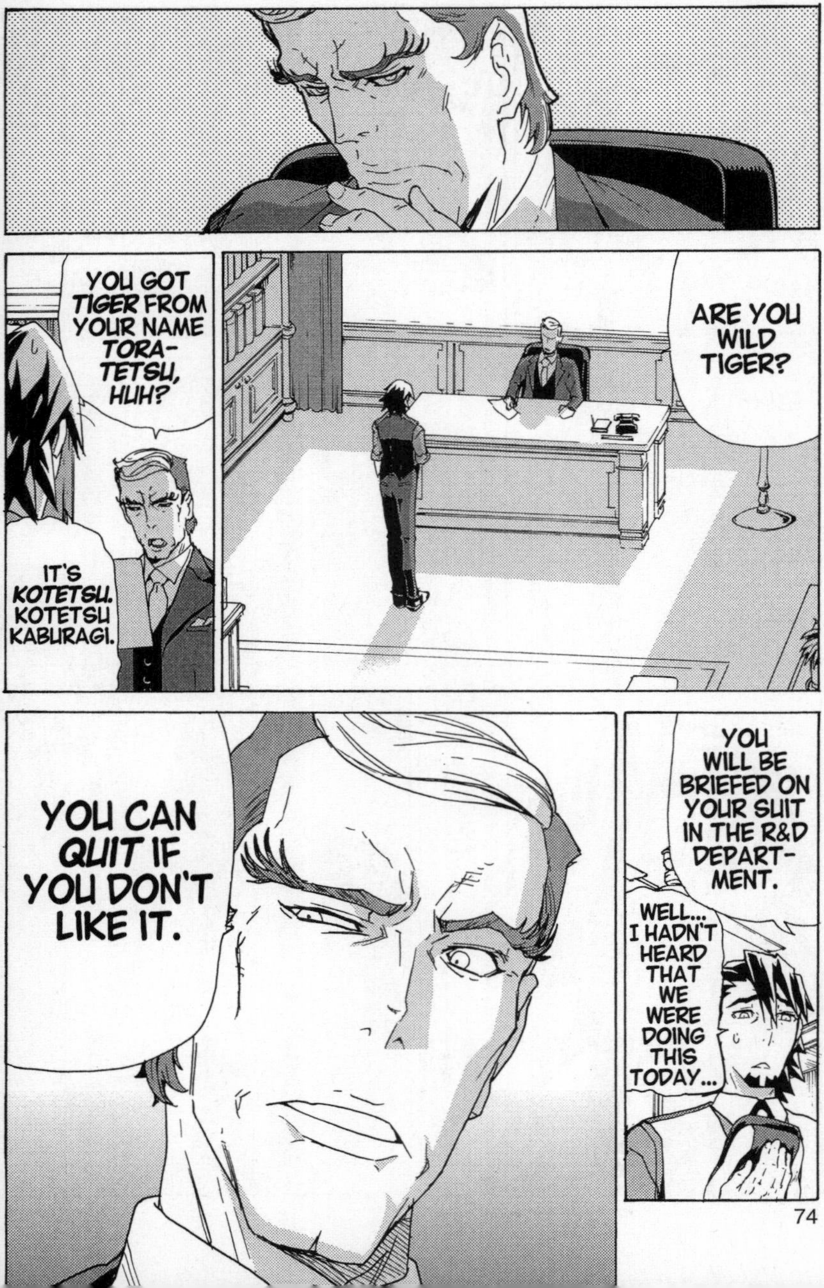
ARE YOU WILD TIGER?
YOU GOT TIGER FROM YOUR NAME TORA-TETSU, HUH?
IT'S KOTETSU. KOTETSU KABURAGI.
YOU WILL BE BRIEFED ON YOUR SUIT IN THE R&D DEPART-MENT.
WELL... I HADN'T HEARD THAT WE WERE DOING THIS TODAY...
YOU CAN QUIT IF YOU DON'T LIKE IT.

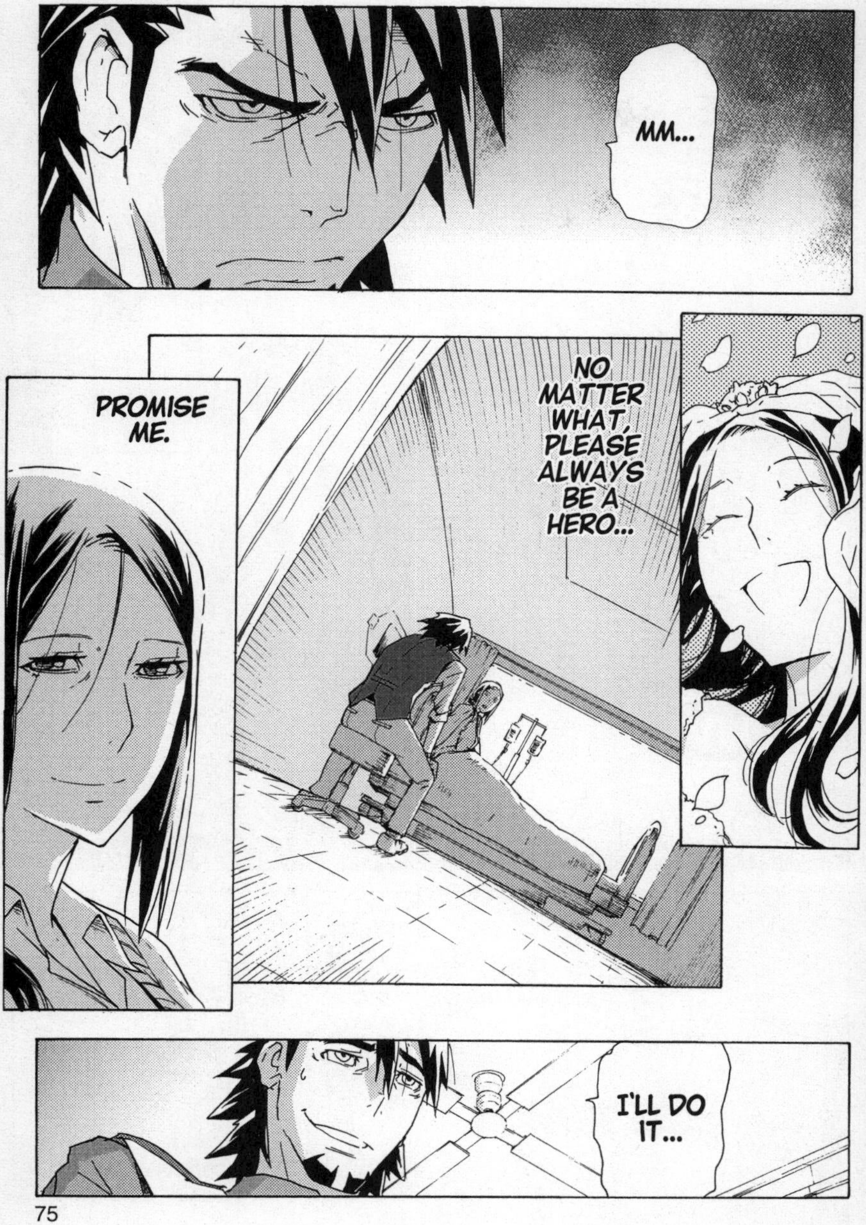
MM...
NO MATTER WHAT, PLEASE ALWAYS BE A HERO...
PROMISE ME.
I'LL DO IT...

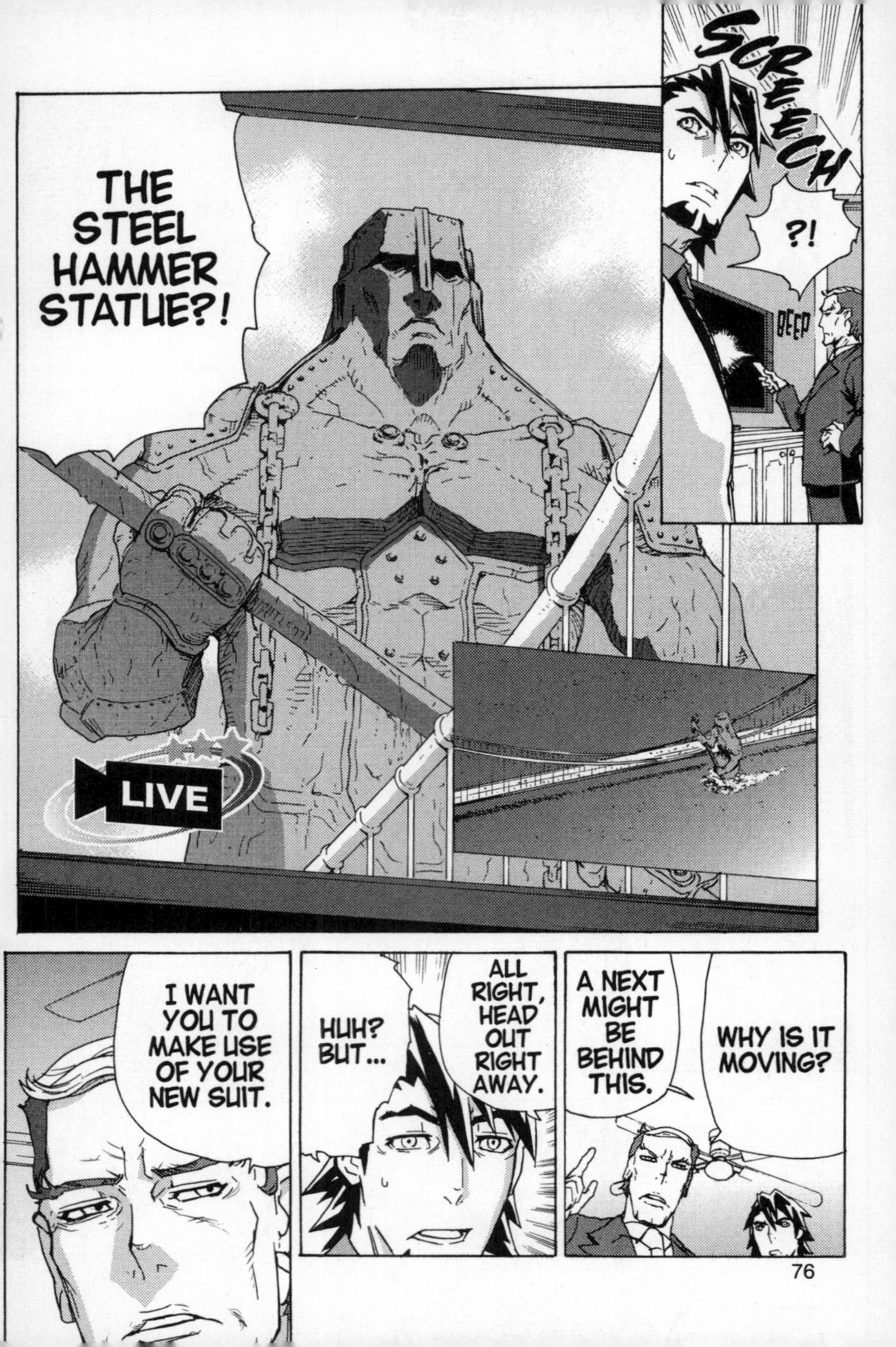
SCREECH
?!
BEEP
THE STEEL HAMMER STATUE?!
LIVE
WHY IS IT MOVING?
A NEXT MIGHT BE BEHIND THIS.
ALL RIGHT, HEAD OUT RIGHT AWAY.
HUH? BUT...
I WANT YOU TO MAKE USE OF YOUR NEW SUIT.

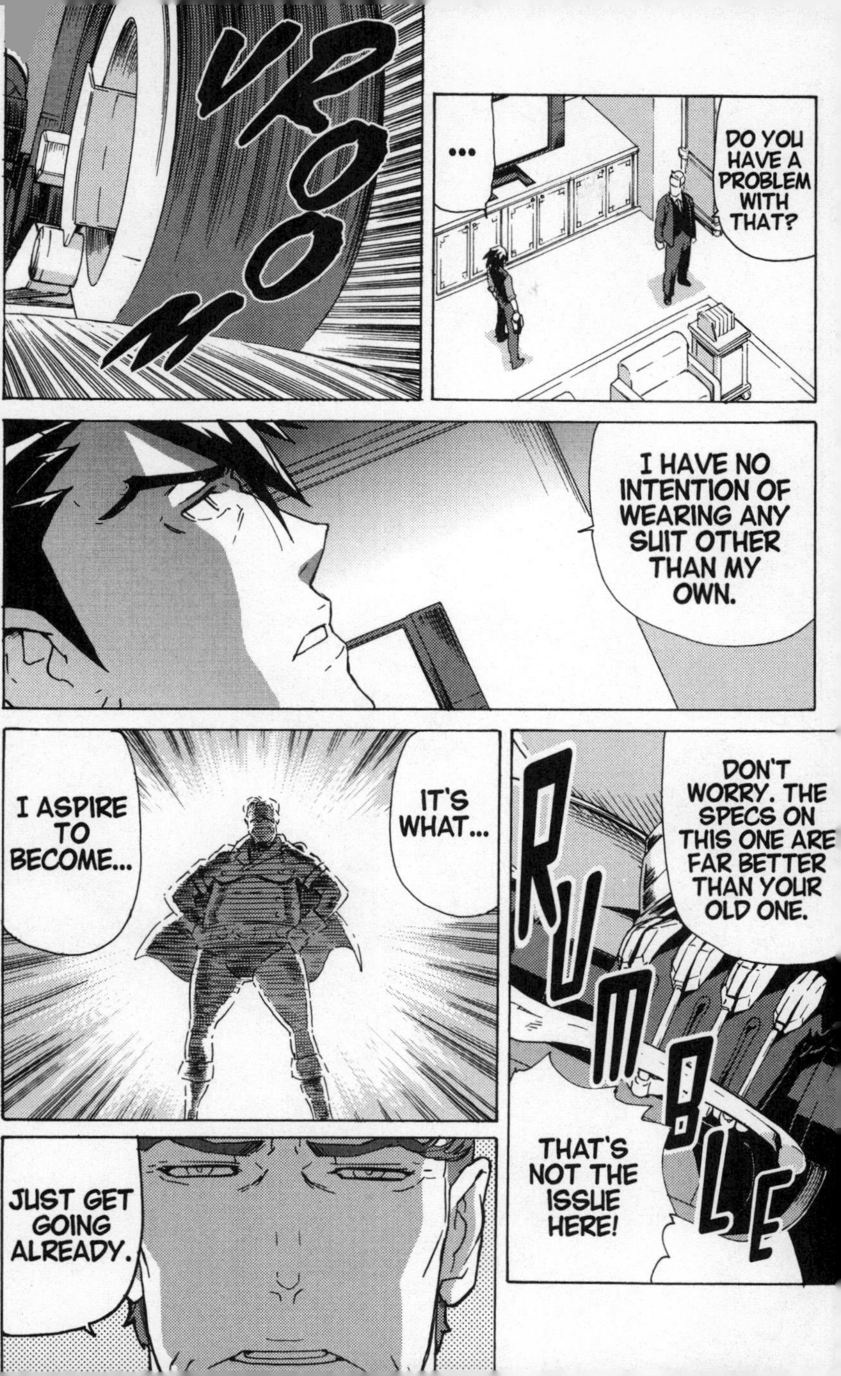
DO YOU HAVE A PROBLEM WITH THAT?
...
VROOM
I HAVE NO INTENTION OF WEARING ANY SUIT OTHER THAN MY OWN.
DON'T WORRY. THE SPECS ON THIS ONE ARE FAR BETTER THAN YOUR OLD ONE.
RUMBLE
THAT'S NOT THE ISSUE HERE!
IT'S WHAT...
I ASPIRE TO BECOME...
JUST GET GOING ALREADY.

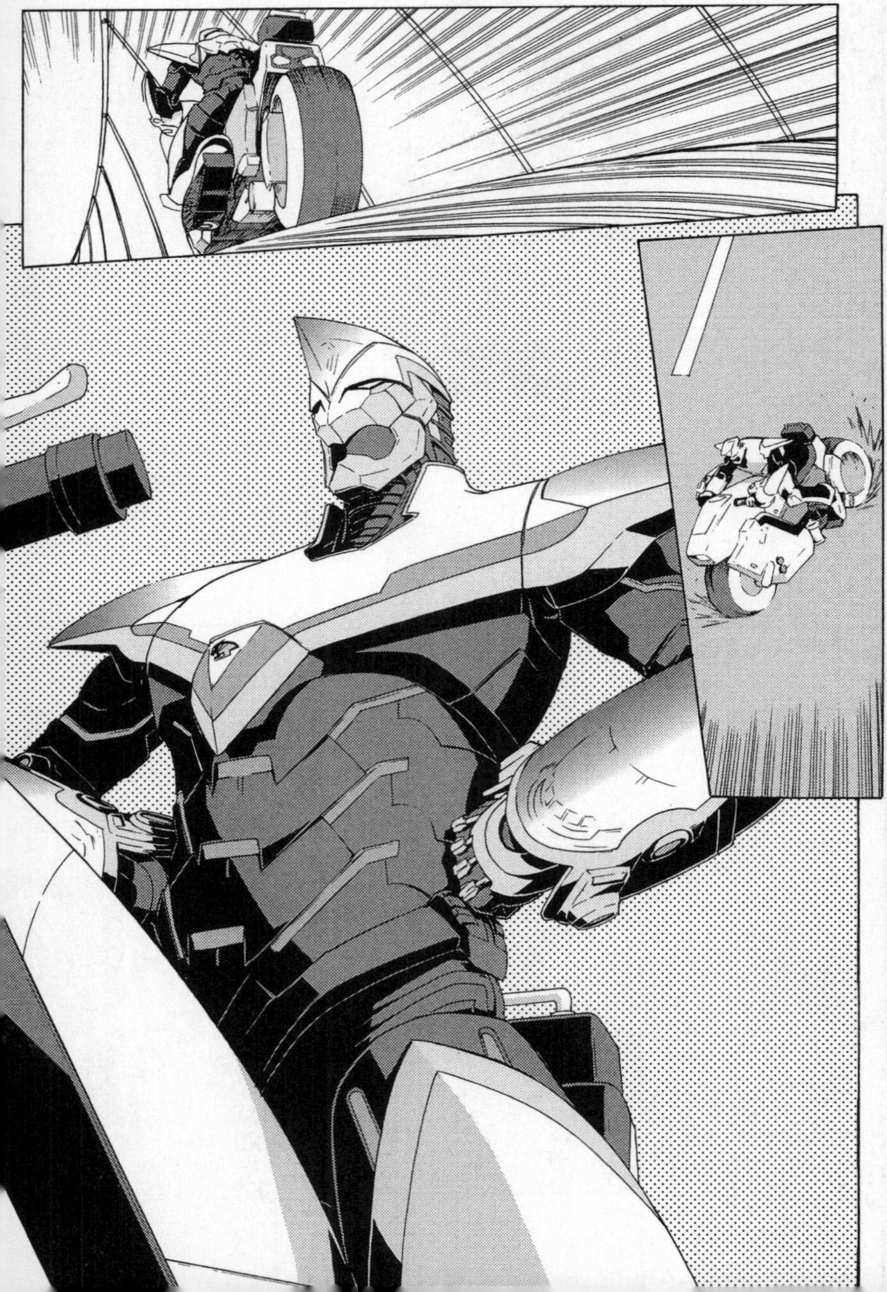

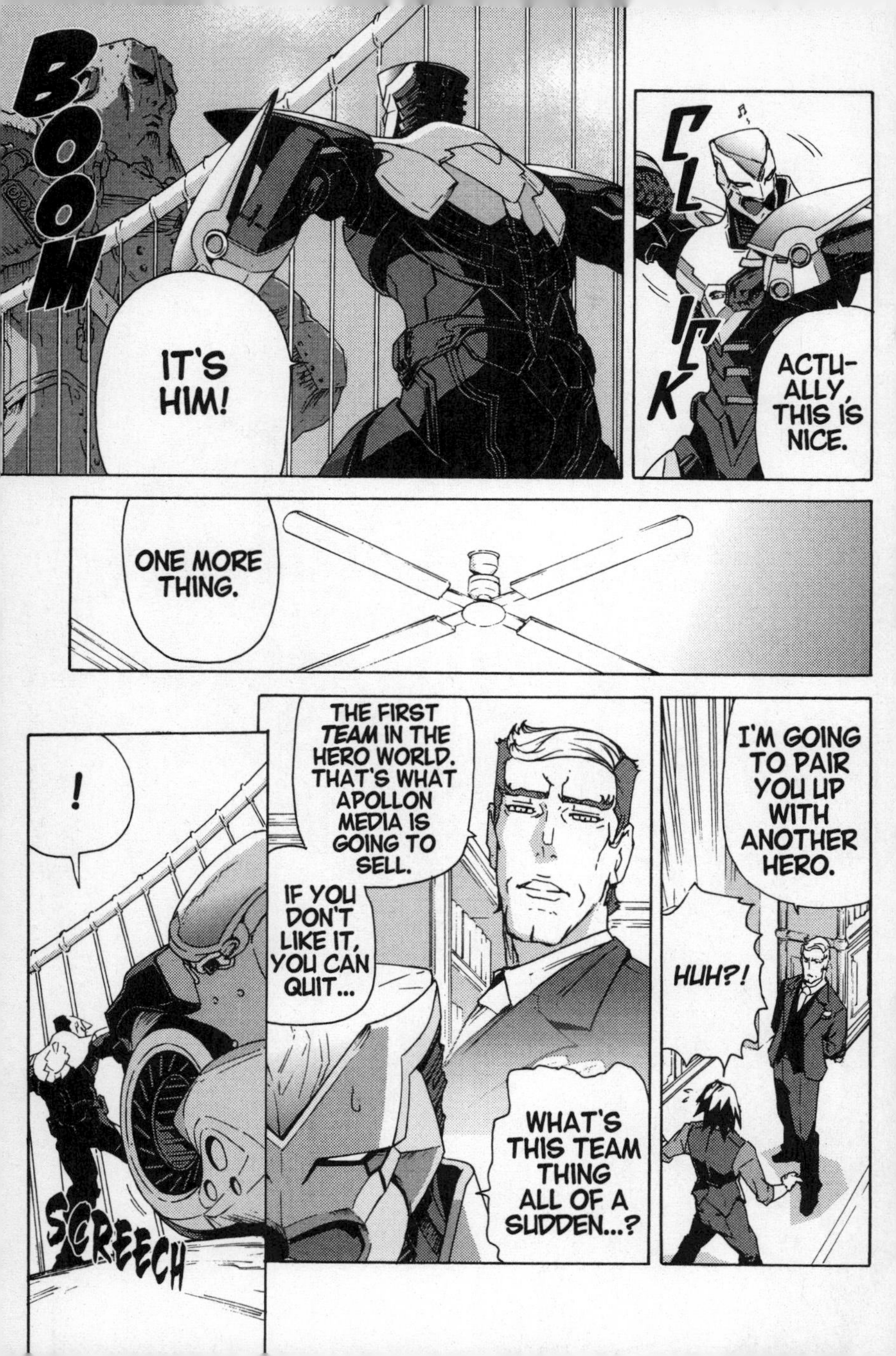
CLICK
ACTUALLY, THIS IS NICE.
BOOM
IT'S HIM!
ONE MORE THING.
I'M GOING TO PAIR YOU UP WITH ANOTHER HERO.
HUH?!
THE FIRST *TEAM* IN THE HERO WORLD. THAT'S WHAT APOLLON MEDIA IS GOING TO SELL.
IF YOU DON'T LIKE IT, YOU CAN QUIT...
WHAT'S THIS TEAM THING ALL OF A SUDDEN...?
!
SCREECH

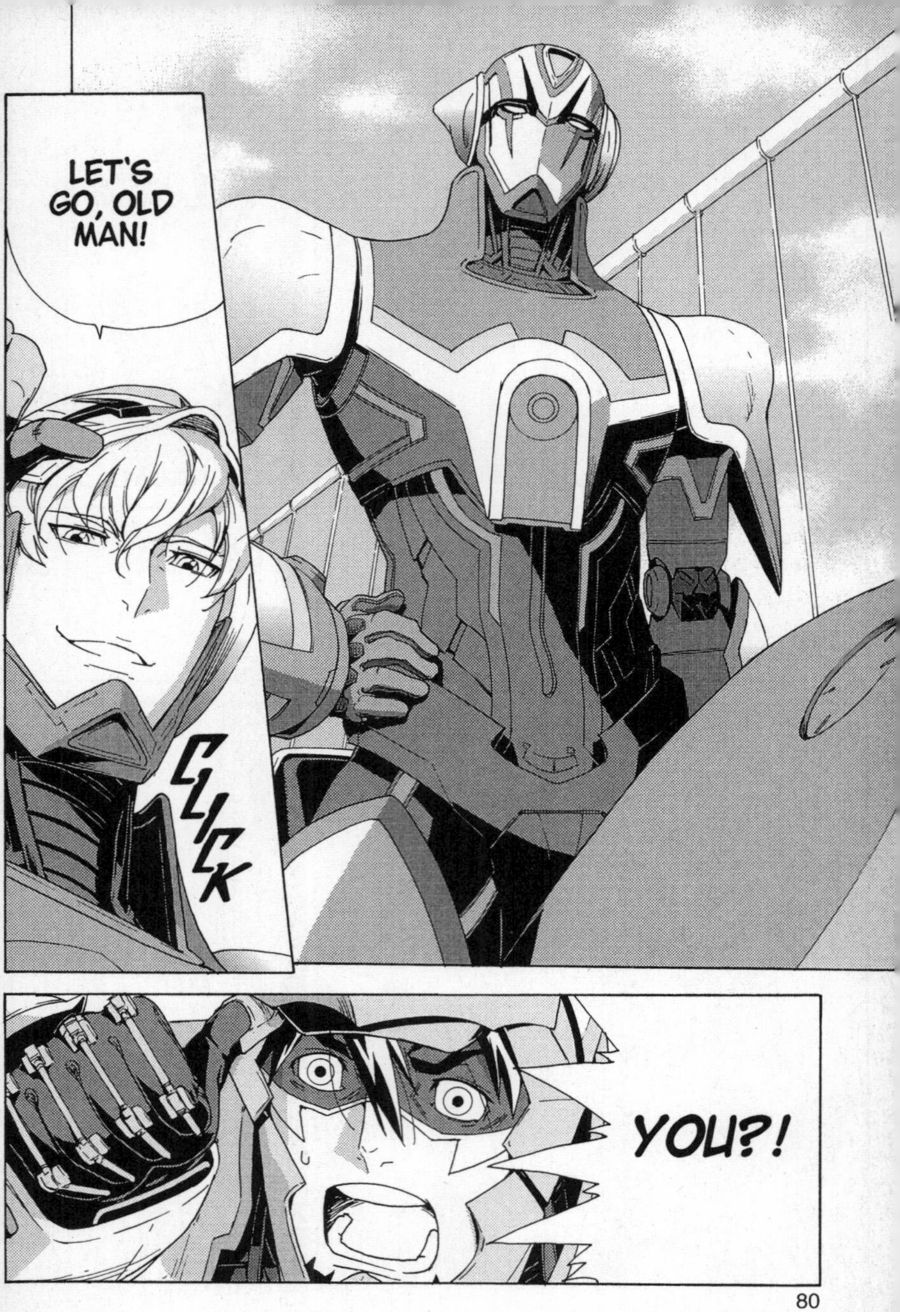
LET'S GO, OLD MAN!
CLICK
YOU?!

TIGER & BUNNY

THE MOVIE

The Beginning

TIGER & BUNNY THE MOVIE The Beginning

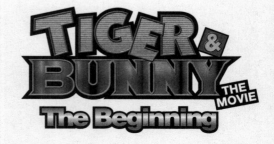

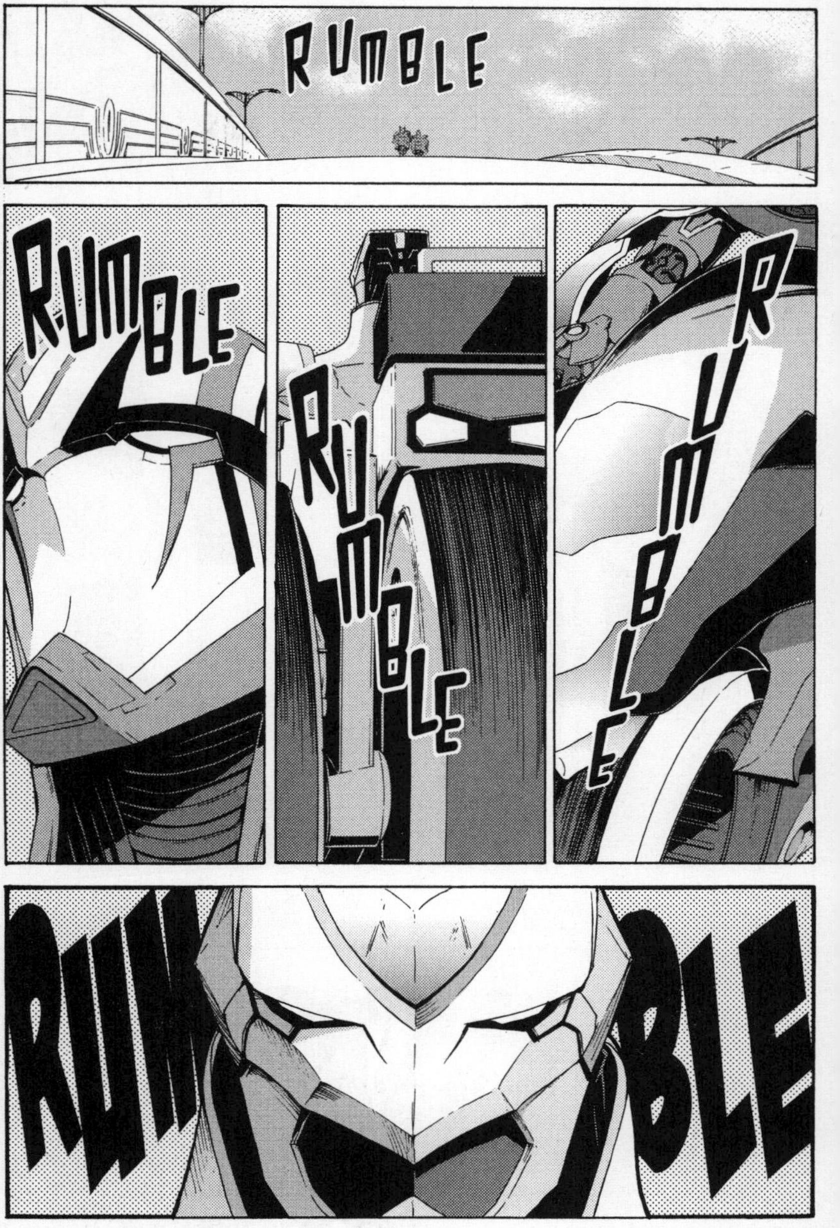
RUMBLE
RUMBLE
RUMBLE
RUMBLE
RUMBLE

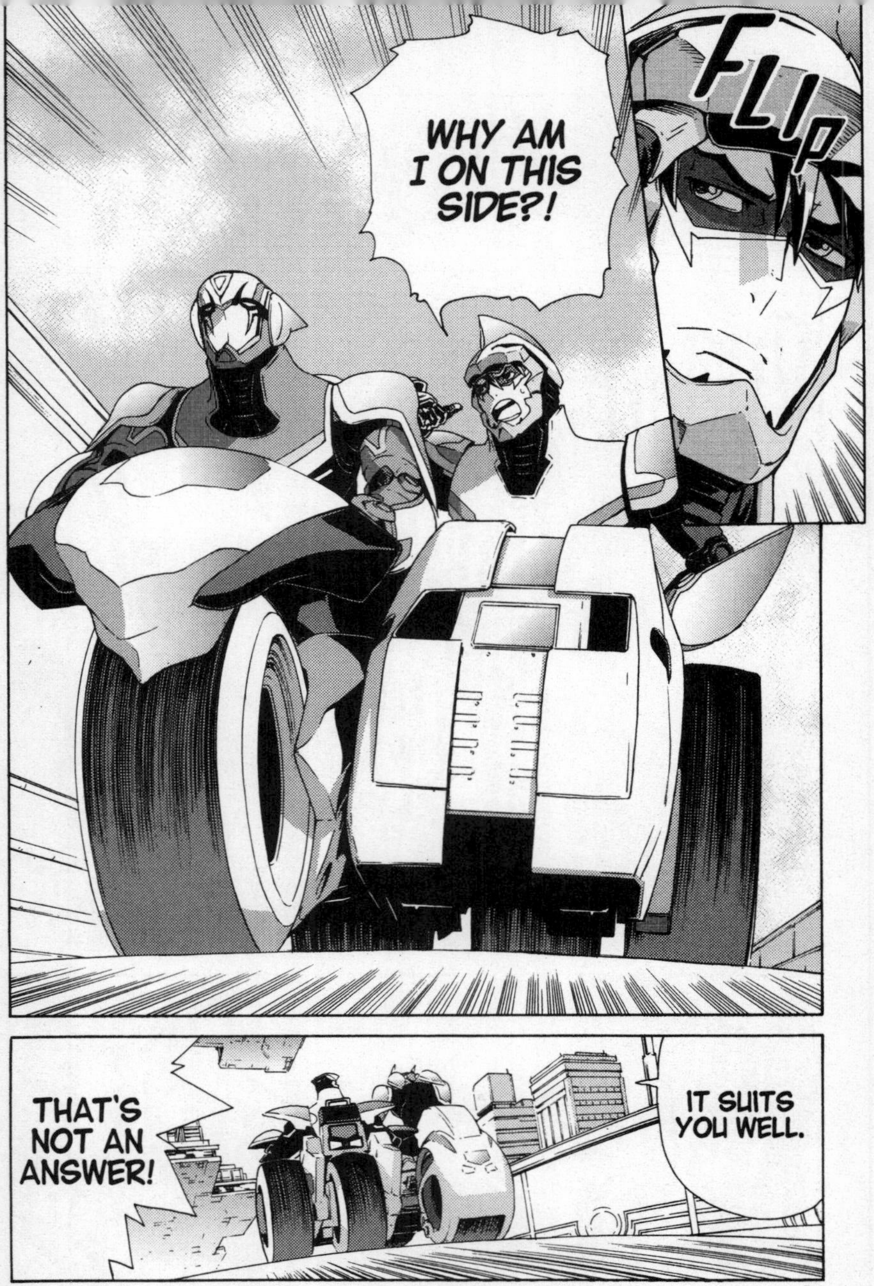
FLIP
WHY AM I ON THIS SIDE?!
IT SUITS YOU WELL.
THAT'S NOT AN ANSWER!

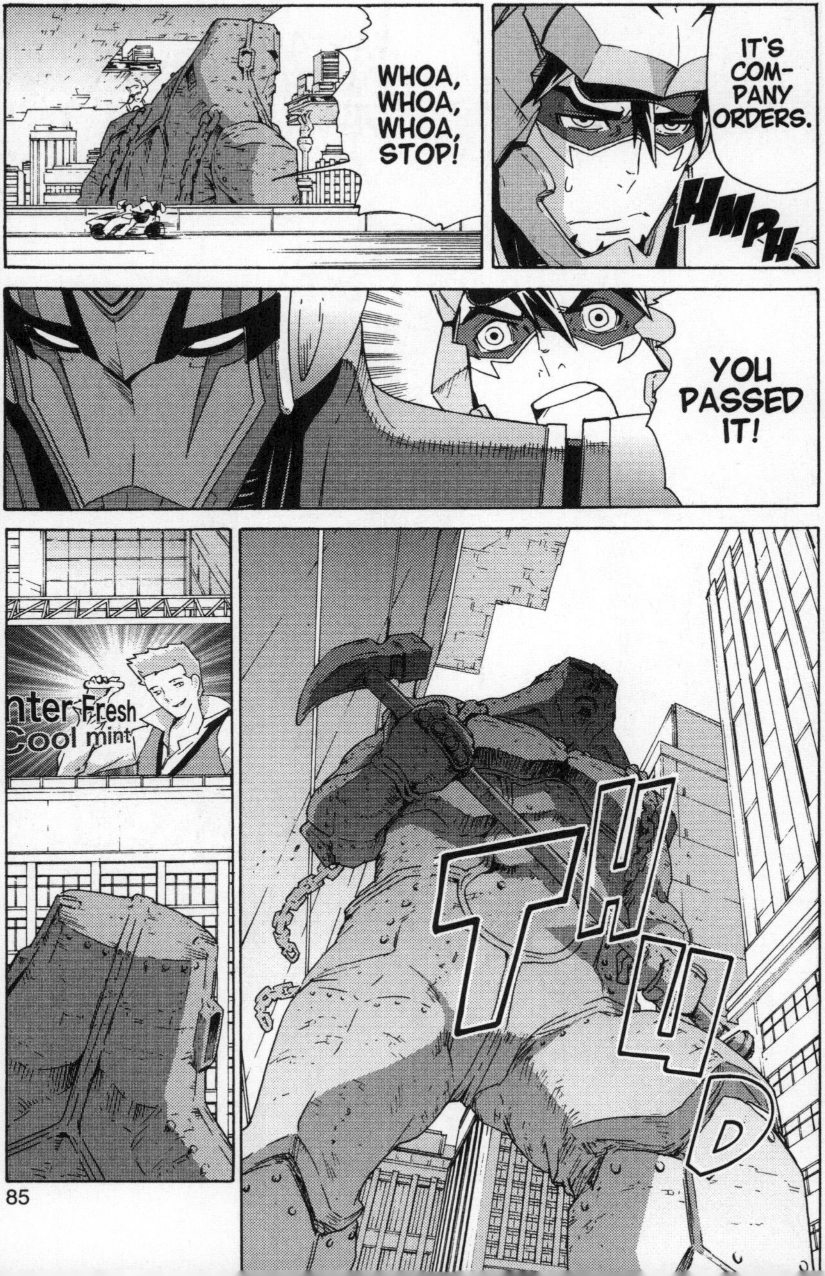
IT'S COMPANY ORDERS.
HMPH
WHOA, WHOA, WHOA, STOP!
YOU PASSED IT!
THUD
nter Fresh
Cool mint

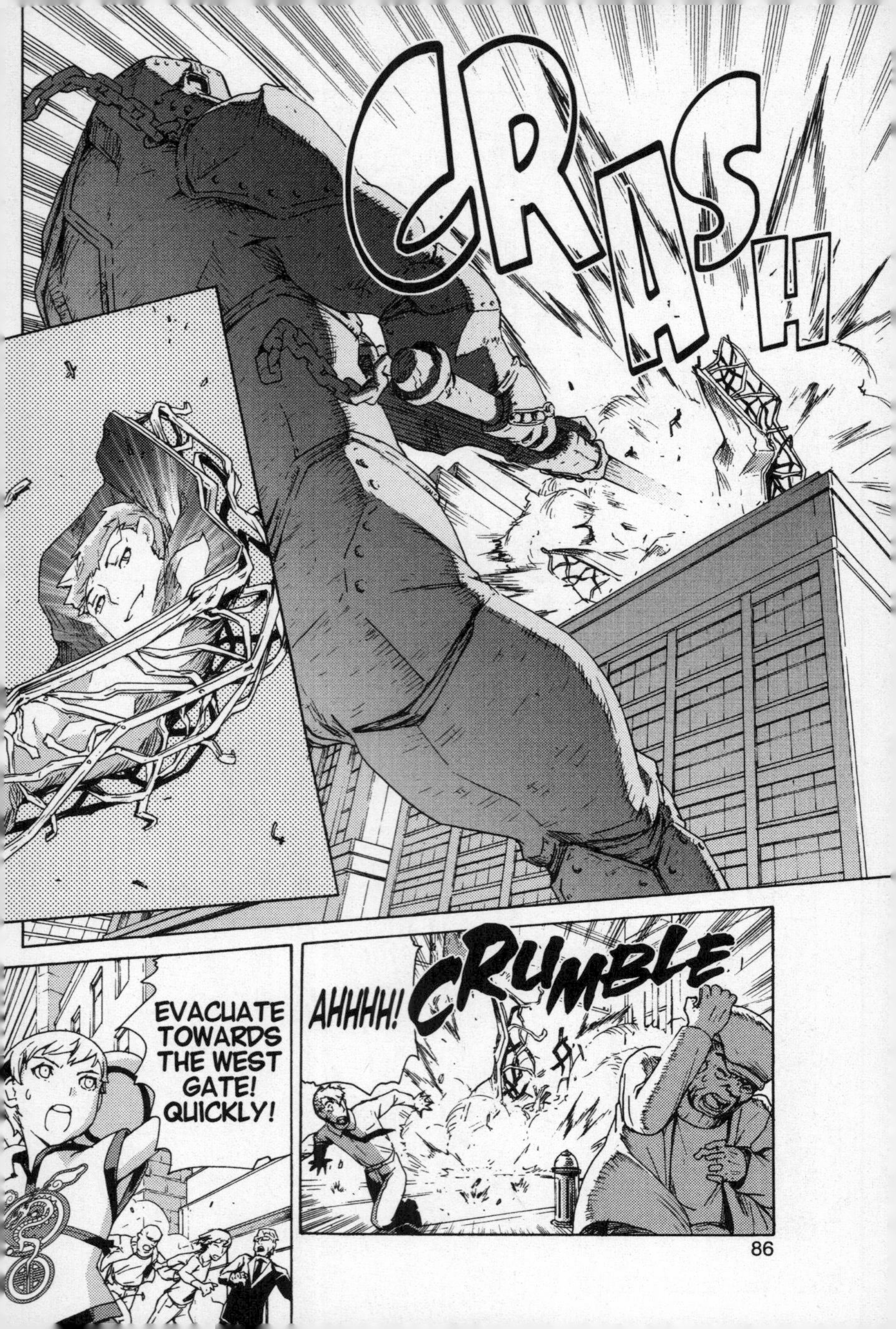
CRASH
AHHHH!
CRUMBLE
EVACUATE TOWARDS THE WEST GATE! QUICKLY!

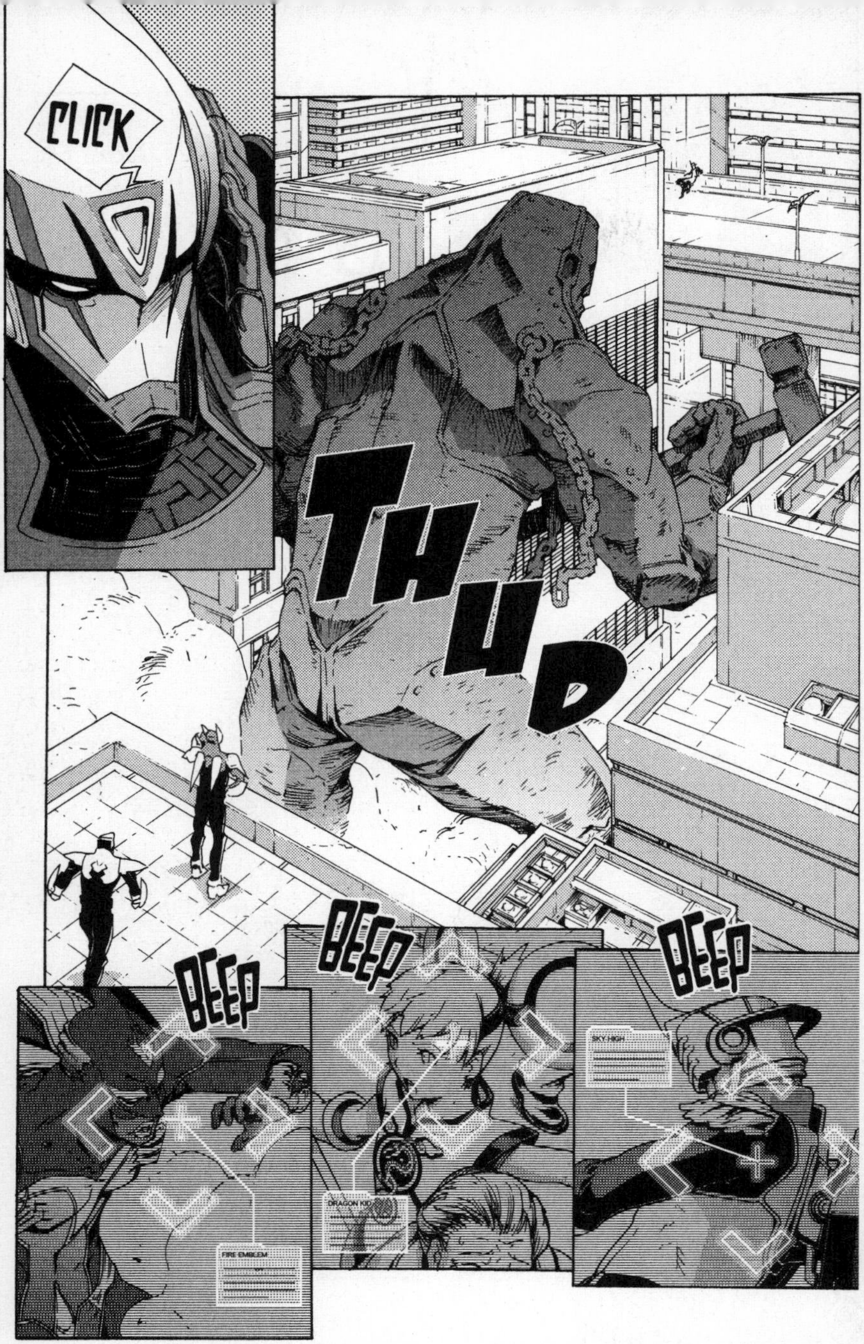
THUD
CLICK
BEEP
SKY HIGH
BEEP
DRAGON KID
BEEP
FIRE EMBLEM

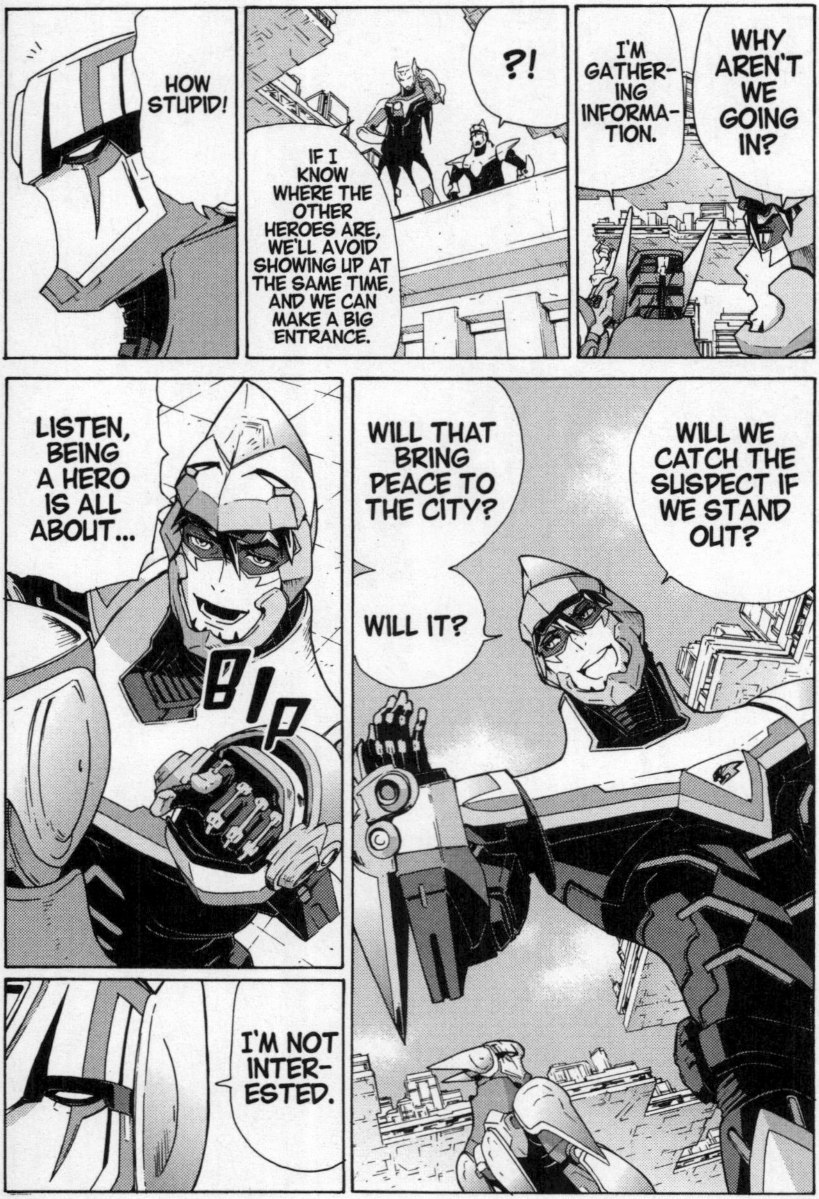
WHY AREN'T WE GOING IN?
I'M GATHERING INFORMATION.
?!
IF I KNOW WHERE THE OTHER HEROES ARE, WE'LL AVOID SHOWING UP AT THE SAME TIME, AND WE CAN MAKE A BIG ENTRANCE.
HOW STUPID!
WILL WE CATCH THE SUSPECT IF WE STAND OUT?
WILL THAT BRING PEACE TO THE CITY?
WILL IT?
LISTEN, BEING A HERO IS ALL ABOUT...
BIP
I'M NOT INTERESTED.

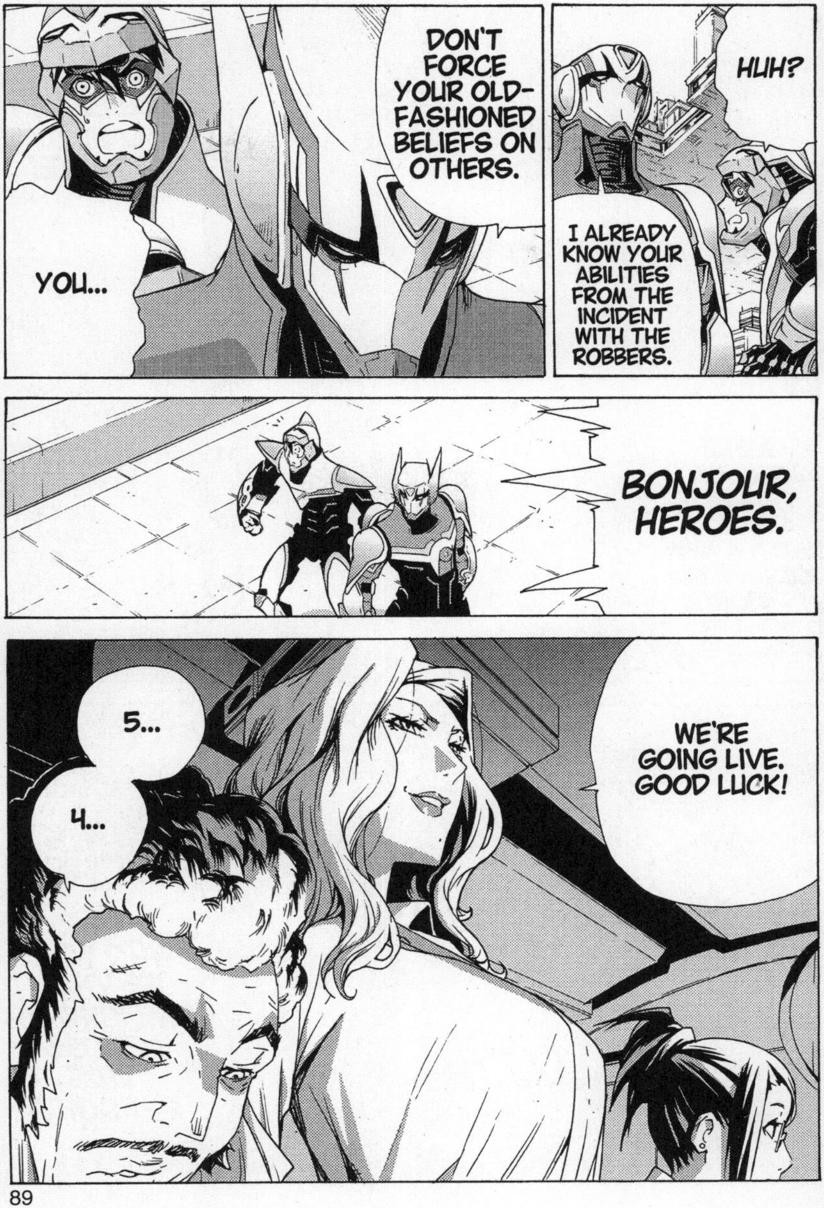
HUH?
I ALREADY KNOW YOUR ABILITIES FROM THE INCIDENT WITH THE ROBBERS.
DON'T FORCE YOUR OLD-FASHIONED BELIEFS ON OTHERS.
YOU...
BONJOUR, HEROES.
WE'RE GOING LIVE. GOOD LUCK!
5...
4...

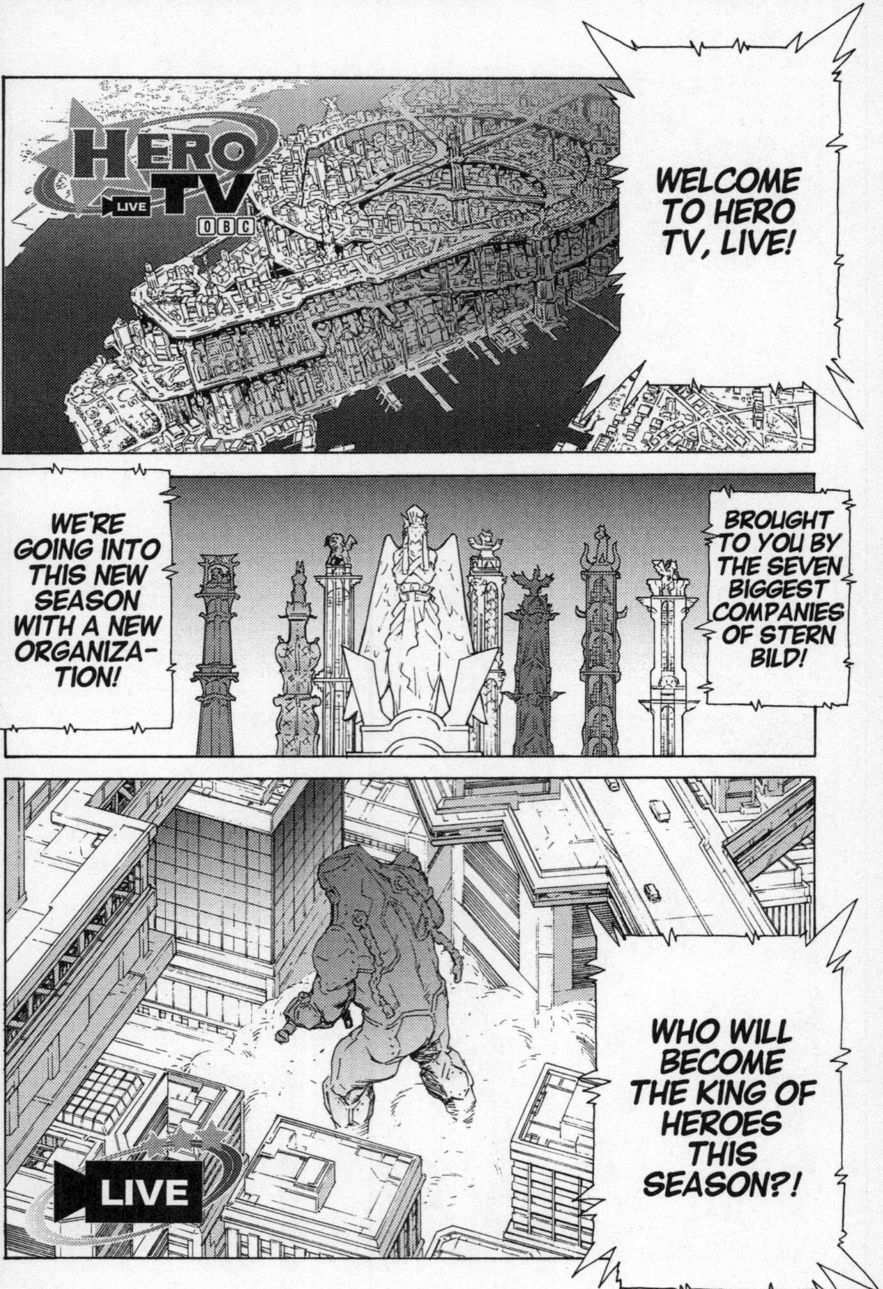
WELCOME TO HERO TV, LIVE!
HERO TV LIVE OBC
BROUGHT TO YOU BY THE SEVEN BIGGEST COMPANIES OF STERN BILD!
WE'RE GOING INTO THIS NEW SEASON WITH A NEW ORGANIZA-TION!
WHO WILL BECOME THE KING OF HEROES THIS SEASON?!
LIVE

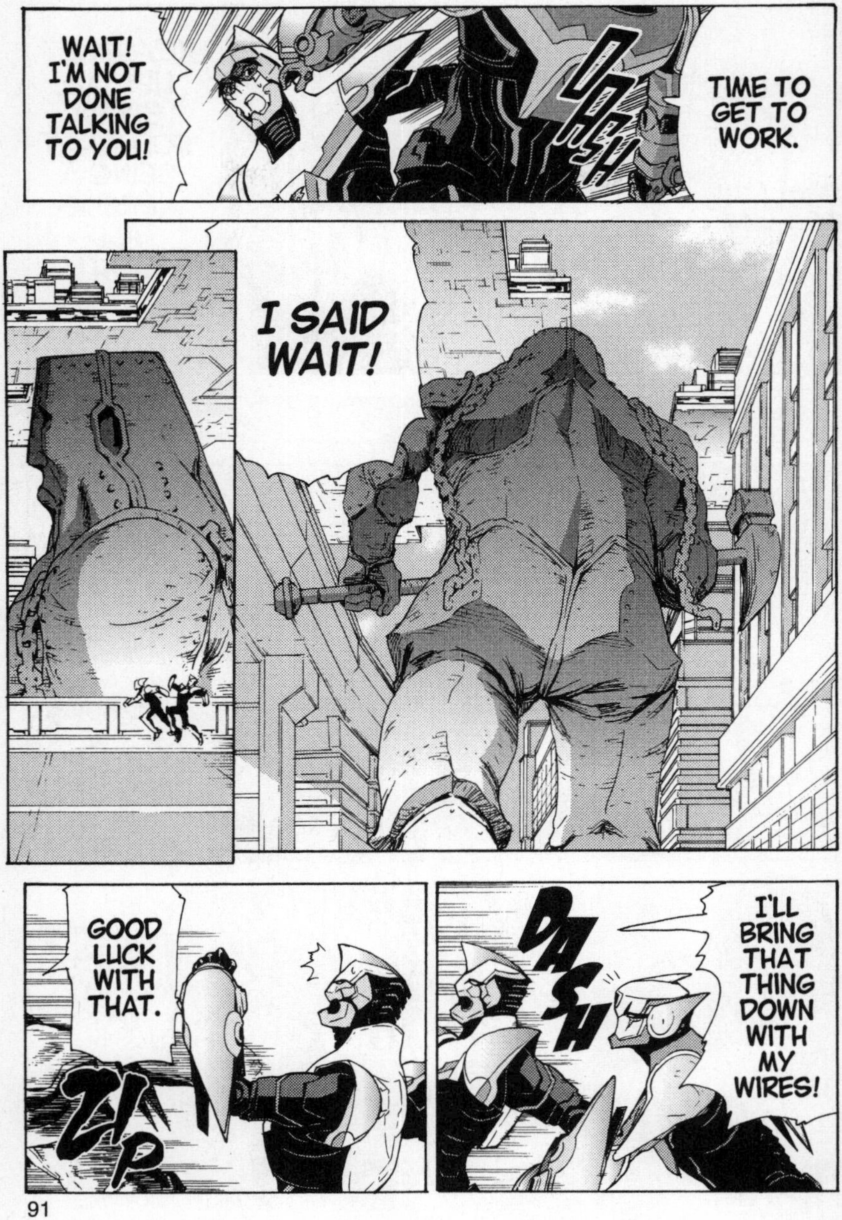
TIME TO GET TO WORK.
DASH
WAIT! I'M NOT DONE TALKING TO YOU!
I SAID WAIT!
I'LL BRING THAT THING DOWN WITH MY WIRES!
DASH
GOOD LUCK WITH THAT.
ZIP

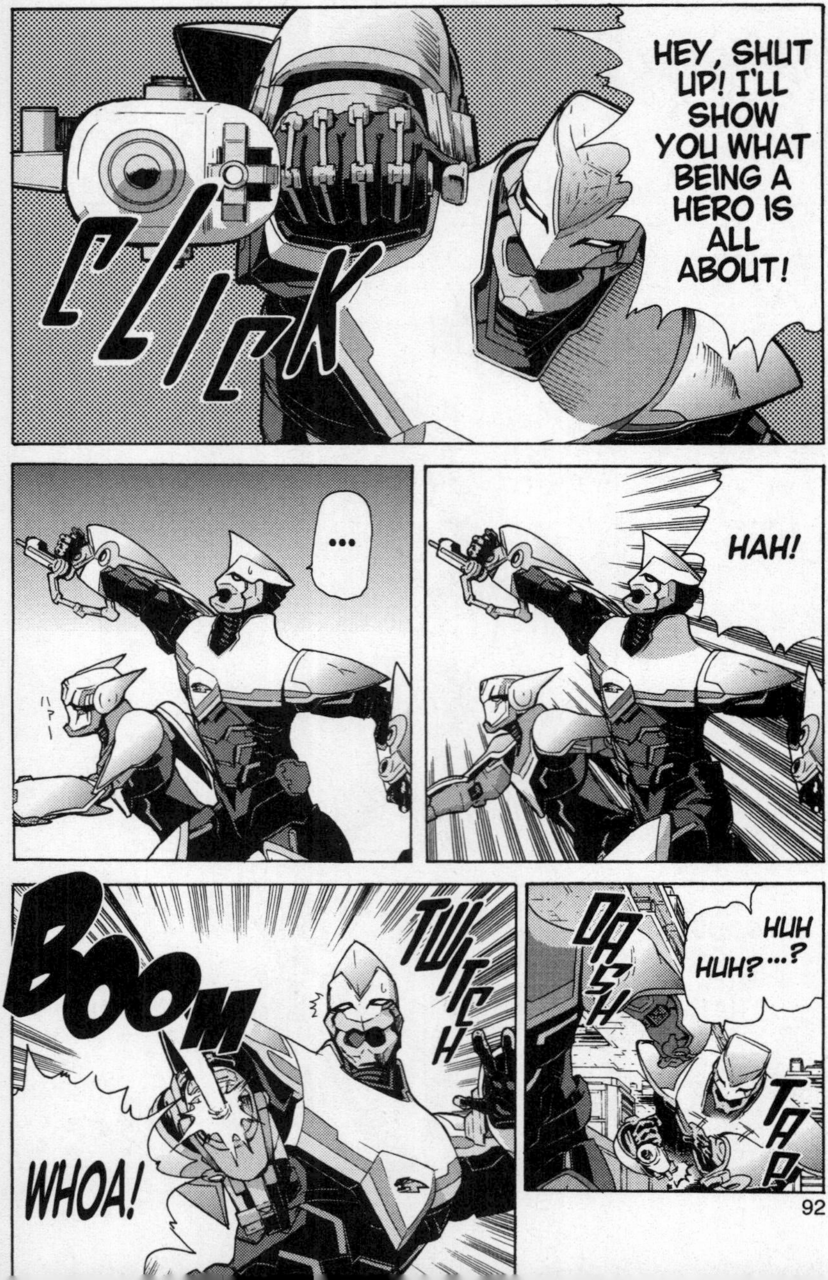
HEY, SHUT UP! I'LL SHOW YOU WHAT BEING A HERO IS ALL ABOUT!
CLICK
HAH!
...
HUH HUH?...?
DASH
TAP
TWITCH
BOOM
WHOA!

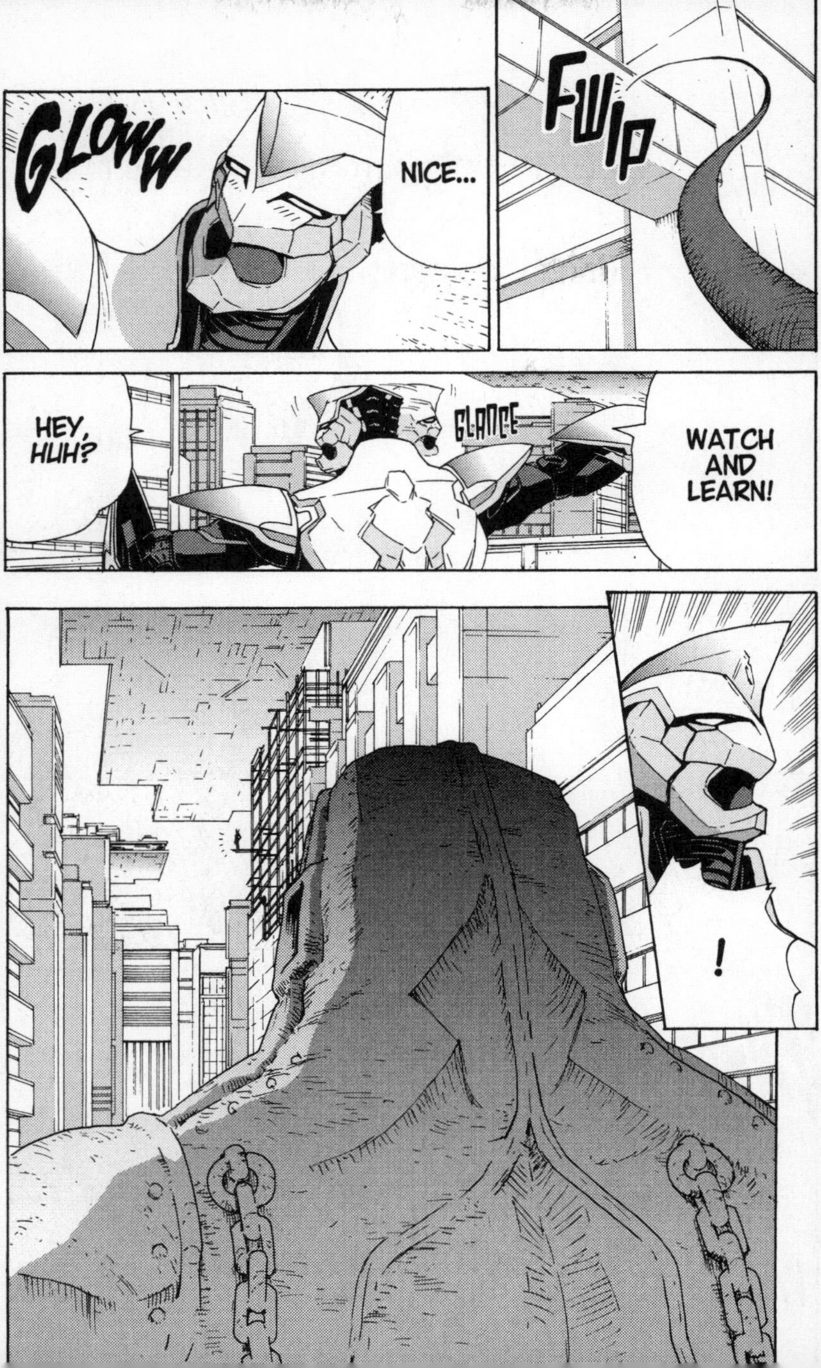
FWIP
GLOWW
NICE...
WATCH AND LEARN!
GLANCE
HEY, HUH?
!

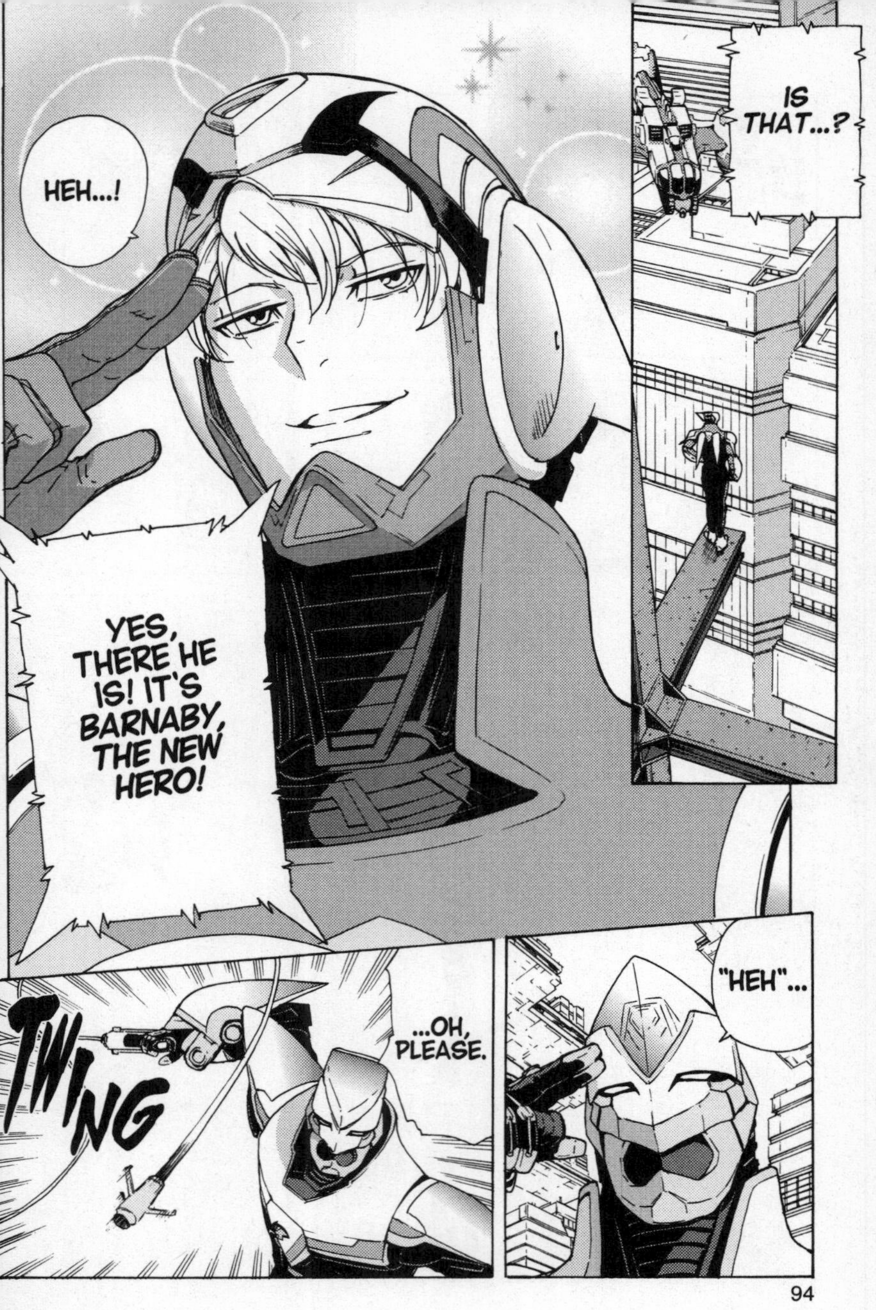
IS THAT...?
HEH...!
YES, THERE HE IS! IT'S BARNABY, THE NEW HERO!
"HEH"...
...OH, PLEASE.
TWING

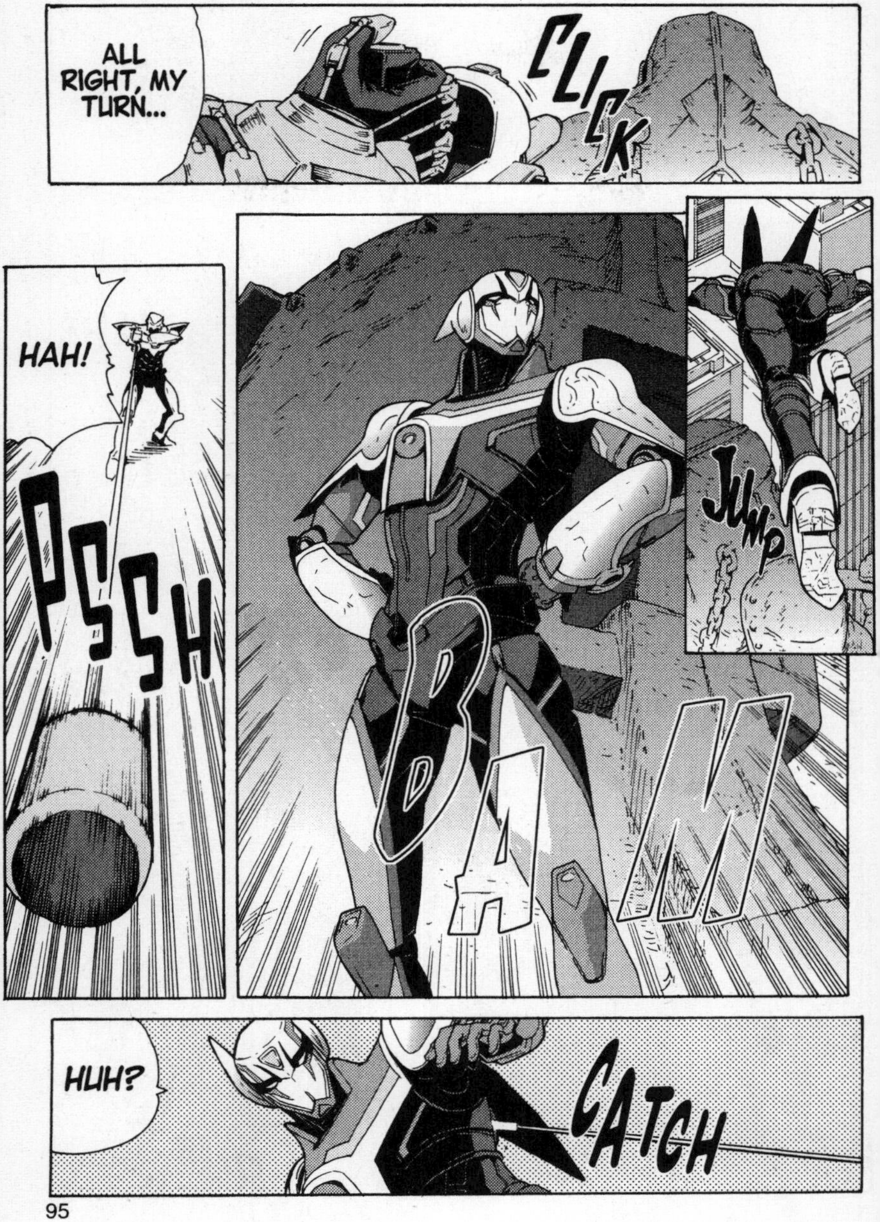
CLICK
ALL RIGHT, MY TURN...
JUMP
BAM
HAH!
PSSH
CATCH
HUH?

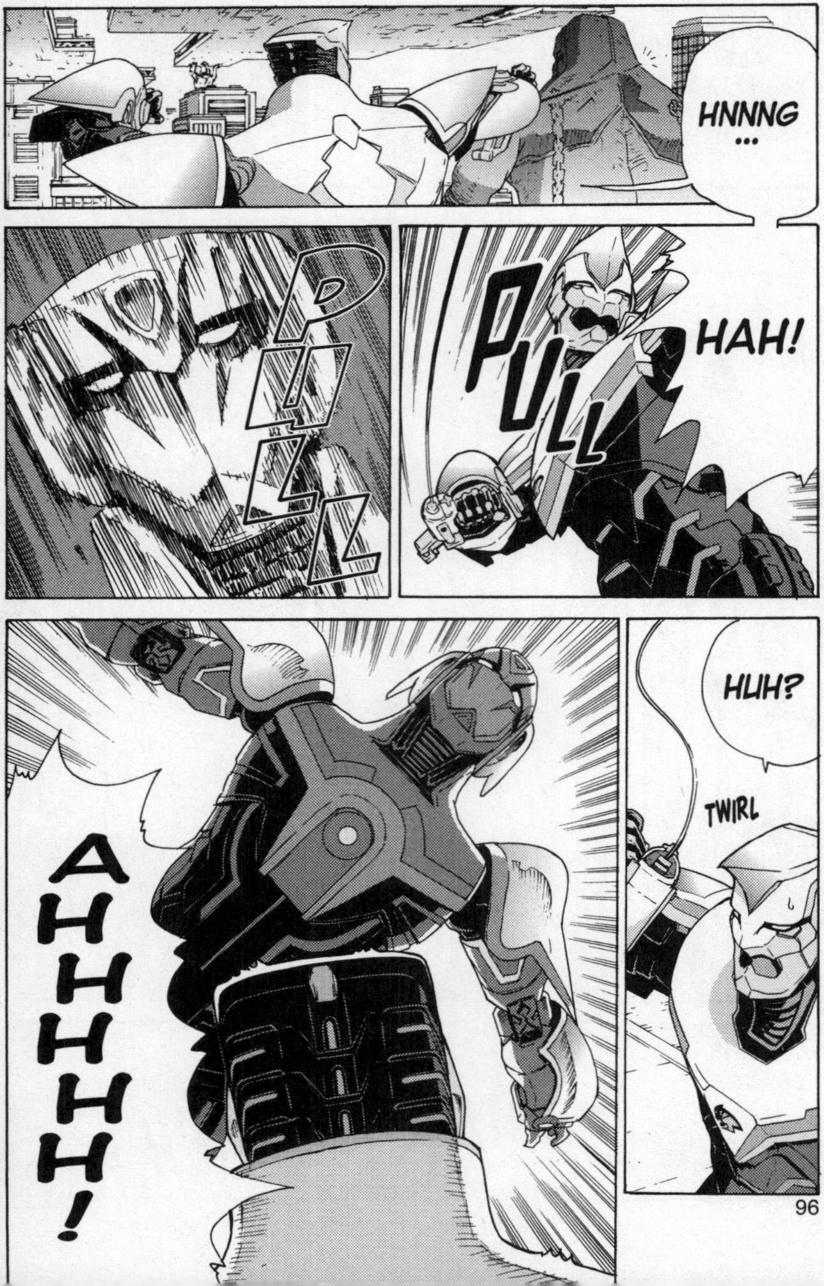
HNNNG ...
PULL
HAH!
PULL
HUH?
TWIRL
AHHHHH!

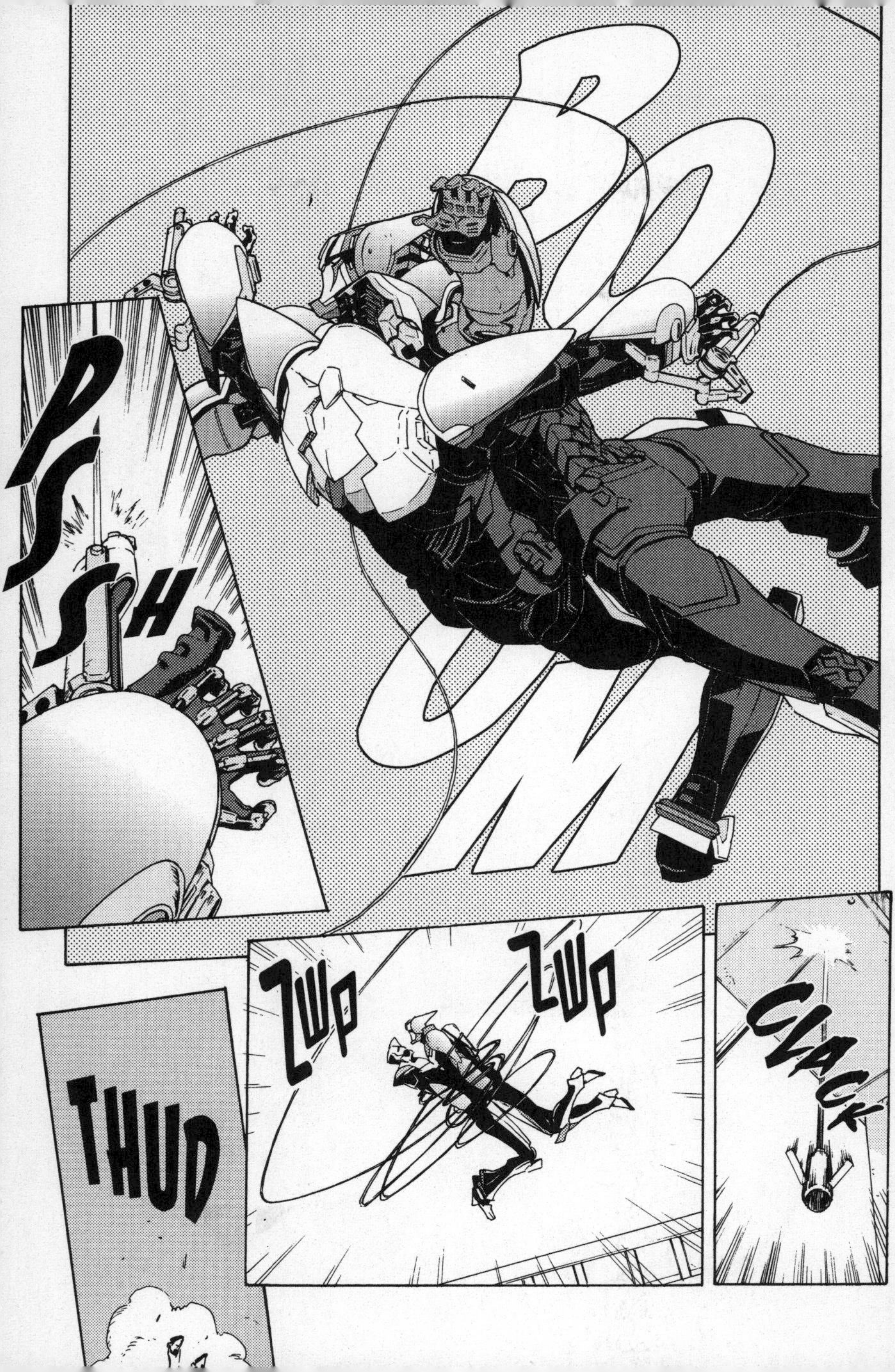
BOOM
PSSH
CLACK
ZWP
ZWP
THUD

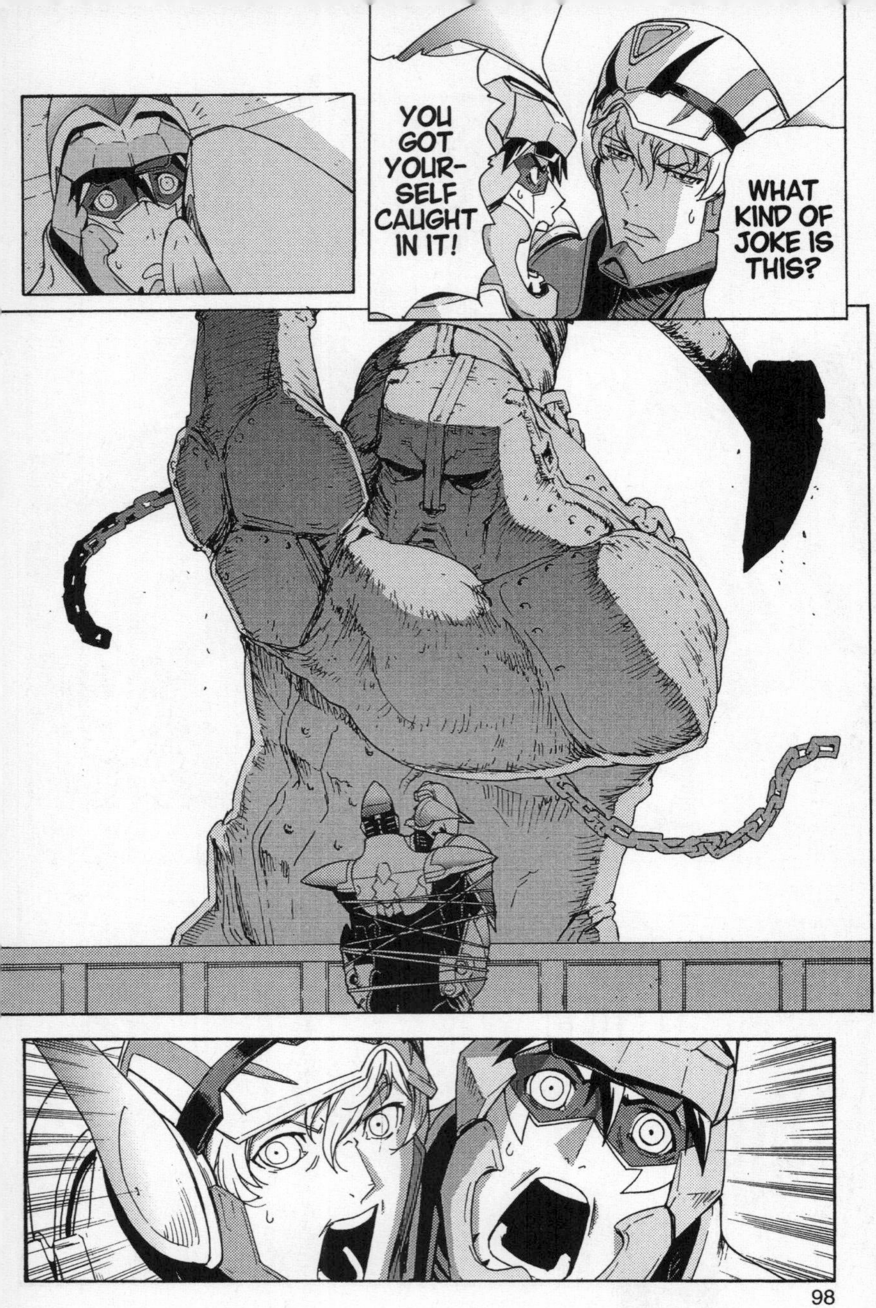
WHAT KIND OF JOKE IS THIS?
YOU GOT YOURSELF CAUGHT IN IT!

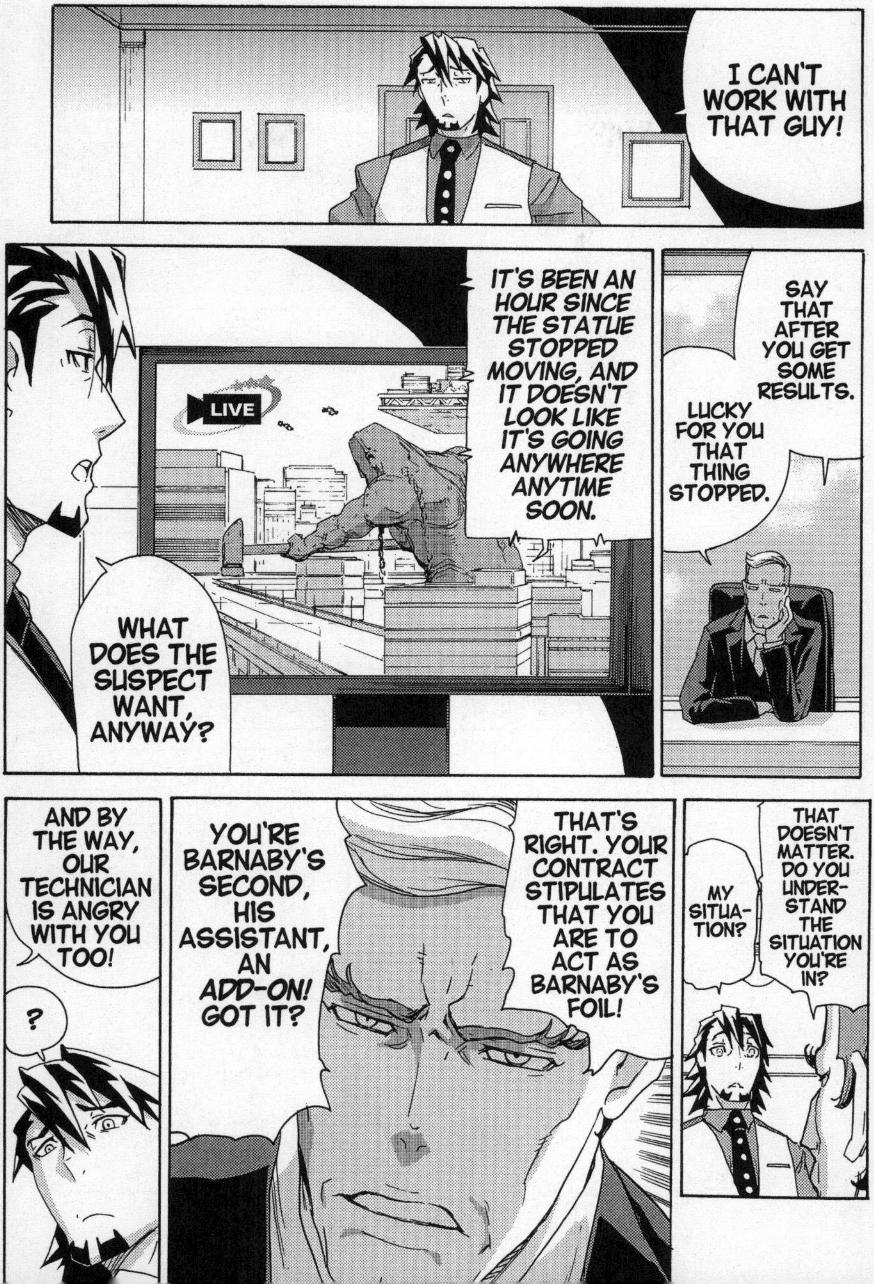
I CAN'T WORK WITH THAT GUY!
SAY THAT AFTER YOU GET SOME RESULTS.
LUCKY FOR YOU THAT THING STOPPED.
LIVE
IT'S BEEN AN HOUR SINCE THE STATUE STOPPED MOVING, AND IT DOESN'T LOOK LIKE IT'S GOING ANYWHERE ANYTIME SOON.
WHAT DOES THE SUSPECT WANT, ANYWAY?
THAT DOESN'T MATTER. DO YOU UNDER-STAND THE SITUATION YOU'RE IN?
MY SITUA-TION?
THAT'S RIGHT. YOUR CONTRACT STIPULATES THAT YOU ARE TO ACT AS BARNABY'S FOIL!
YOU'RE BARNABY'S SECOND, HIS ASSISTANT, AN ADD-ON! GOT IT?
AND BY THE WAY, OUR TECHNICIAN IS ANGRY WITH YOU TOO!
?

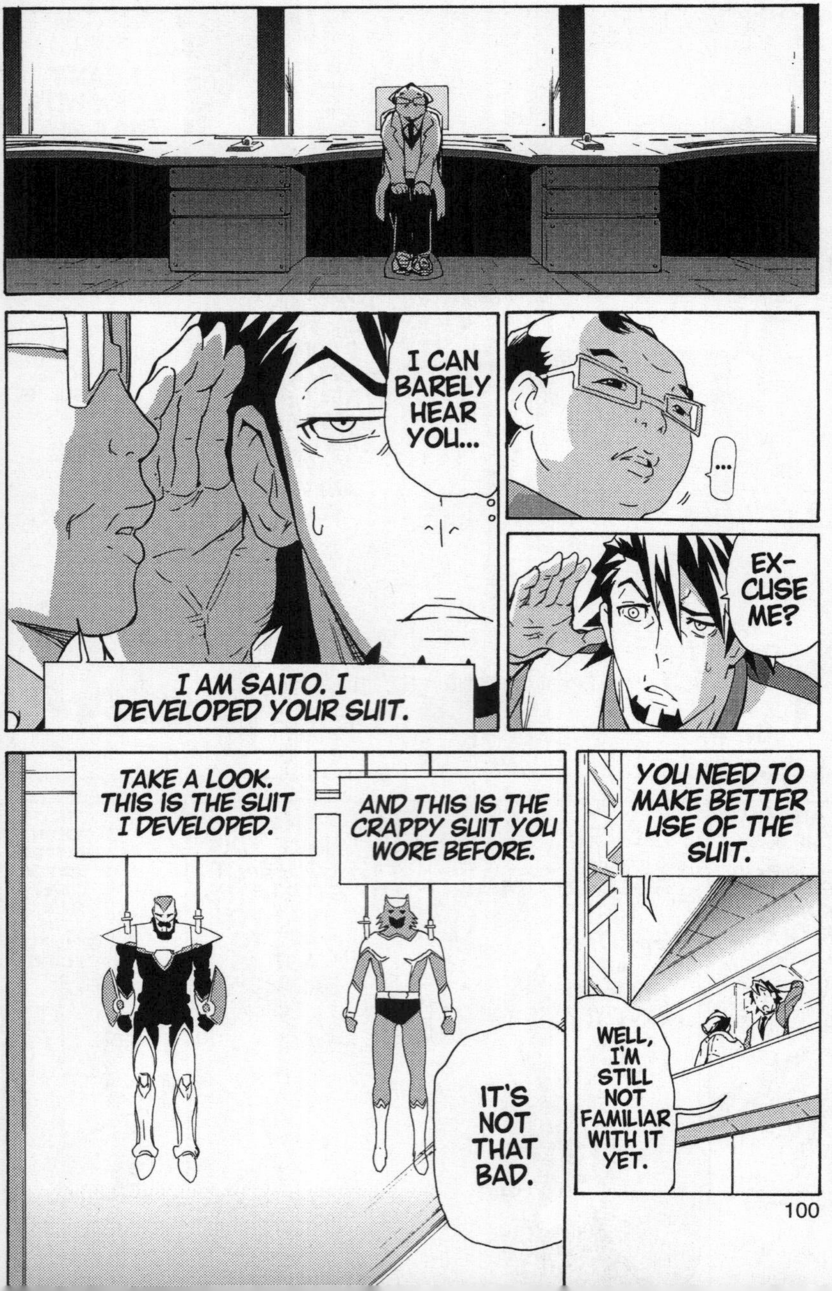
...
EX-CUSE ME?
I CAN BARELY HEAR YOU...
I AM SAITO. I DEVELOPED YOUR SUIT.
YOU NEED TO MAKE BETTER USE OF THE SUIT.
WELL, I'M STILL NOT FAMILIAR WITH IT YET.
TAKE A LOOK. THIS IS THE SUIT I DEVELOPED.
AND THIS IS THE CRAPPY SUIT YOU WORE BEFORE.
IT'S NOT THAT BAD.

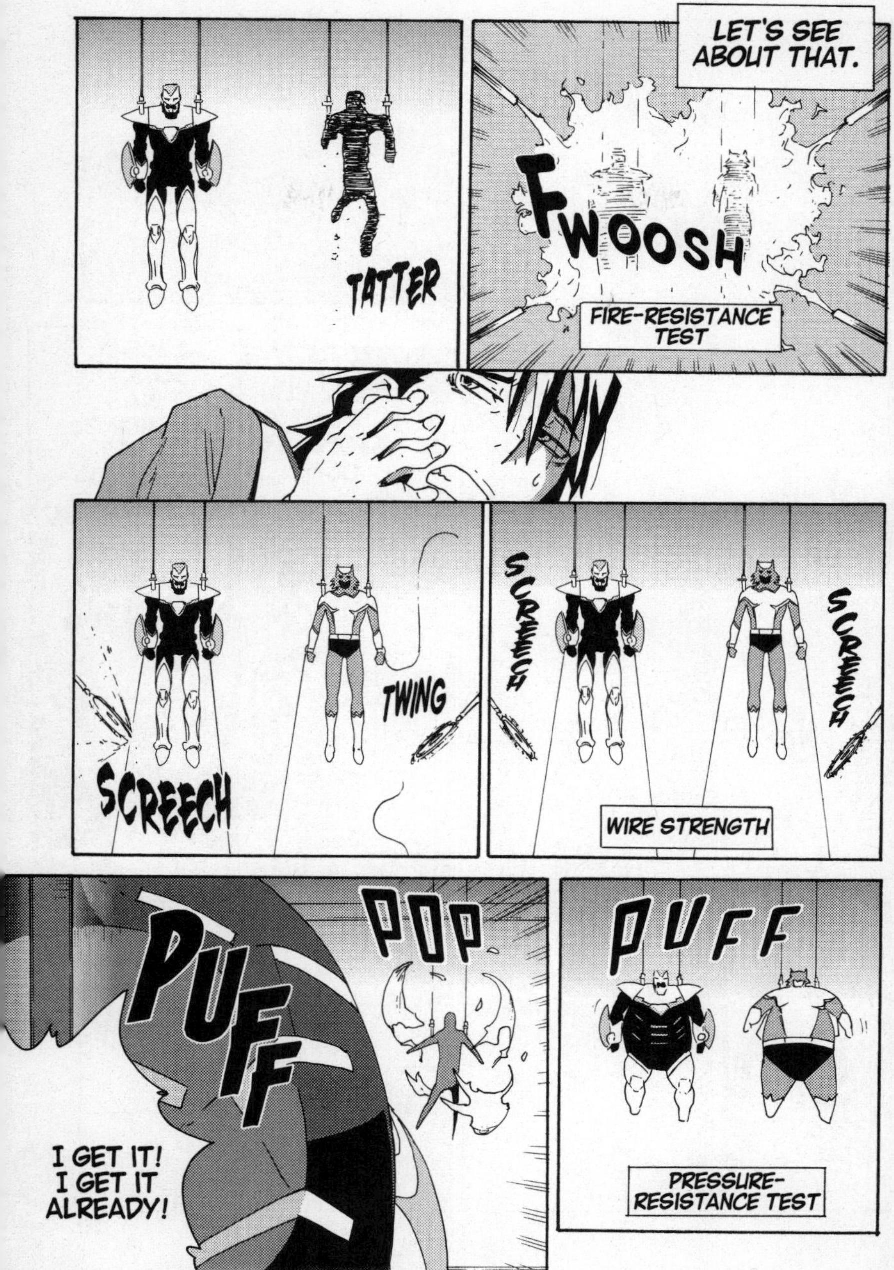
LET'S SEE ABOUT THAT.
FWOOSH
FIRE-RESISTANCE TEST
TATTER
SCREECH
SCREECH
WIRE STRENGTH
TWING
SCREECH
PUFF
PRESSURE-RESISTANCE TEST
POP
PUFF
I GET IT! I GET IT ALREADY!

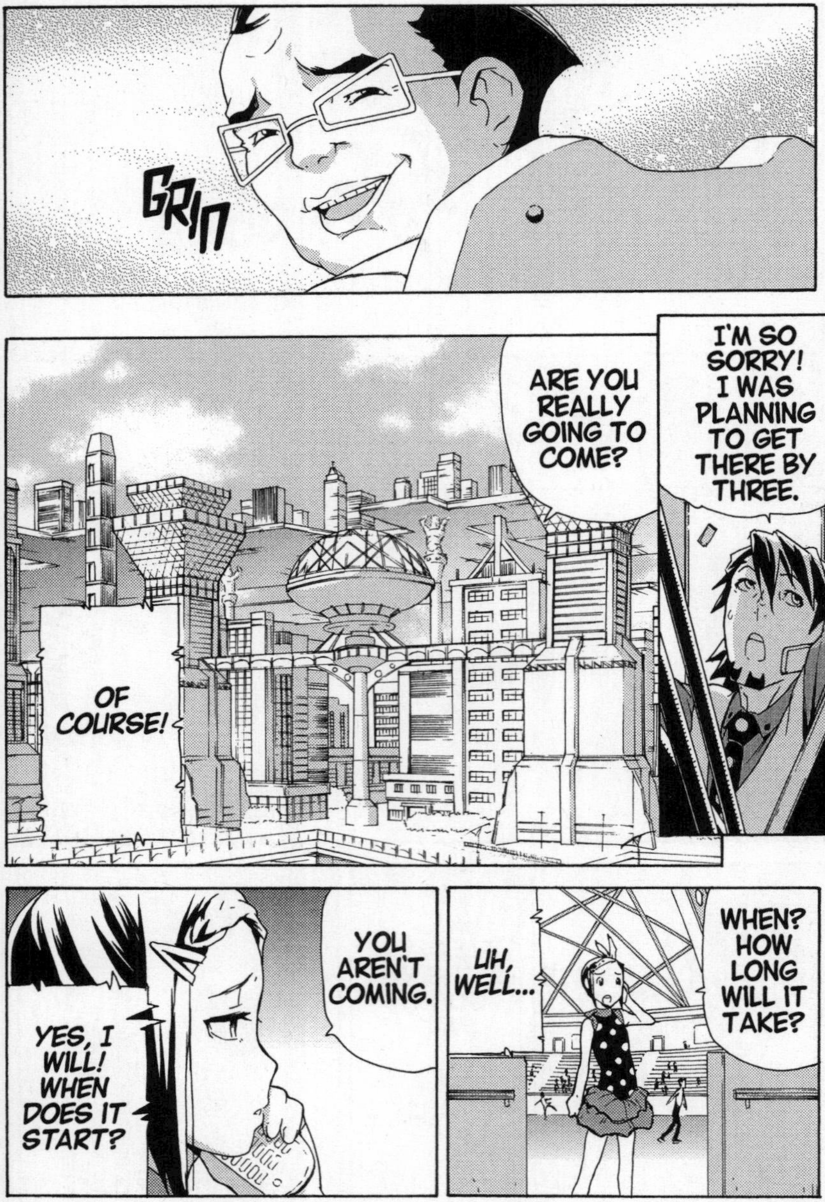
GRIN
I'M SO SORRY! I WAS PLANNING TO GET THERE BY THREE.
ARE YOU REALLY GOING TO COME?
OF COURSE!
WHEN? HOW LONG WILL IT TAKE?
UH, WELL...
YOU AREN'T COMING.
YES, I WILL! WHEN DOES IT START?

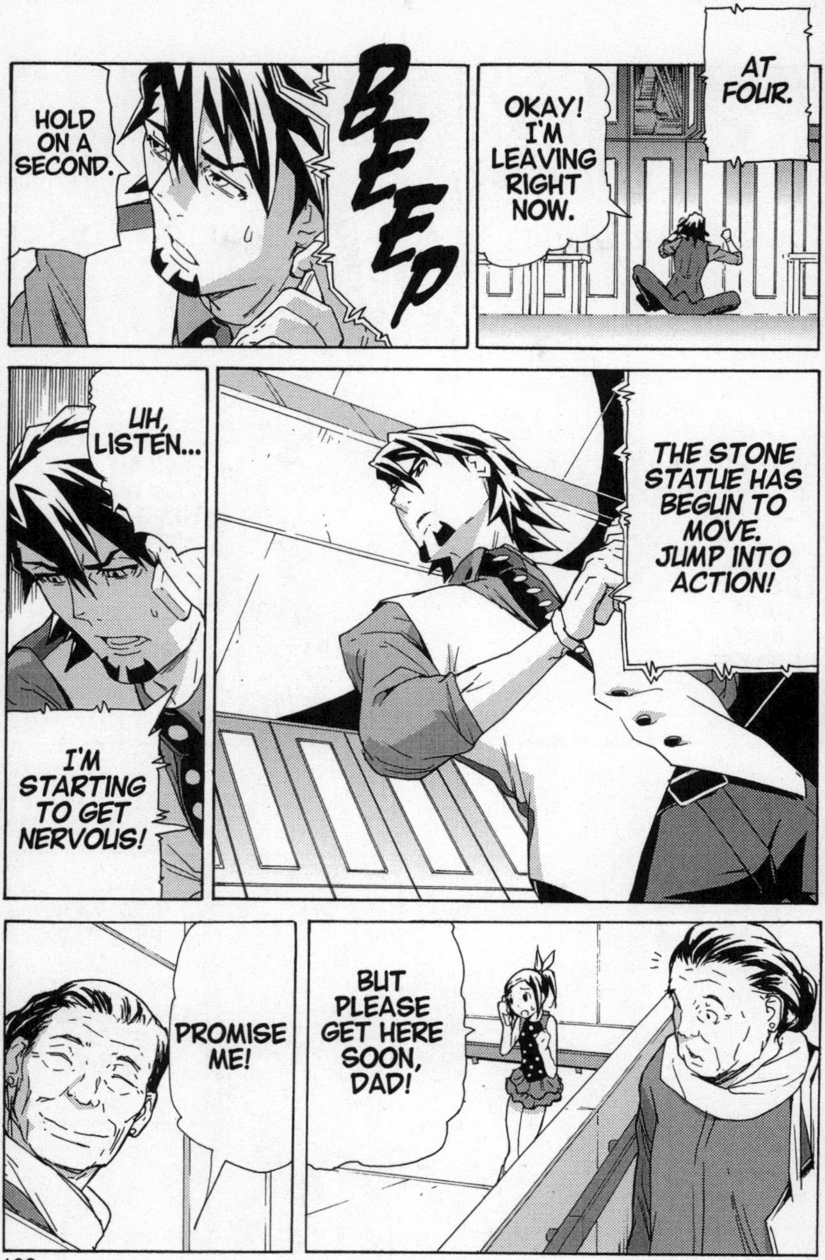
AT FOUR.
OKAY! I'M LEAVING RIGHT NOW.
BEEP
HOLD ON A SECOND.
THE STONE STATUE HAS BEGUN TO MOVE. JUMP INTO ACTION!
UH, LISTEN...
I'M STARTING TO GET NERVOUS!
BUT PLEASE GET HERE SOON, DAD!
PROMISE ME!

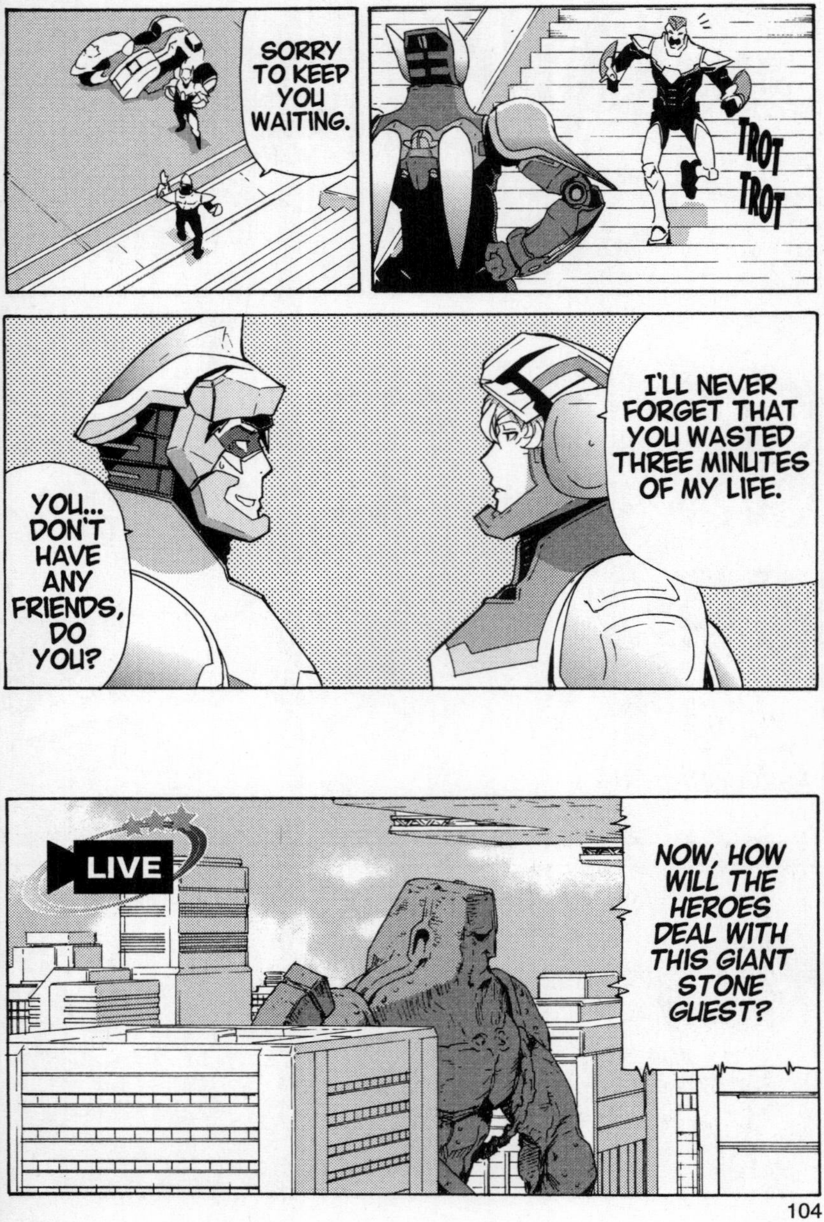
TROT
TROT
SORRY TO KEEP YOU WAITING.
I'LL NEVER FORGET THAT YOU WASTED THREE MINUTES OF MY LIFE.
YOU... DON'T HAVE ANY FRIENDS, DO YOU?
NOW, HOW WILL THE HEROES DEAL WITH THIS GIANT STONE GUEST?
LIVE

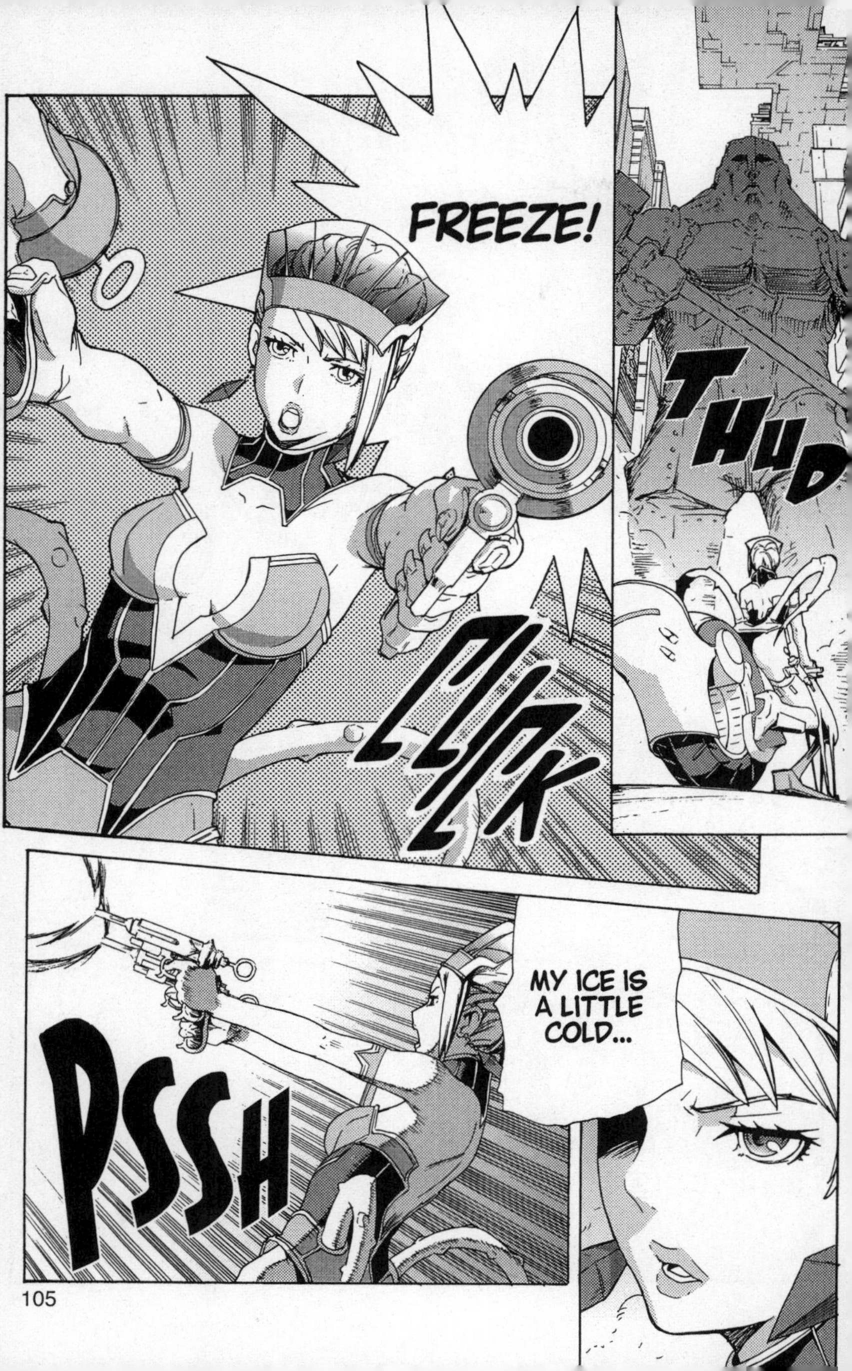
THUD
FREEZE!
CLICK
MY ICE IS A LITTLE COLD...
PSSH

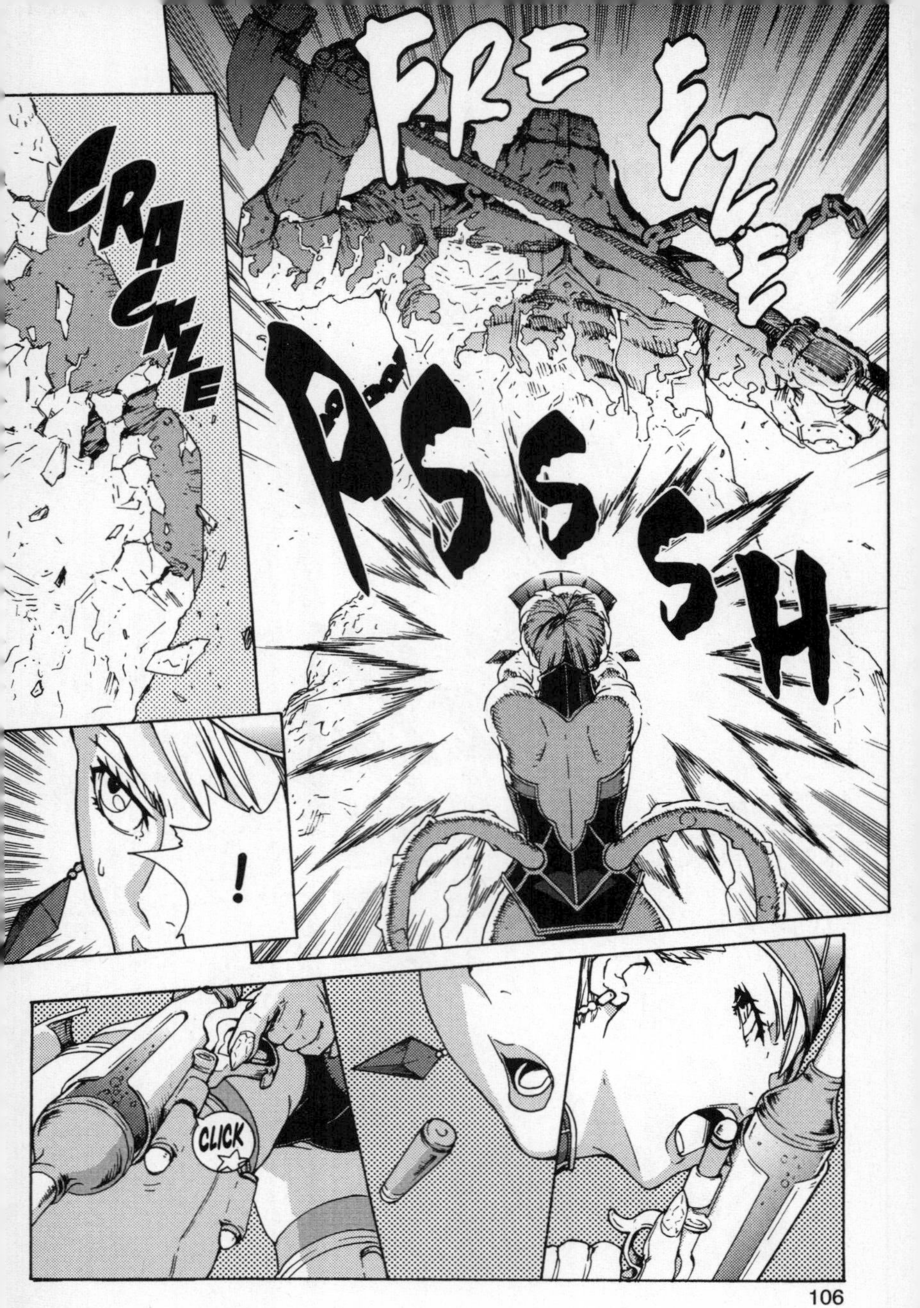
FREEZE
PSSSH
CRACKLE
!
CLICK

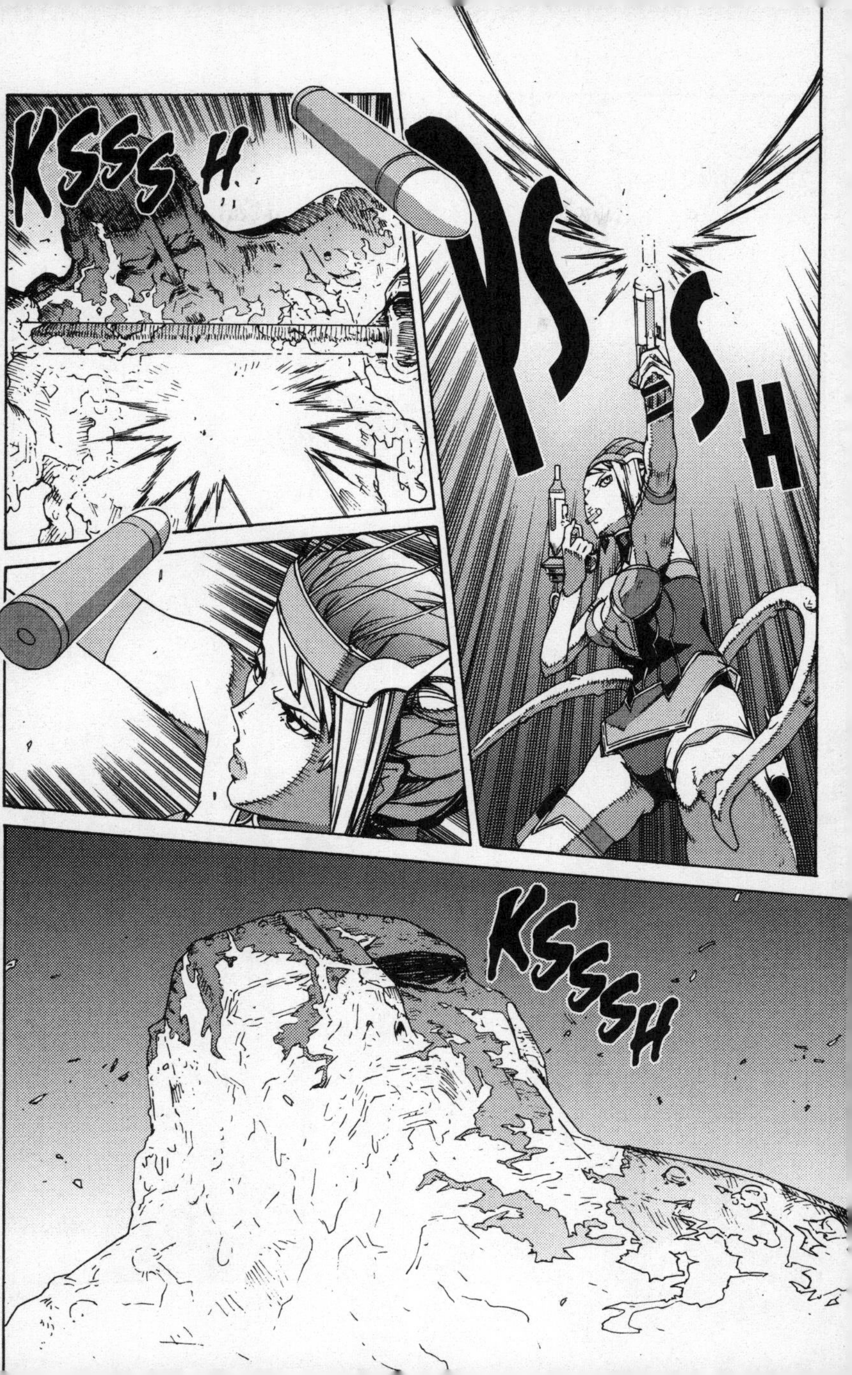
YSSSH
KSSSH
KSSSH

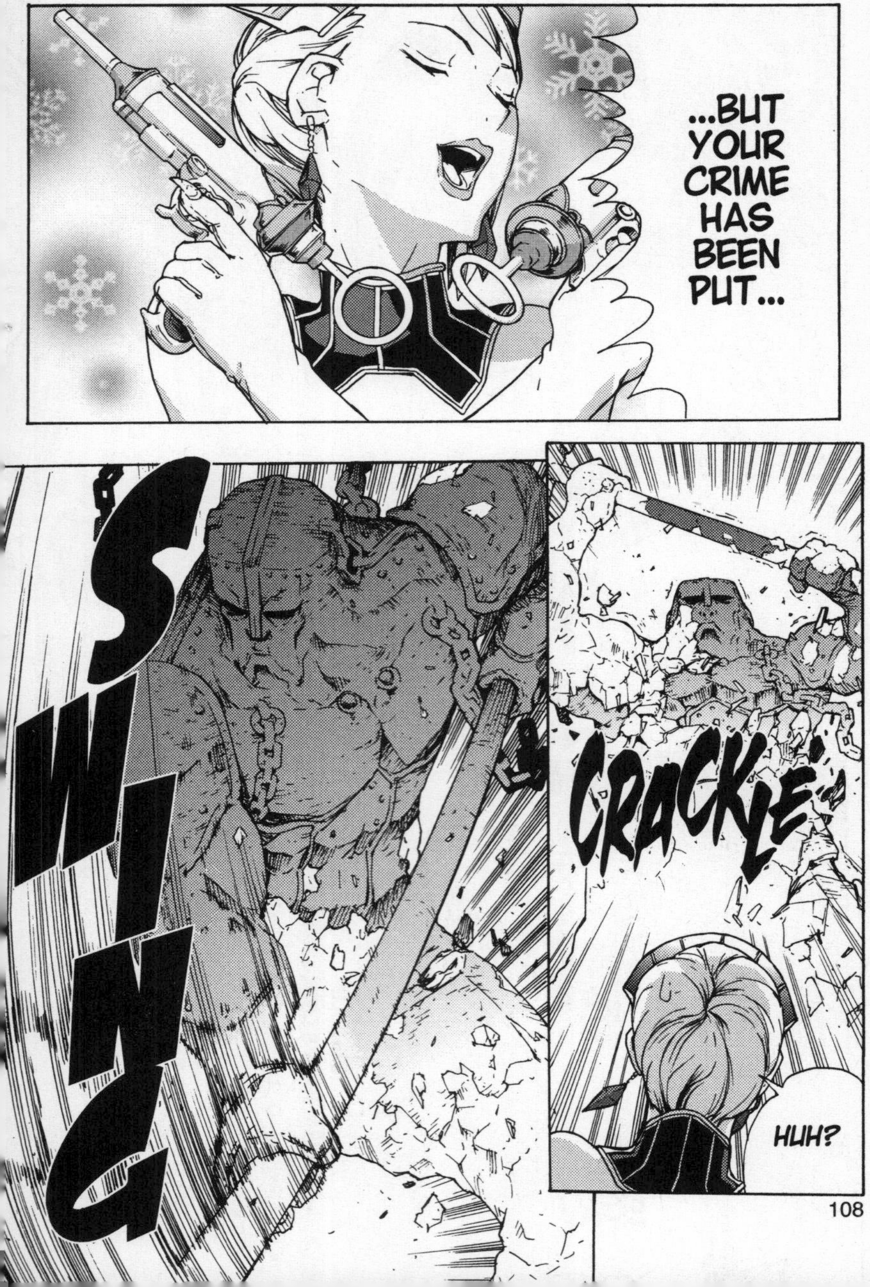
...BUT YOUR CRIME HAS BEEN PUT...
CRACKLE
HUH?
SWING

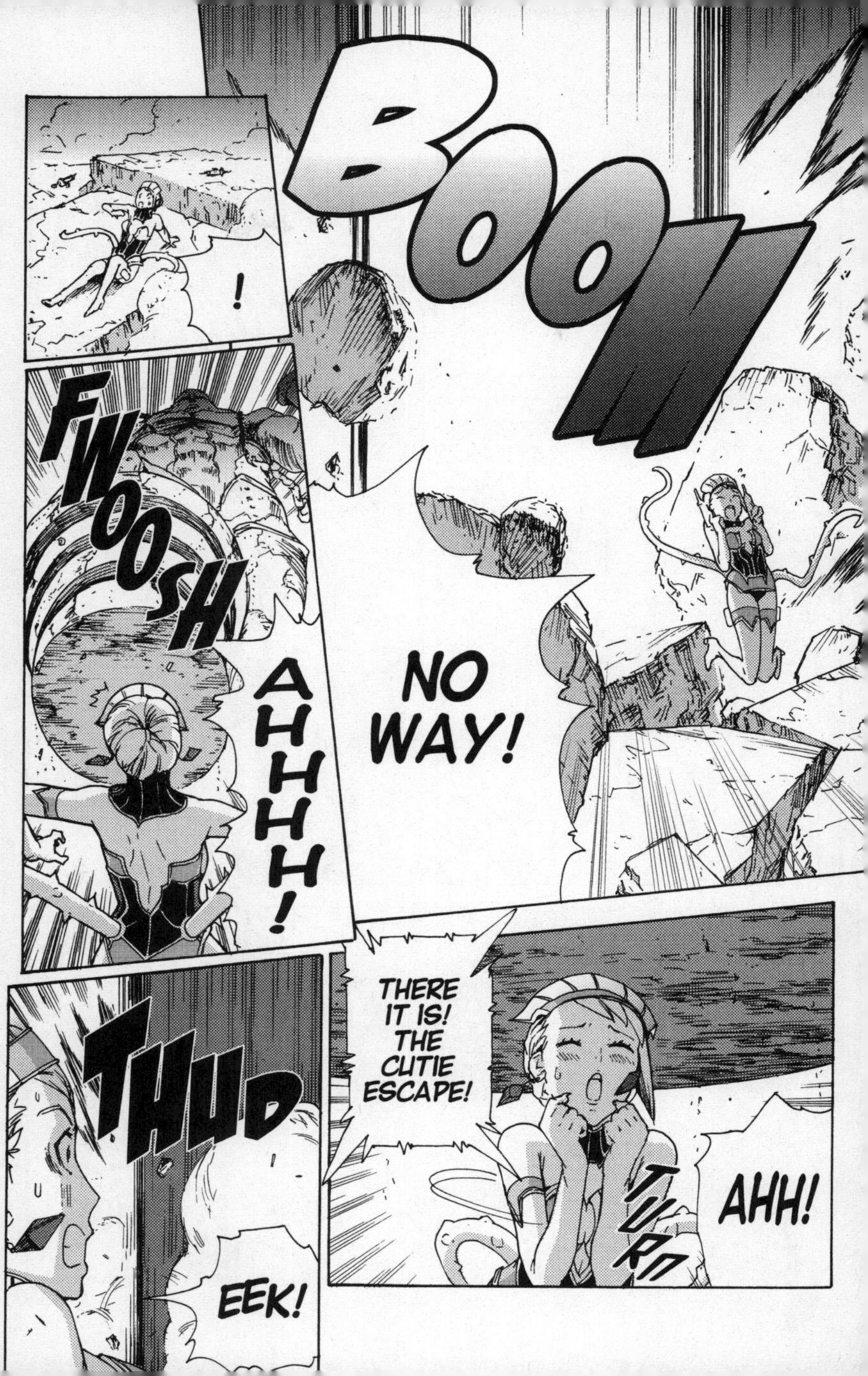
BOOM
NO WAY!
!
FWOOSH
AHHHH!
THERE IT IS! THE CUTIE ESCAPE!
AHH!
TURN
THUD
EEK!

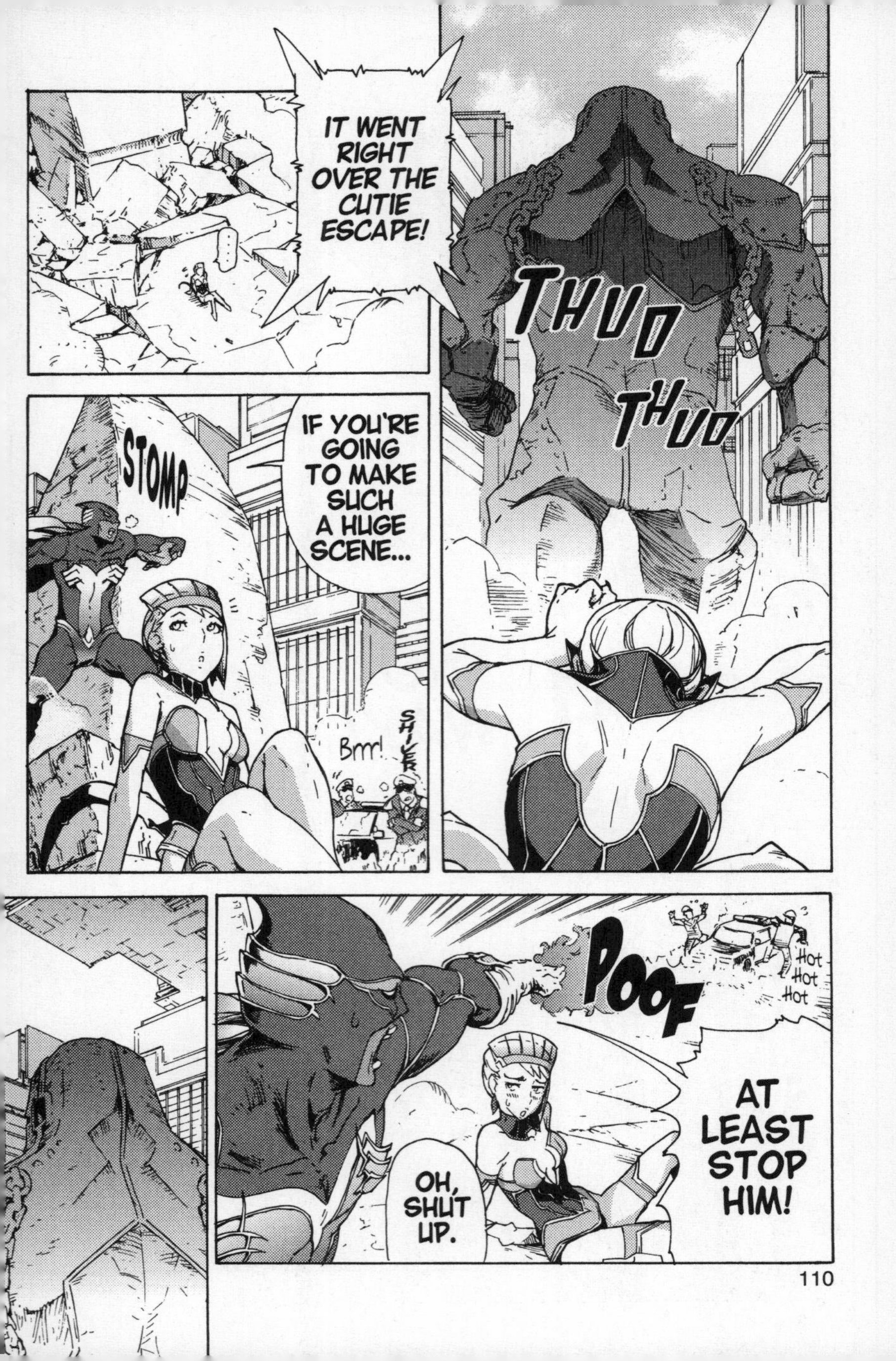
THUD
THUD
IT WENT RIGHT OVER THE CUTIE ESCAPE!
...
IF YOU'RE GOING TO MAKE SUCH A HUGE SCENE...
STOMP
Brrr!
SHIVER
POOF
Hot Hot Hot
AT LEAST STOP HIM!
OH, SHUT UP.

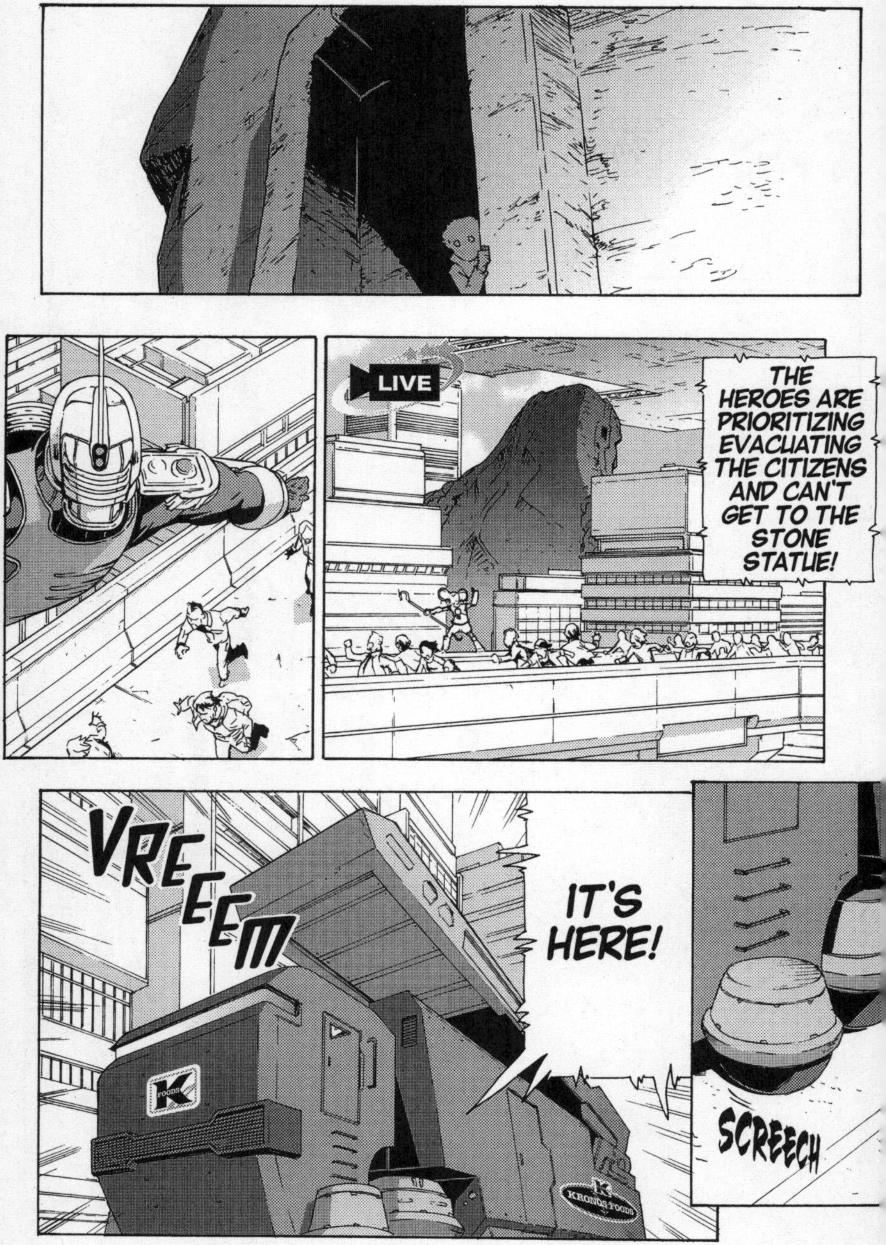
LIVE
THE HEROES ARE PRIORITIZING EVACUATING THE CITIZENS AND CAN'T GET TO THE STONE STATUE!
SCREECH
VREEEM
IT'S HERE!
K FOODS
KRONOS FOODS

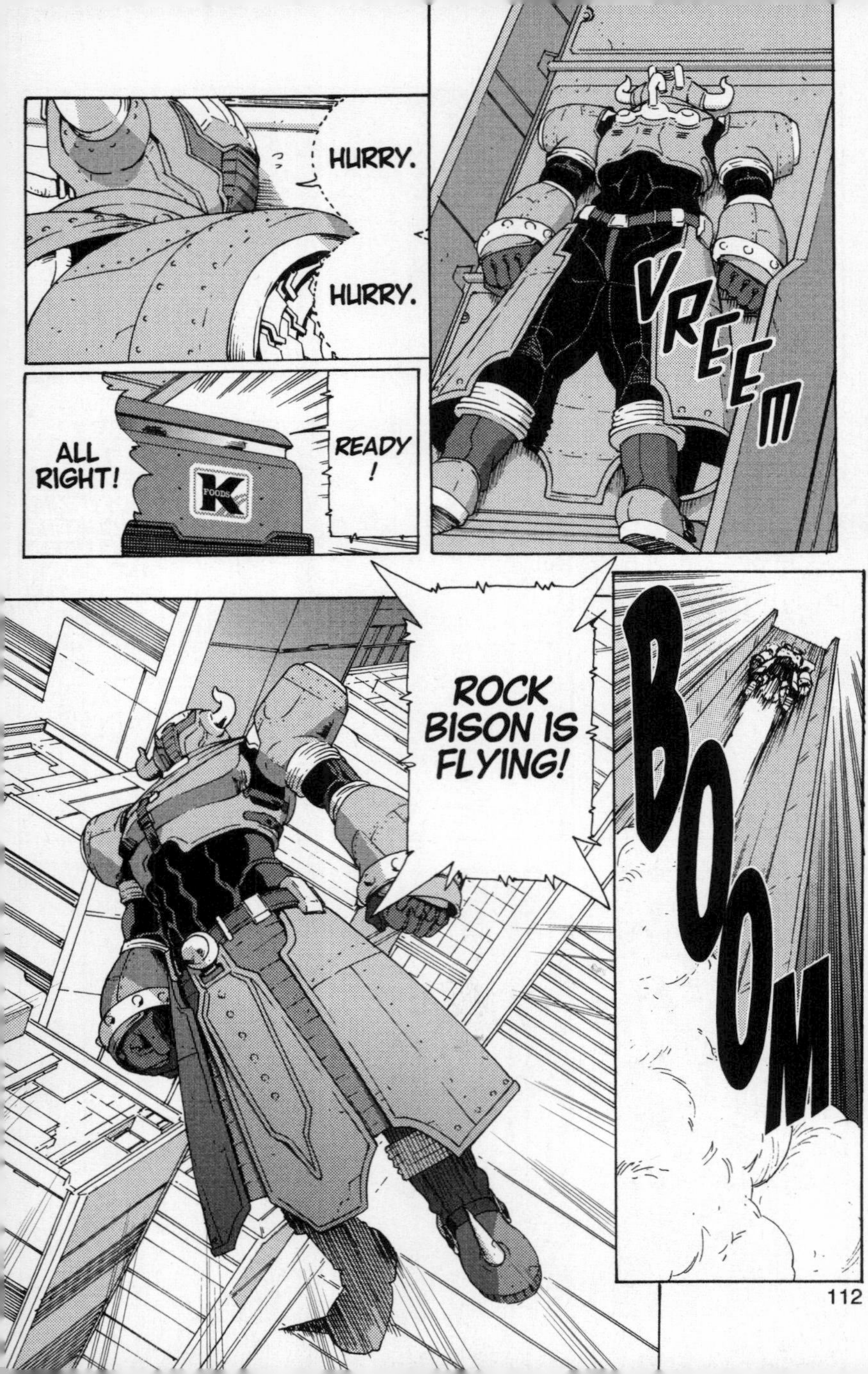
VREEM
HURRY.
HURRY.
READY!
ALL RIGHT!
BOOOM
ROCK BISON IS FLYING!

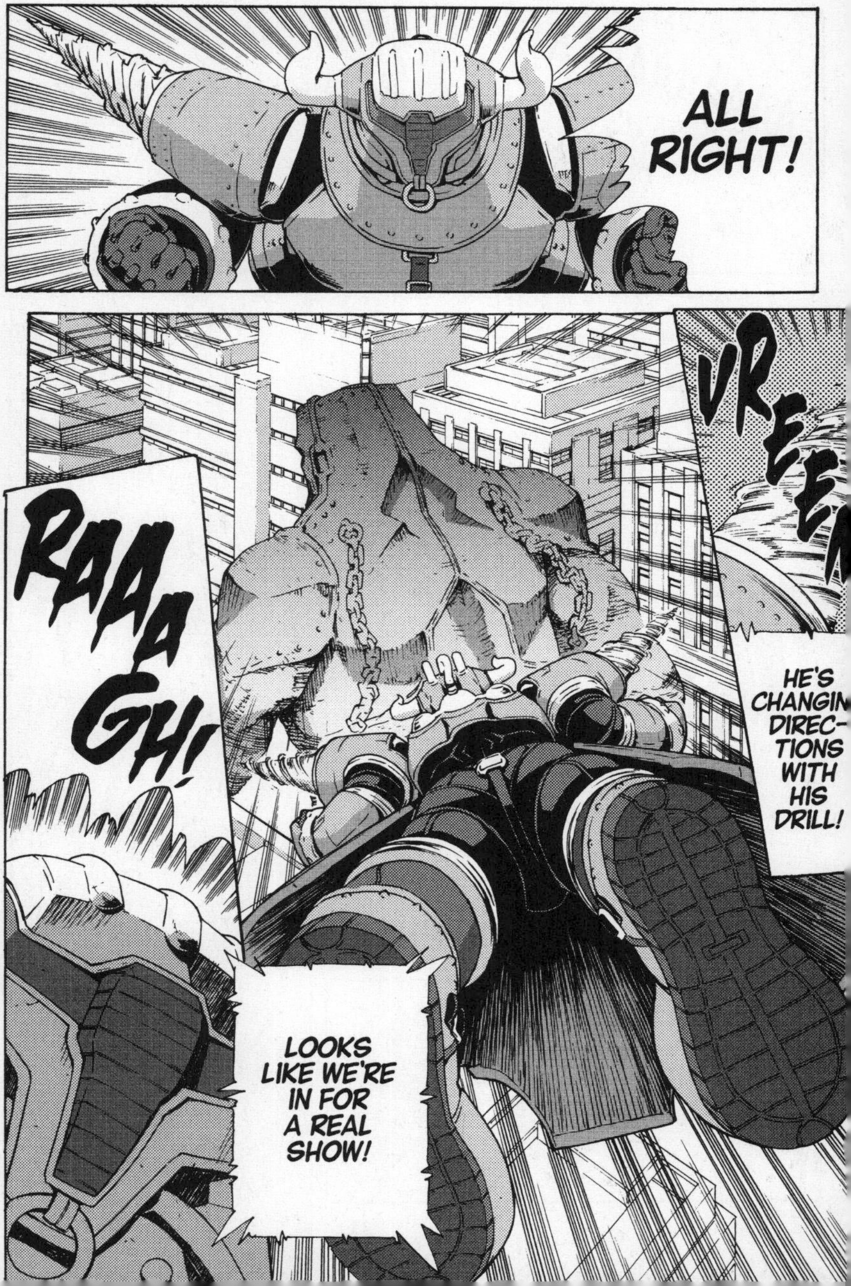
ALL RIGHT!
VREEN
HE'S CHANGIN DIREC-TIONS WITH HIS DRILL!
RAAAGH!
LOOKS LIKE WE'RE IN FOR A REAL SHOW!

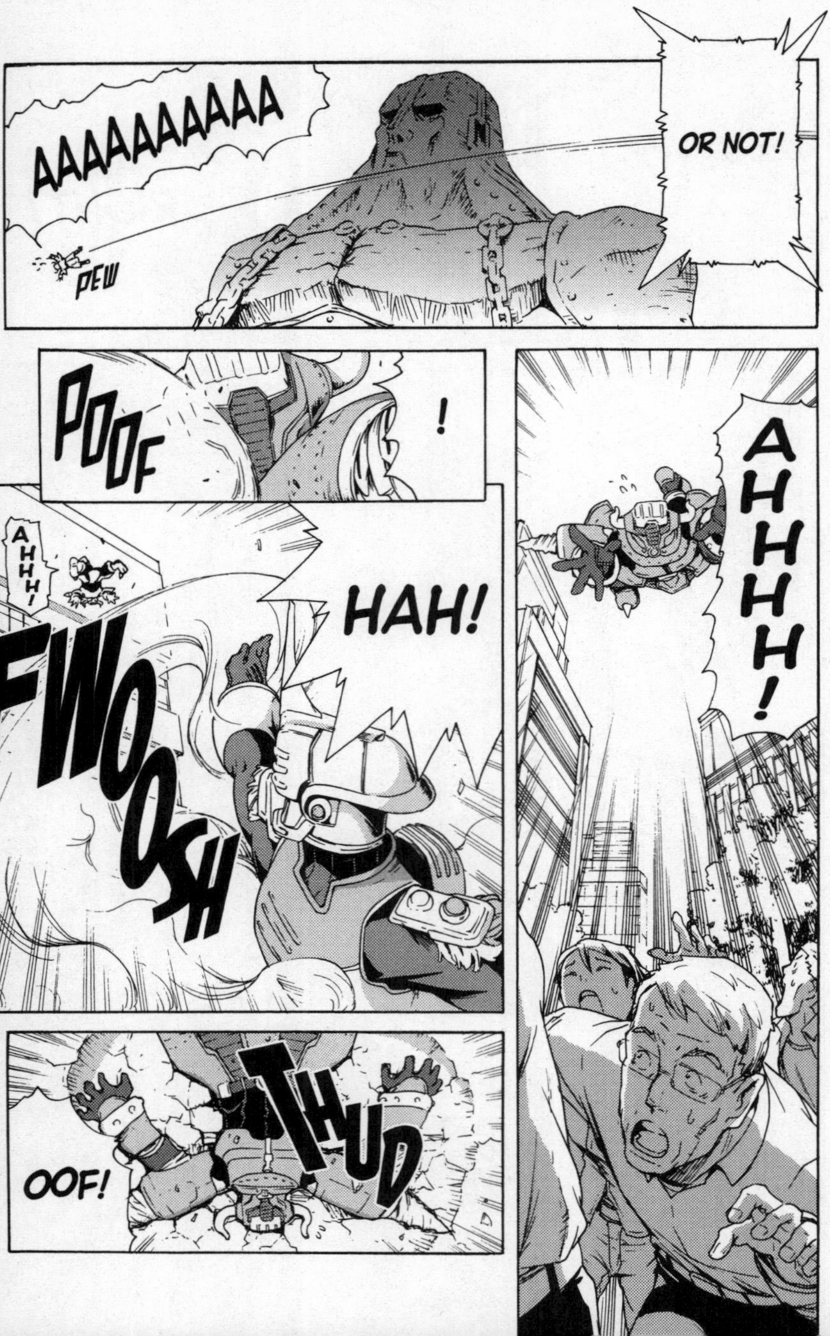
OR NOT!
AAAAAAAAA
PEW
AHHHH!
POOF
!
HAH!
AHHH!
FWOOSH
THUD
OOF!

UH OH!

AHHH!

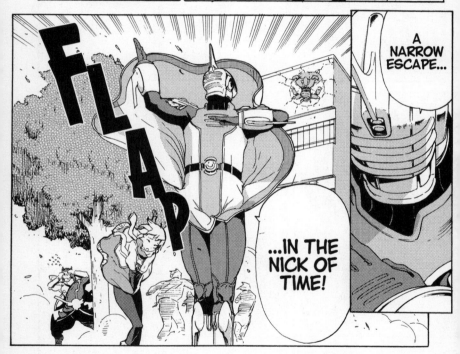

A NARROW ESCAPE...

...IN THE NICK OF TIME!

VREEN

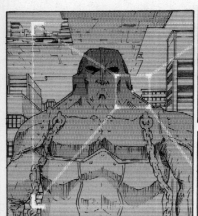

BEEP

!

BEEP

...

DASH

A KID?!

ZIP

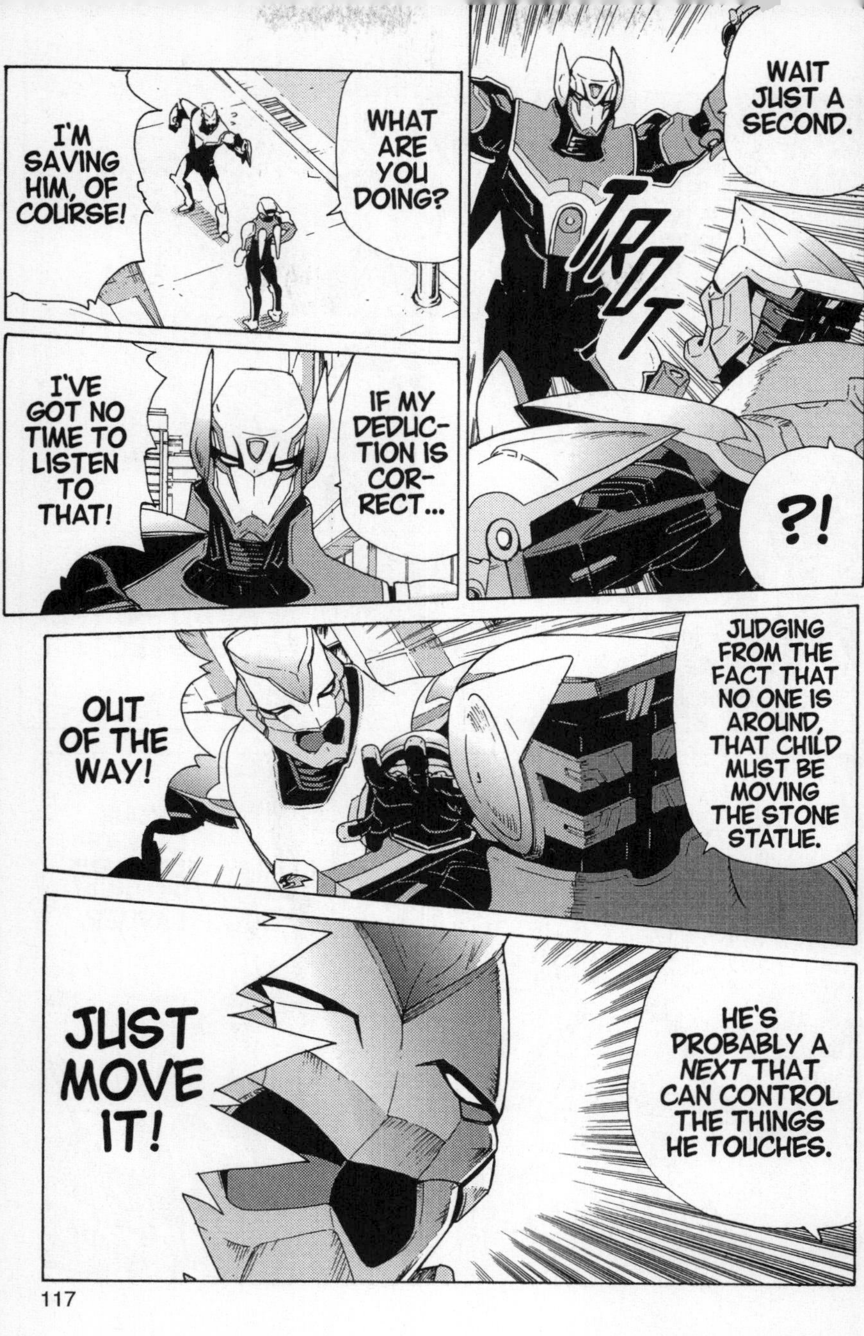
WAIT JUST A SECOND.
TROT
?!
WHAT ARE YOU DOING?
I'M SAVING HIM, OF COURSE!
IF MY DEDUCTION IS CORRECT...
I'VE GOT NO TIME TO LISTEN TO THAT!
JUDGING FROM THE FACT THAT NO ONE IS AROUND, THAT CHILD MUST BE MOVING THE STONE STATUE.
OUT OF THE WAY!
HE'S PROBABLY A *NEXT* THAT CAN CONTROL THE THINGS HE TOUCHES.
JUST MOVE IT!

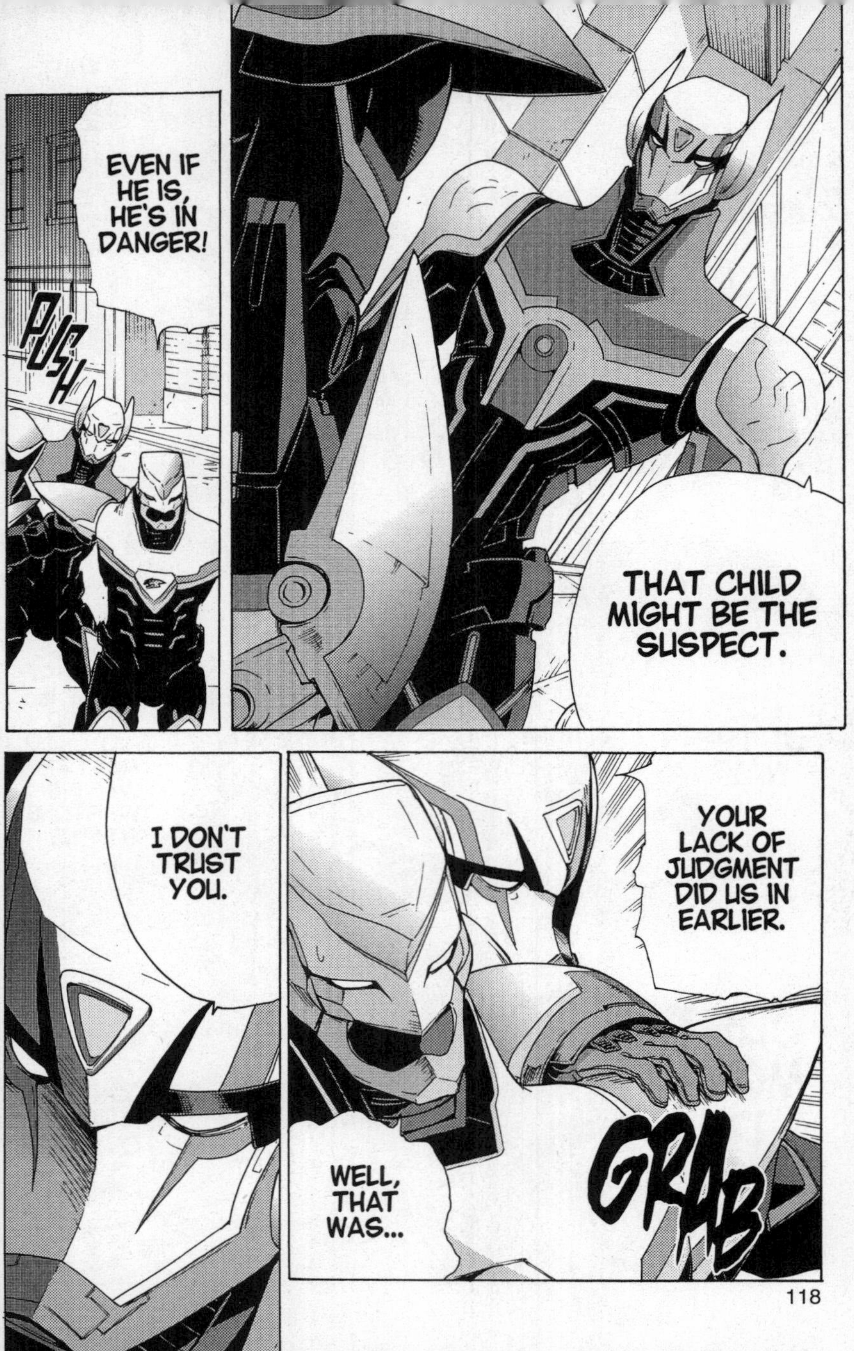
THAT CHILD MIGHT BE THE SUSPECT.
EVEN IF HE IS, HE'S IN DANGER!
PUSH
YOUR LACK OF JUDGMENT DID US IN EARLIER.
GRAB
WELL, THAT WAS...
I DON'T TRUST YOU.

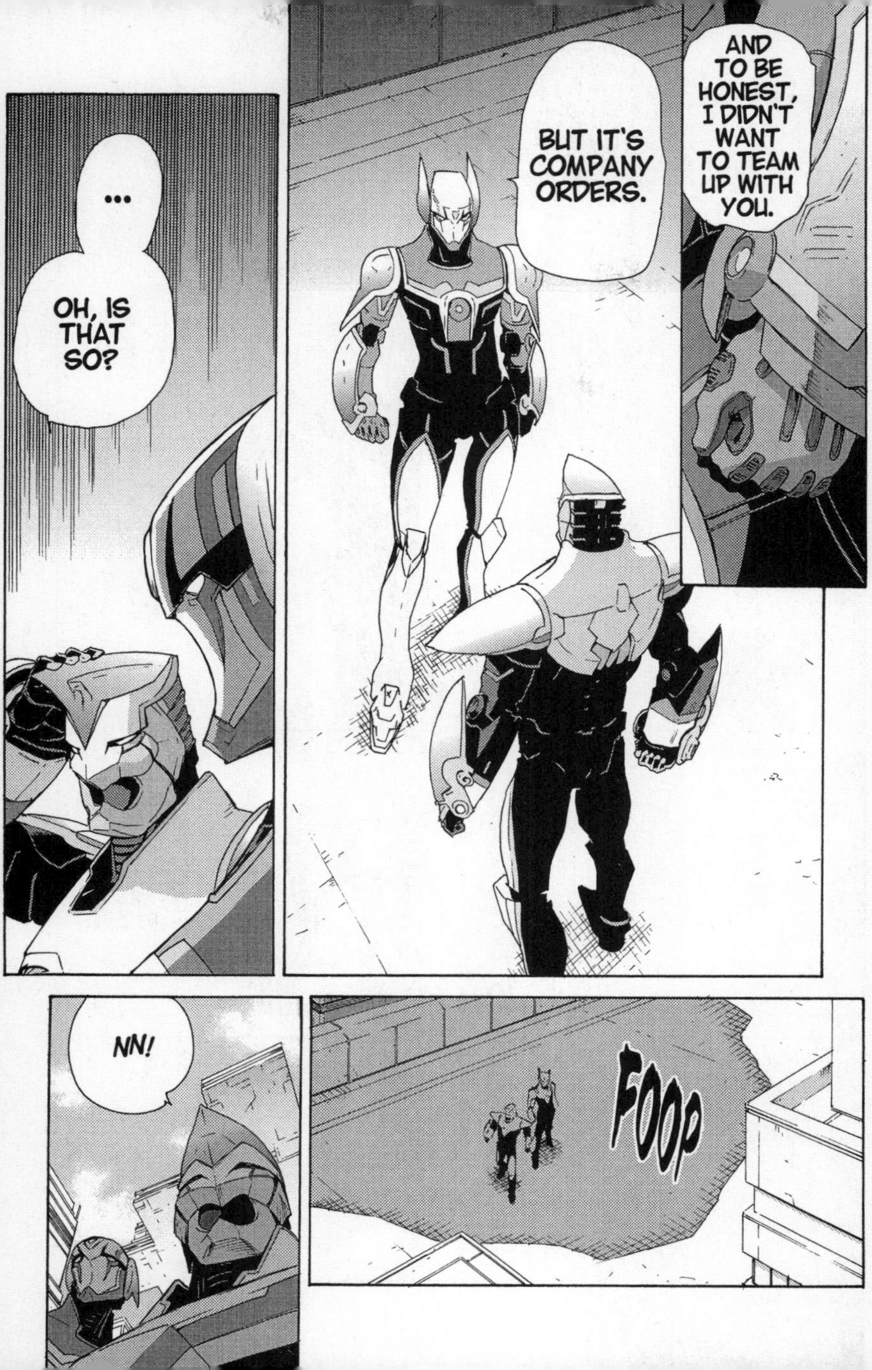
BUT IT'S COMPANY ORDERS.
AND TO BE HONEST, I DIDN'T WANT TO TEAM UP WITH YOU.
...
OH, IS THAT SO?
FOOP
NN!

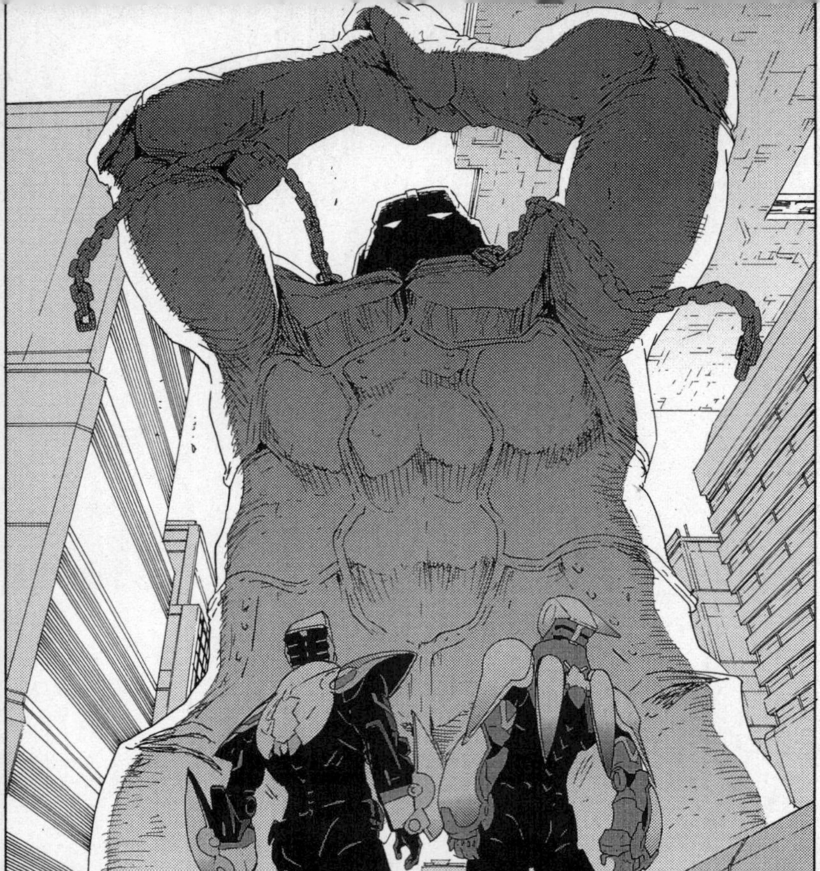
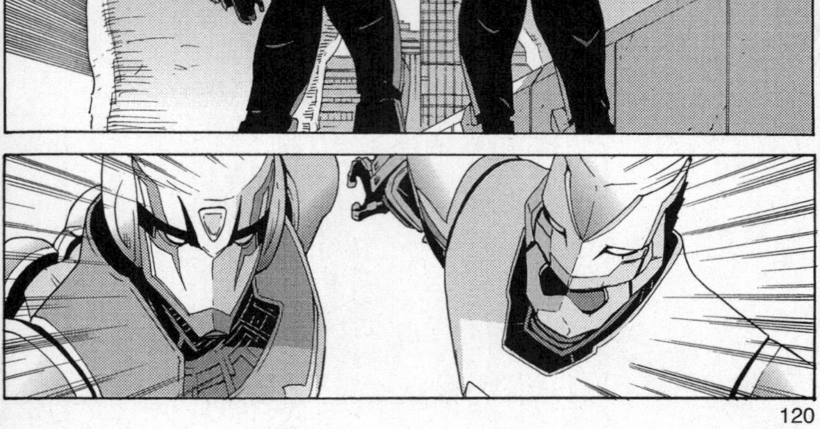

TIGER & BUNNY THE MOVIE

The Beginning

TIGER & BUNNY THE MOVIE
The Beginning

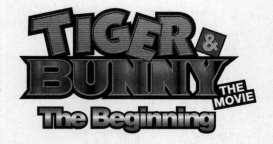

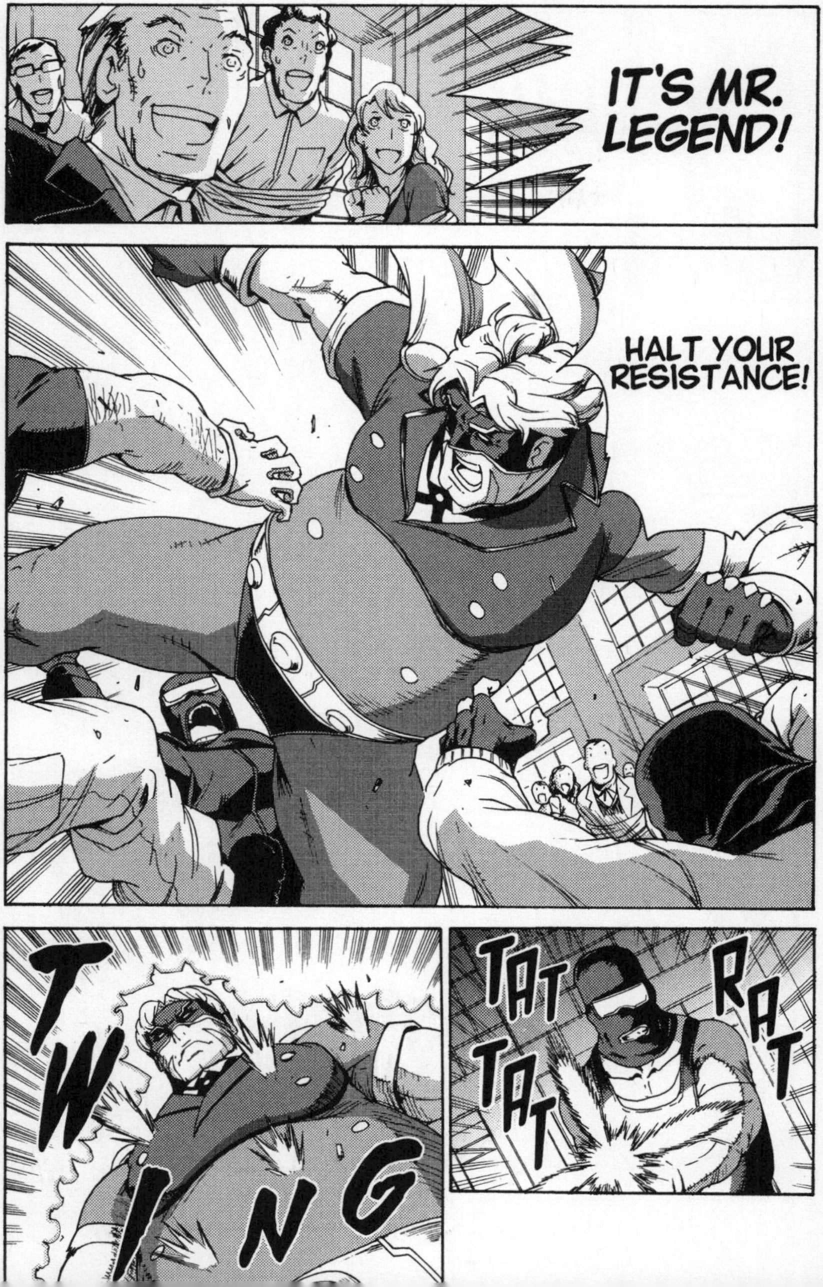
IT'S MR. LEGEND!
HALT YOUR RESISTANCE!
RAT
TAT
TAT
TWING

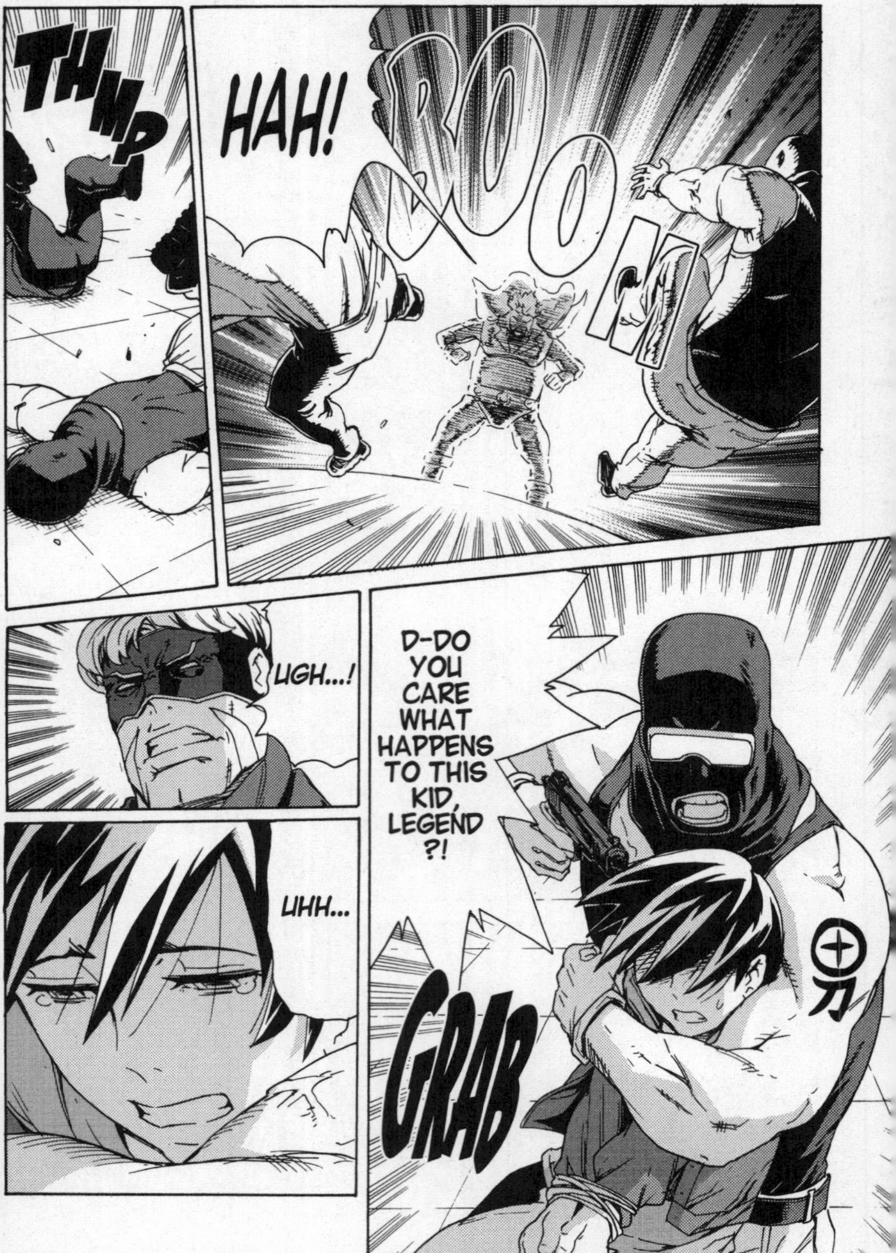
HAH!
BOOM
THMP
D-DO YOU CARE WHAT HAPPENS TO THIS KID, LEGEND?!
GRAB
UGH...!
UHH...

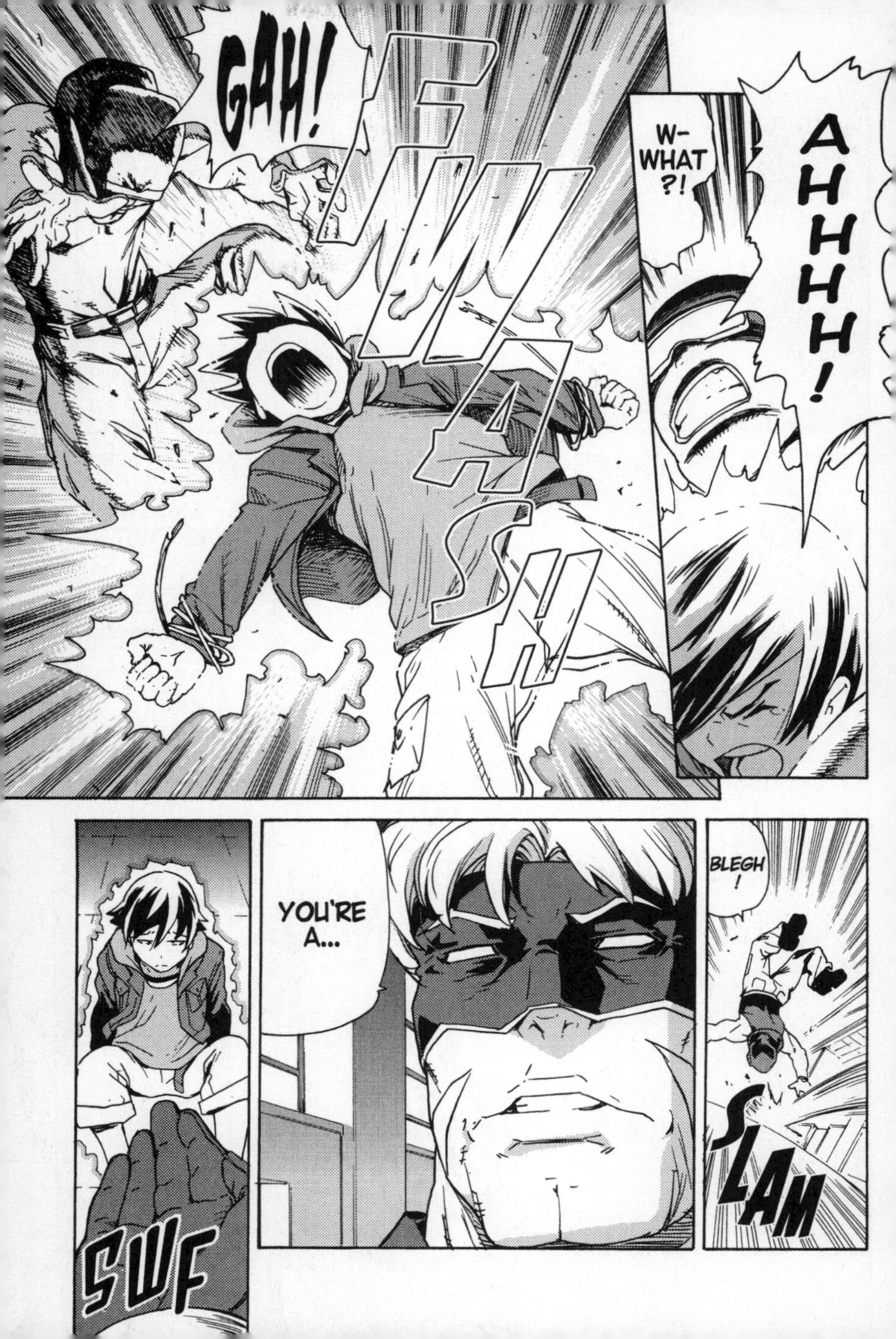
AHHHH!
W-WHAT?!
FWASH
GAH!
BLEGH!
SLAM
YOU'RE A...
SWF

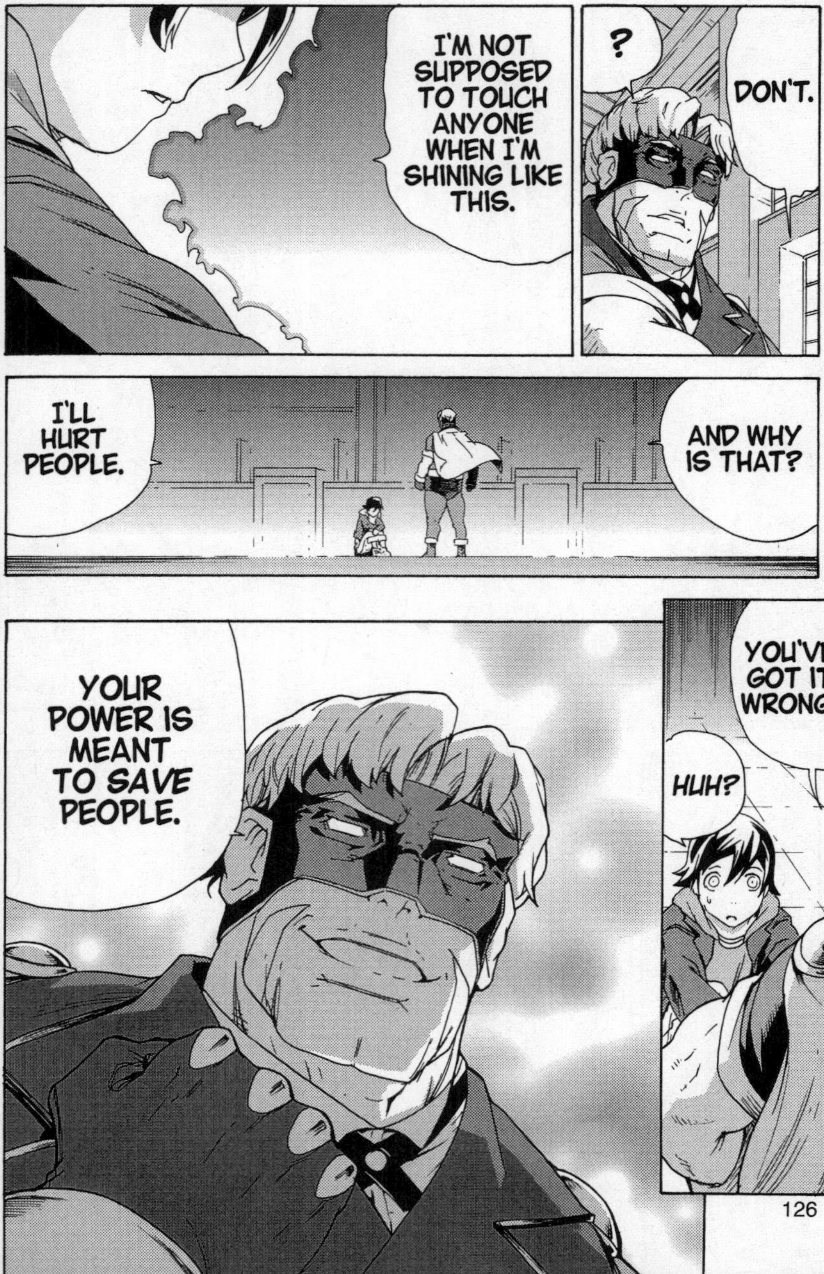
?
DON'T.
I'M NOT SUPPOSED TO TOUCH ANYONE WHEN I'M SHINING LIKE THIS.
AND WHY IS THAT?
I'LL HURT PEOPLE.
YOU'VE GOT IT WRONG.
HUH?
YOUR POWER IS MEANT TO SAVE PEOPLE.

YOU SAVED ME. THAT MAKES YOU A HERO TOO!

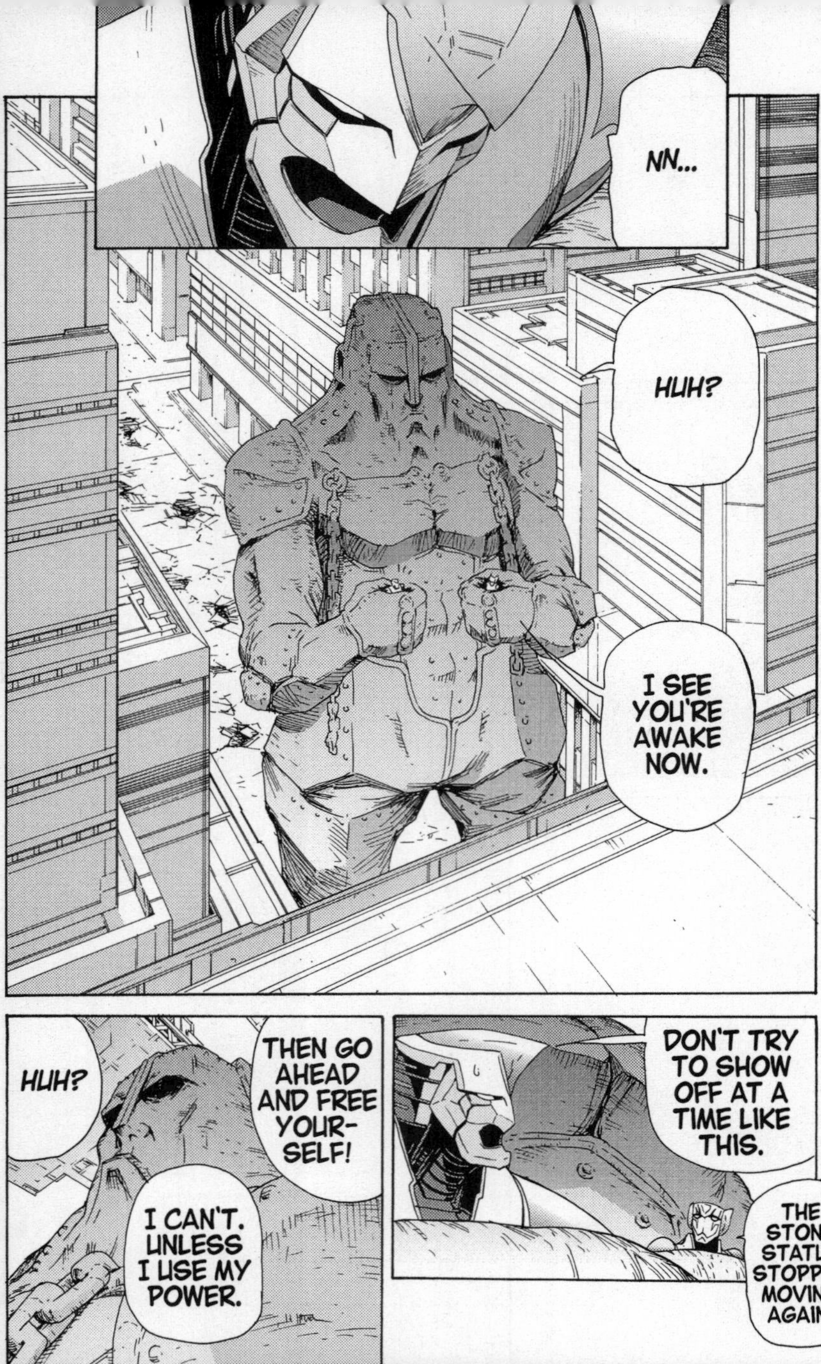
NN...
HUH?
I SEE YOU'RE AWAKE NOW.
DON'T TRY TO SHOW OFF AT A TIME LIKE THIS.
THE STONE STATUE STOPPED MOVING AGAIN.
THEN GO AHEAD AND FREE YOUR-SELF!
HUH?
I CAN'T. UNLESS I USE MY POWER.

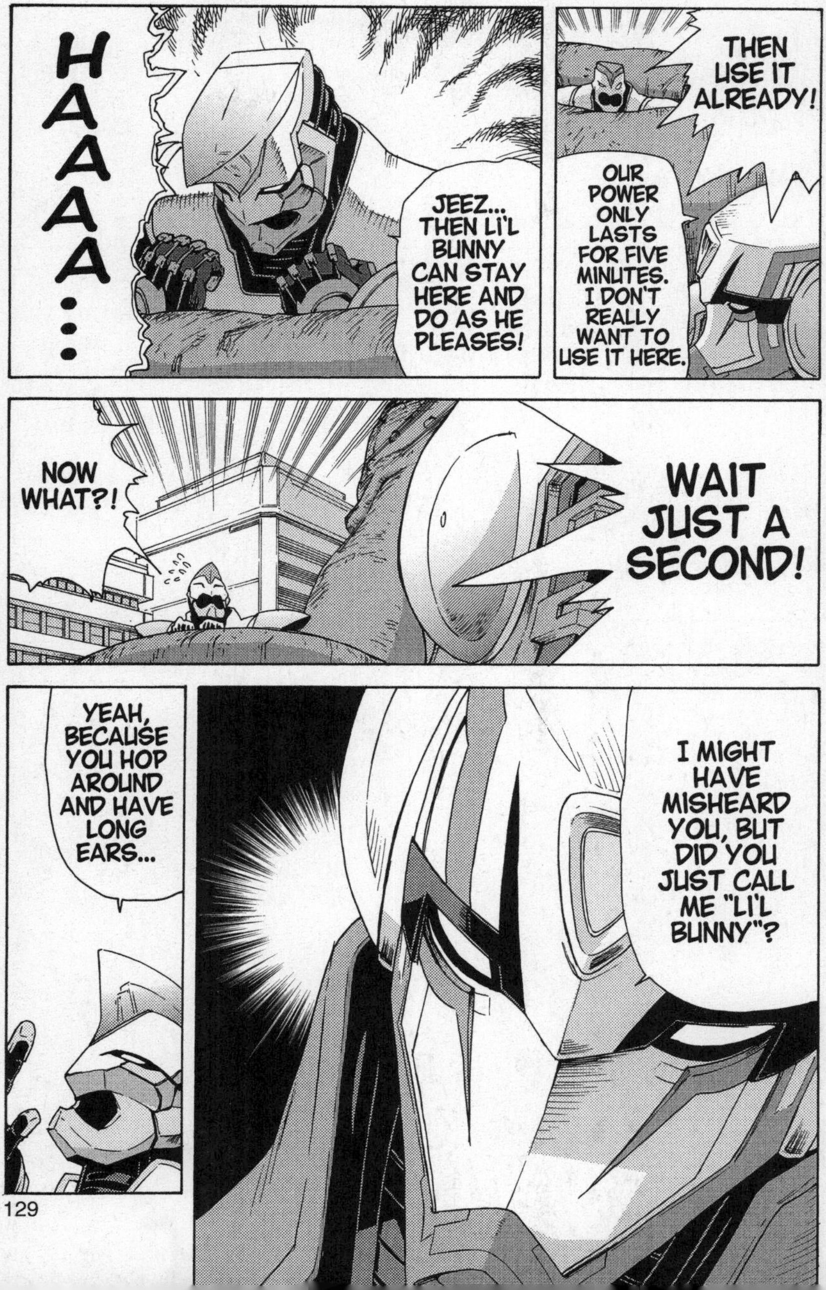
THEN USE IT ALREADY!
OUR POWER ONLY LASTS FOR FIVE MINUTES. I DON'T REALLY WANT TO USE IT HERE.
HAAAA...
JEEZ... THEN LI'L BUNNY CAN STAY HERE AND DO AS HE PLEASES!
WAIT JUST A SECOND!
NOW WHAT?!
I MIGHT HAVE MISHEARD YOU, BUT DID YOU JUST CALL ME "LI'L BUNNY"?
YEAH, BECAUSE YOU HOP AROUND AND HAVE LONG EARS...

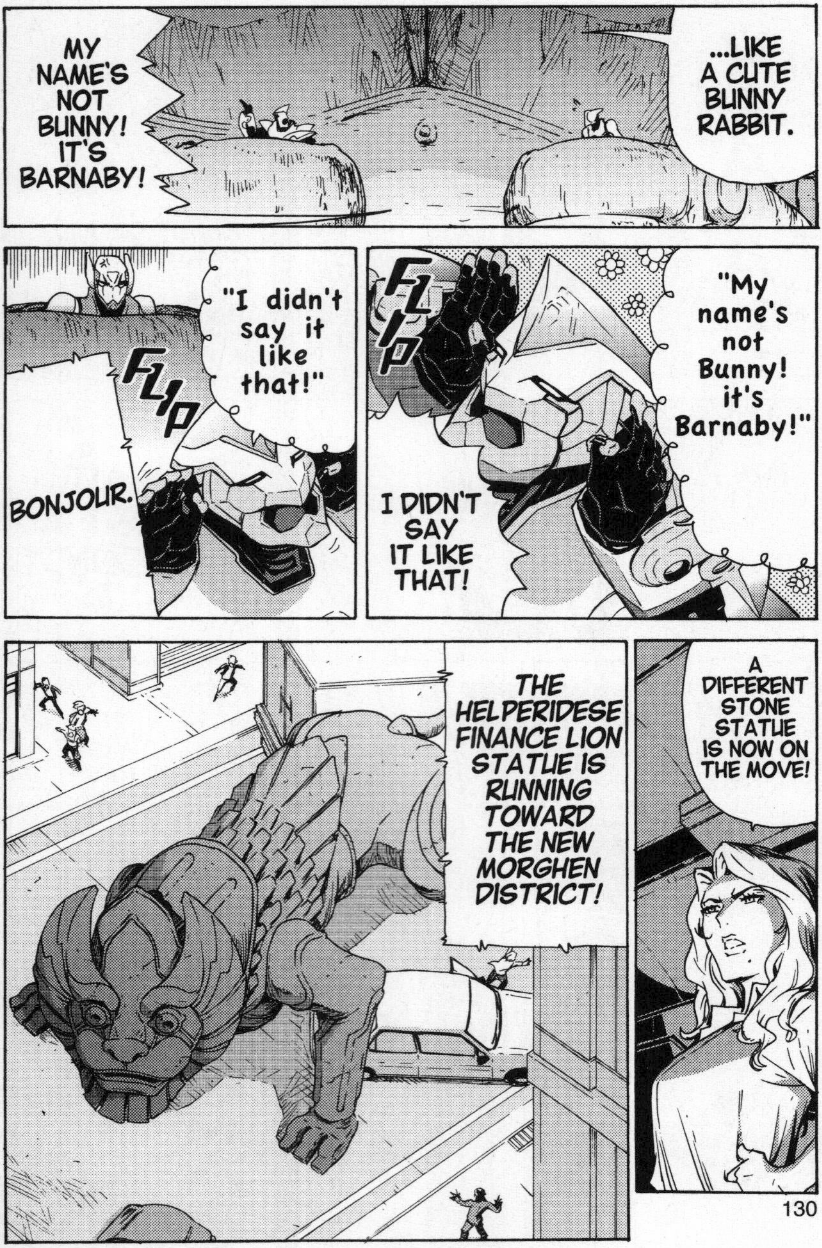
...LIKE A CUTE BUNNY RABBIT.
MY NAME'S NOT BUNNY! IT'S BARNABY!
"My name's not Bunny! it's Barnaby!"
FLIP
I DIDN'T SAY IT LIKE THAT!
"I didn't say it like that!"
FLIP
BONJOUR.
A DIFFERENT STONE STATUE IS NOW ON THE MOVE!
THE HELPERIDESE FINANCE LION STATUE IS RUNNING TOWARD THE NEW MORGHEN DISTRICT!

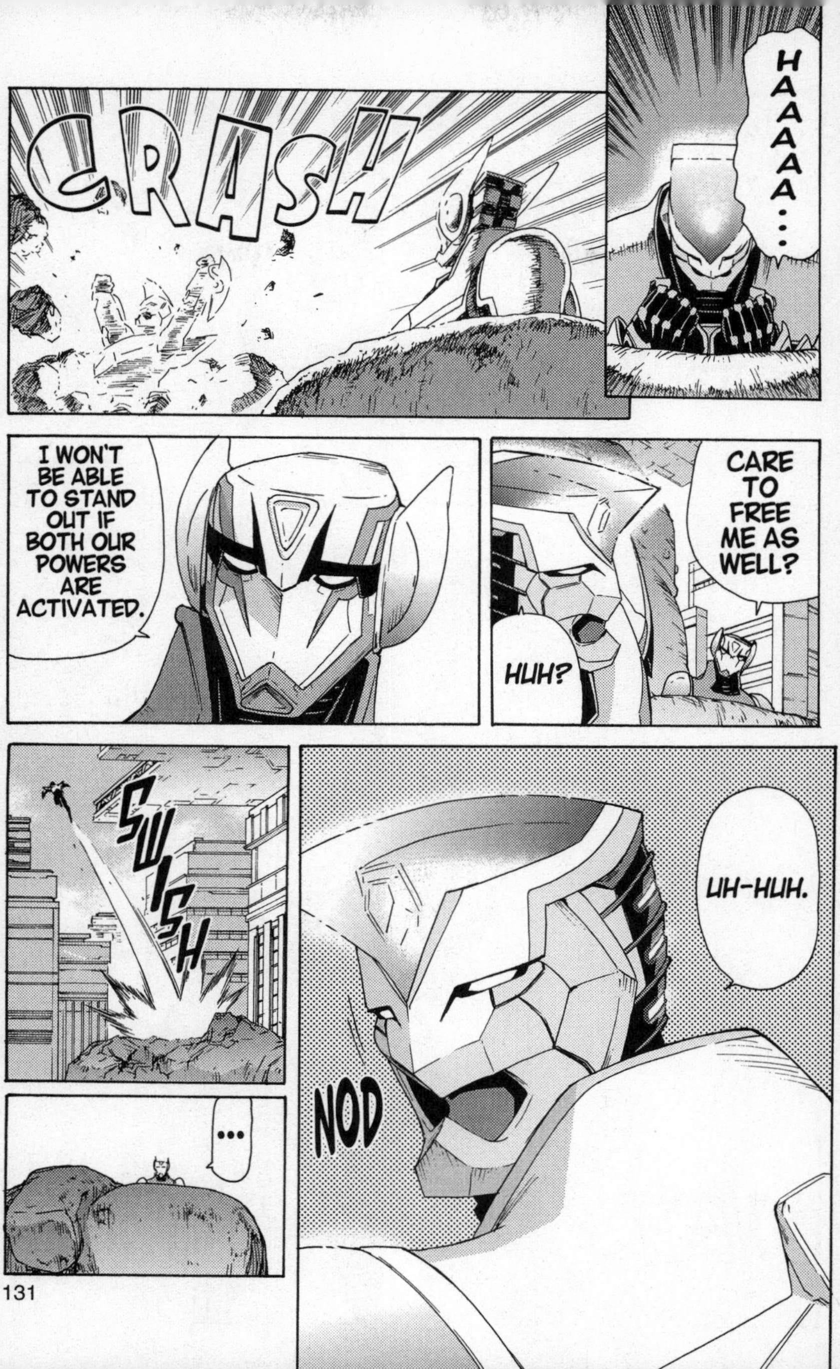
HAAAAA...
CRASH
CARE TO FREE ME AS WELL?
HUH?
I WON'T BE ABLE TO STAND OUT IF BOTH OUR POWERS ARE ACTIVATED.
UH-HUH.
NOD
SWISH
...

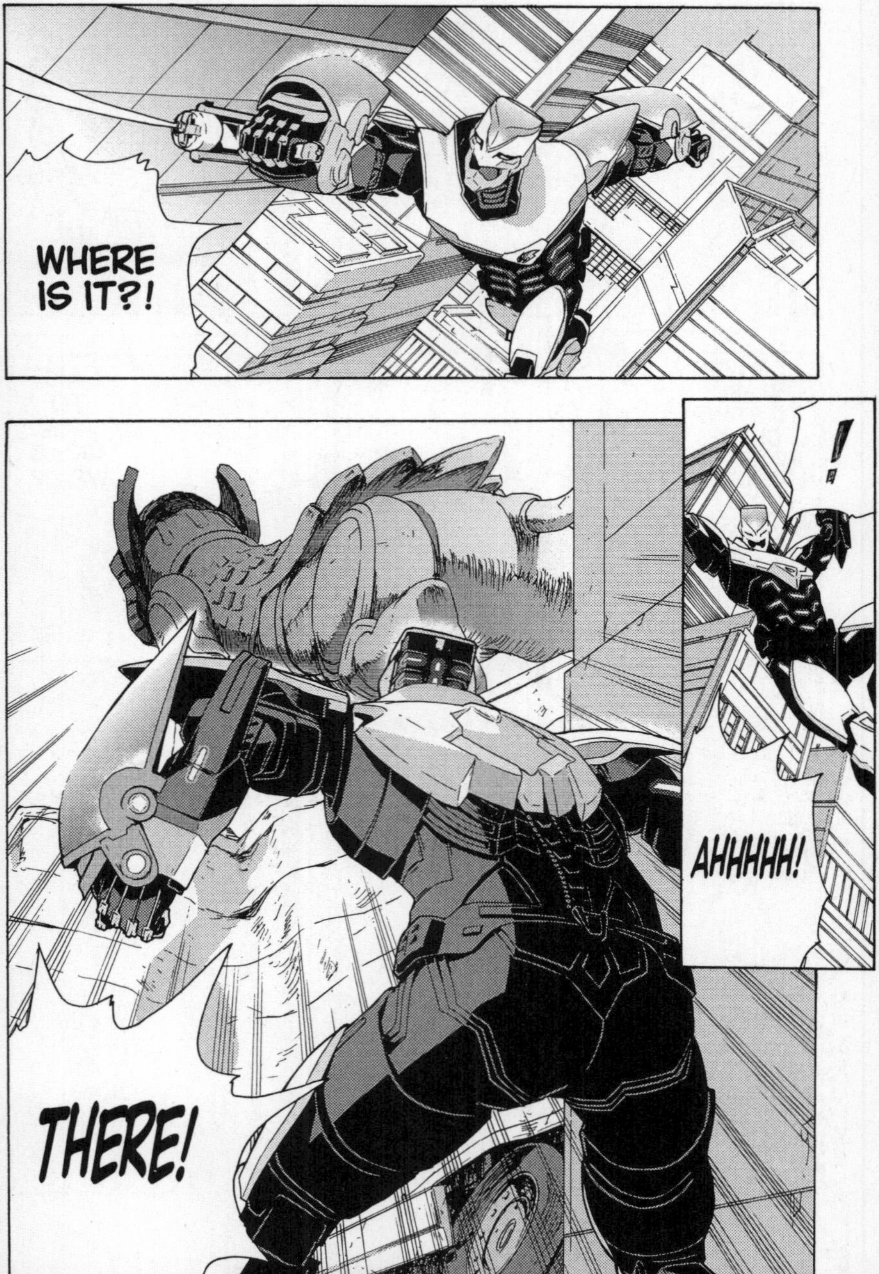
WHERE IS IT?!
!
AHHHHH!
THERE!

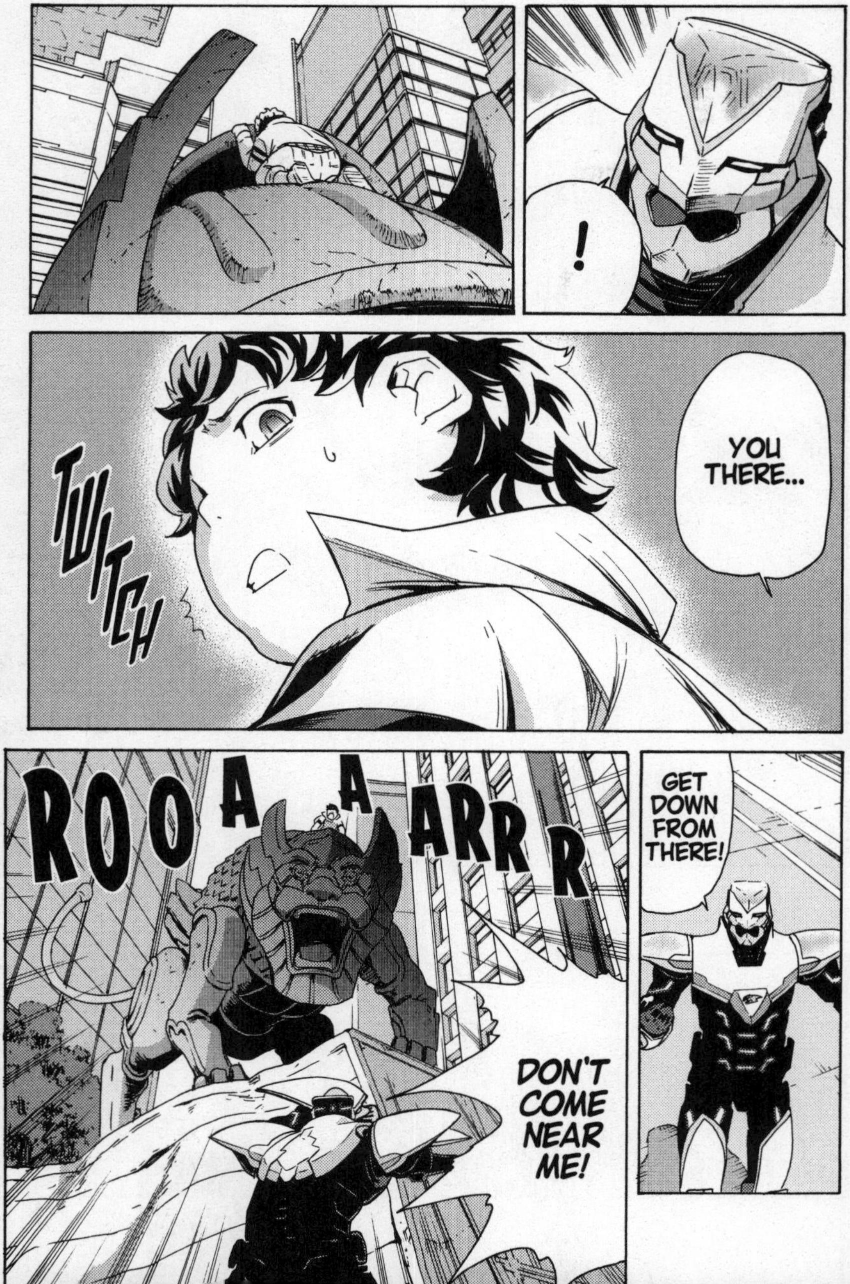
!
YOU THERE...
TWITCH
GET DOWN FROM THERE!
ROOAAARRR
DON'T COME NEAR ME!

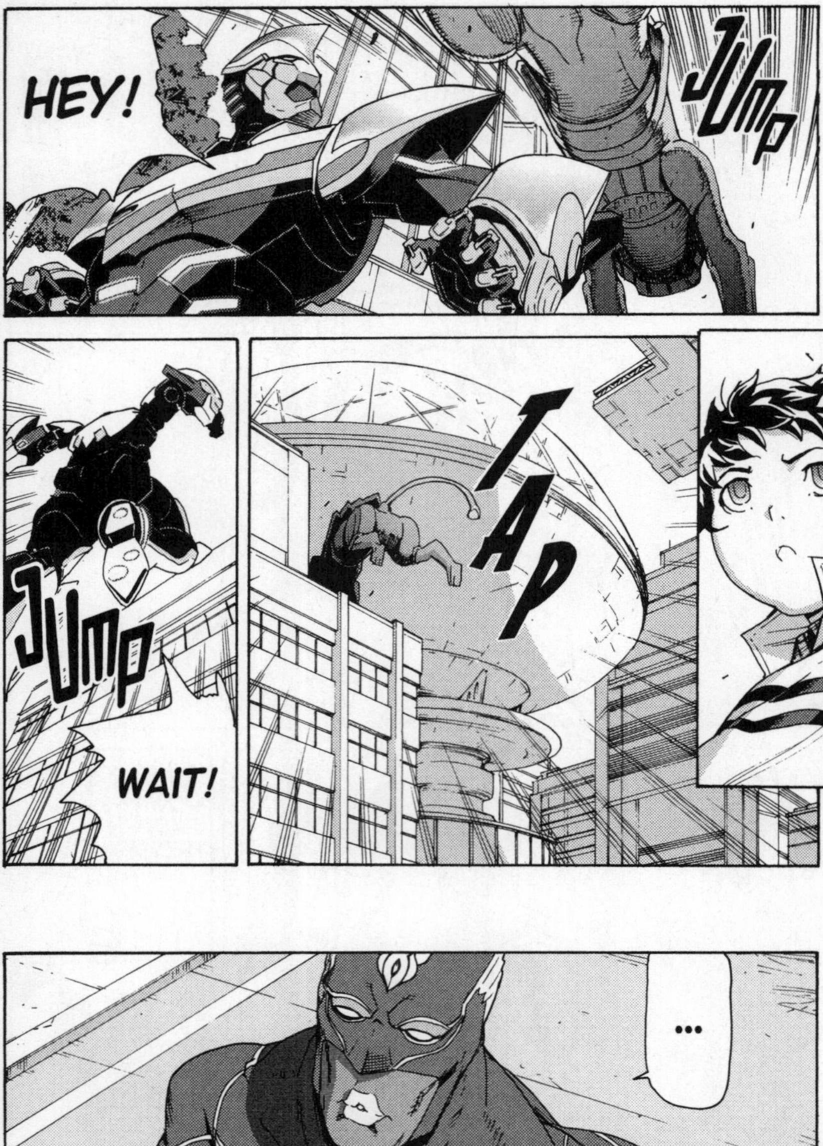
JUMP
HEY!
TAP
JUMP
WAIT!
...

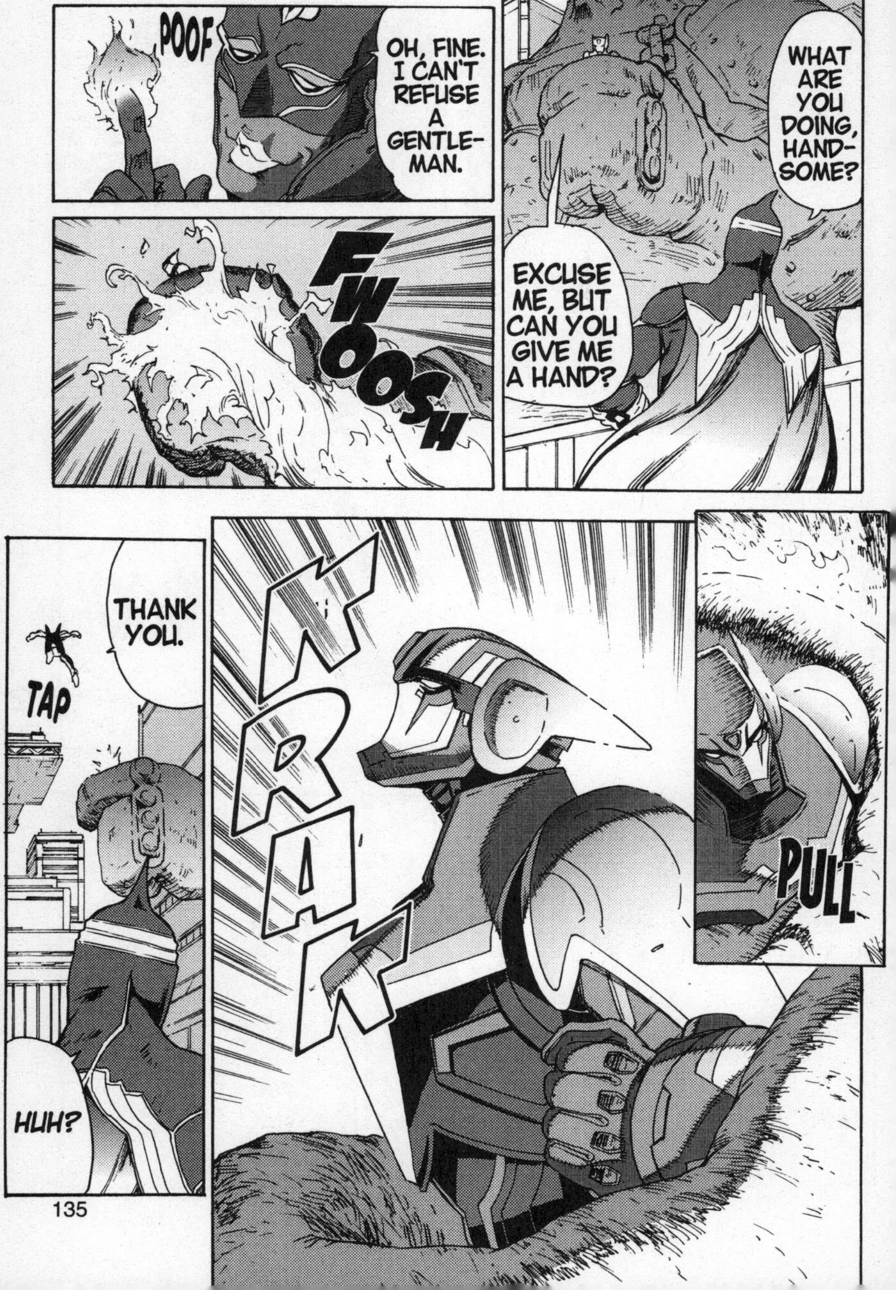
WHAT ARE YOU DOING, HANDSOME?
EXCUSE ME, BUT CAN YOU GIVE ME A HAND?
OH, FINE. I CAN'T REFUSE A GENTLEMAN.
POOF
FWOOSH
PULL
KRAK
THANK YOU.
TAP
HUH?

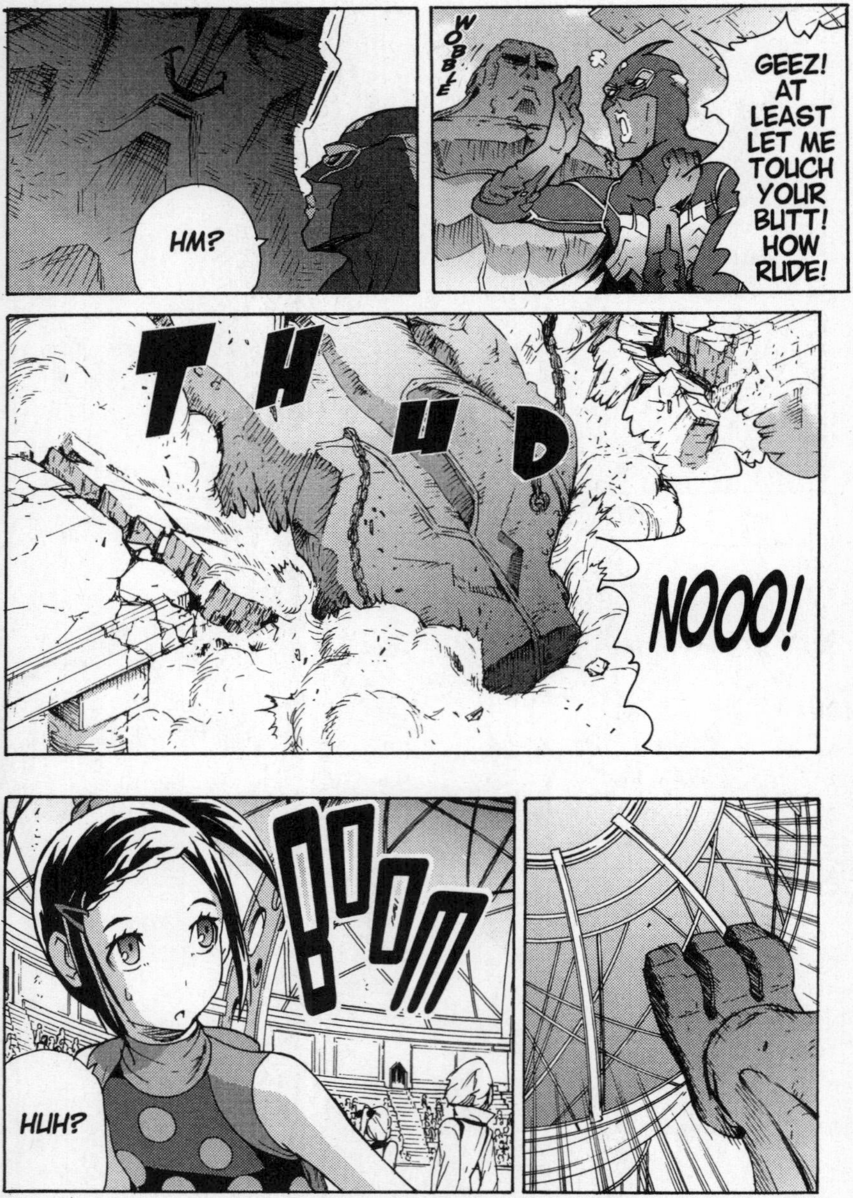
GEEZ! AT LEAST LET ME TOUCH YOUR BUTT! HOW RUDE!
WOBBLE
HM?
THUD
NOOO!
BOOM
HUH?

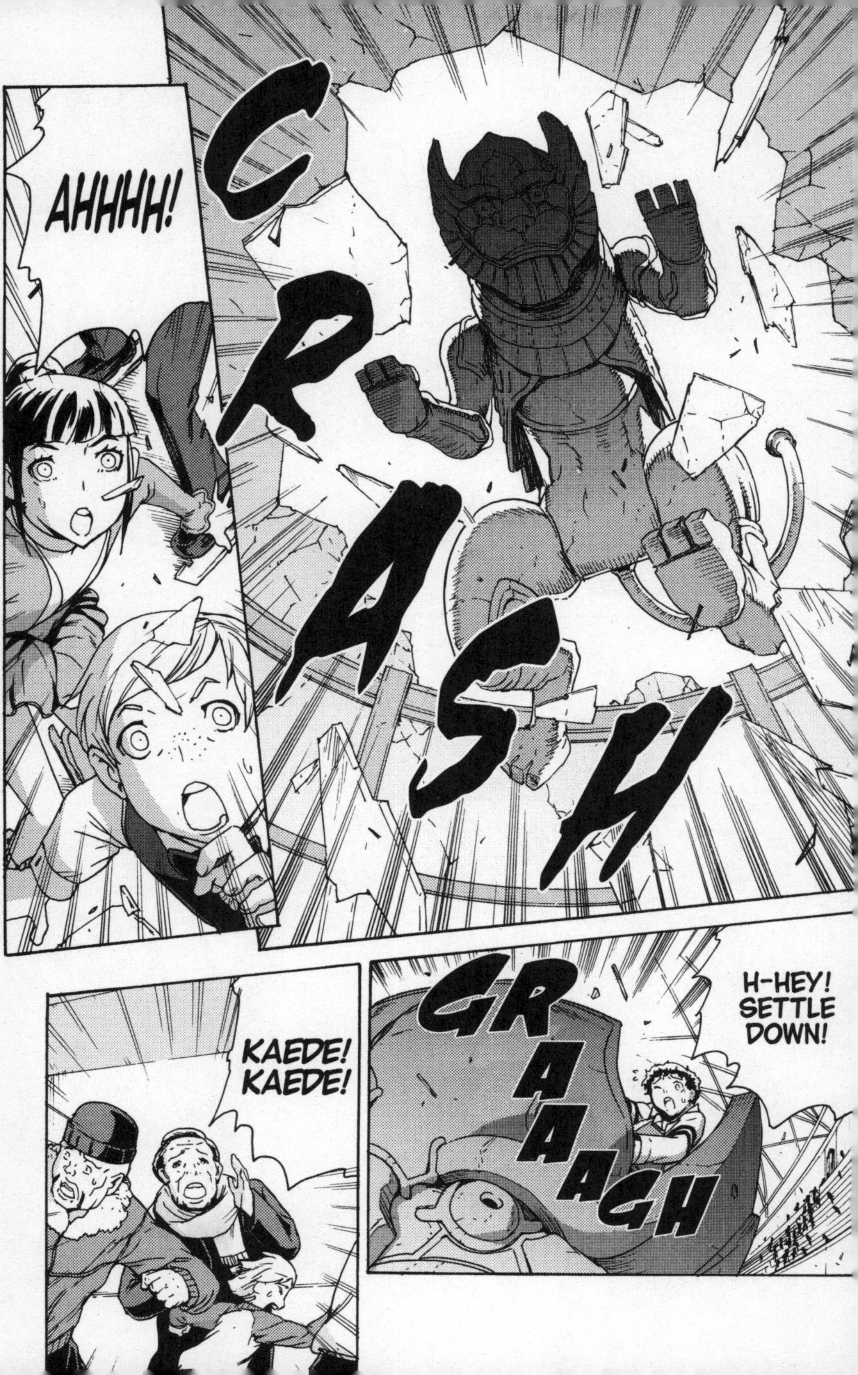
CRASH
AHHHH!
H-HEY! SETTLE DOWN!
GRAAAAGH
KAEDE! KAEDE!

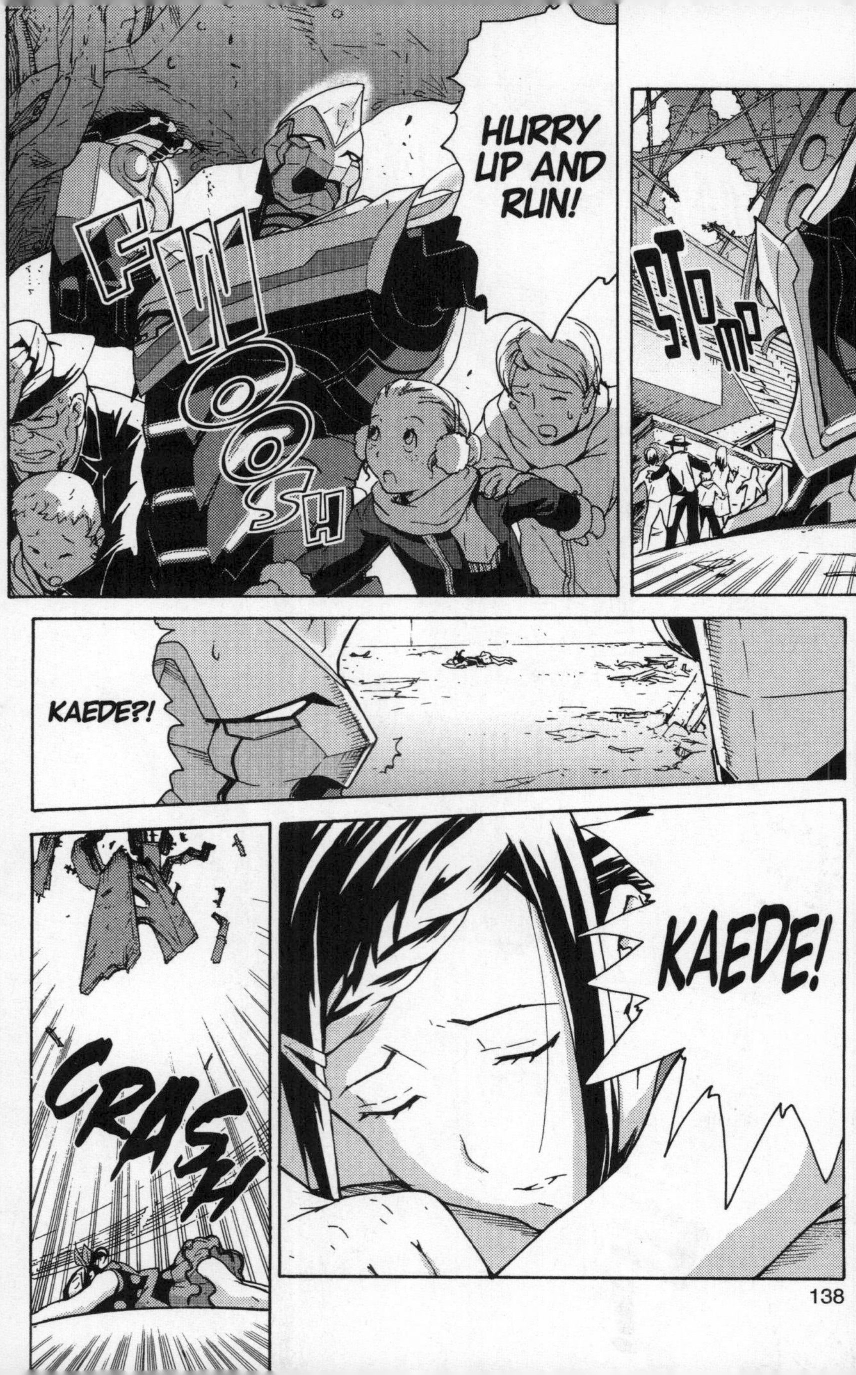
STOMP
HURRY UP AND RUN!
FWOOOOSH
KAEDE?!
KAEDE!
CRASH

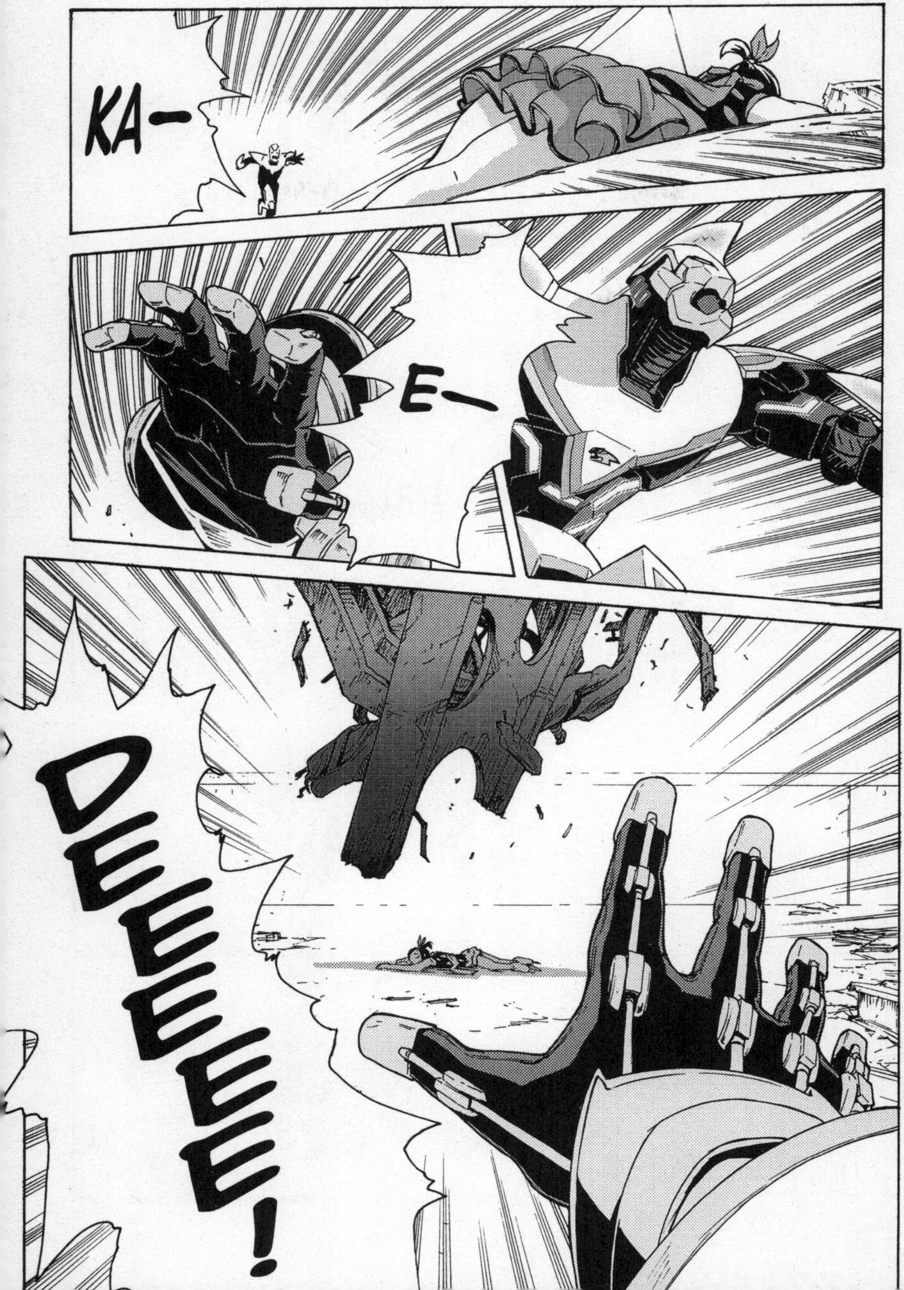
KA–
E–
DEEEEEE!

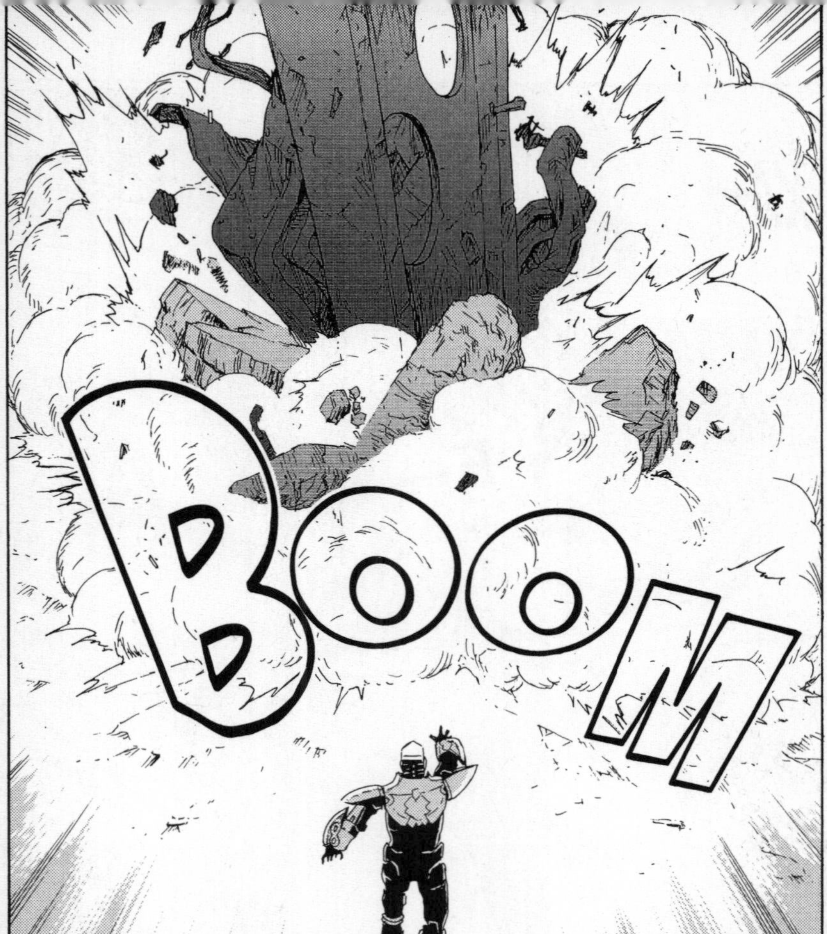
BOOM
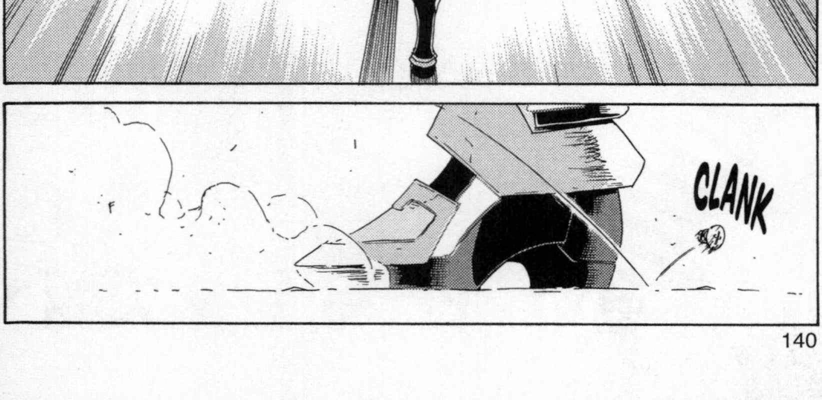
CLANK

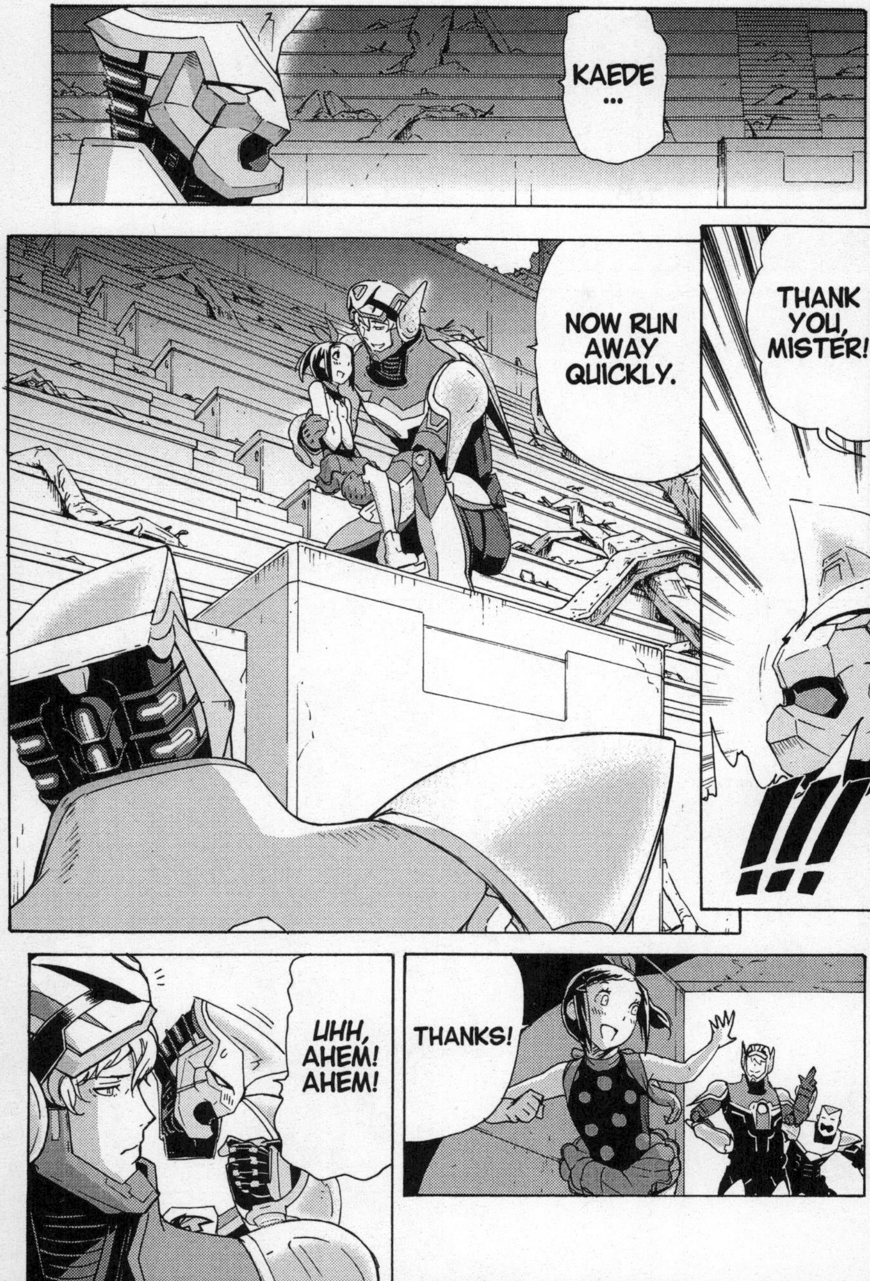
KAEDE ...
THANK YOU, MISTER!
!!!
NOW RUN AWAY QUICKLY.
THANKS!
UHH, AHEM! AHEM!

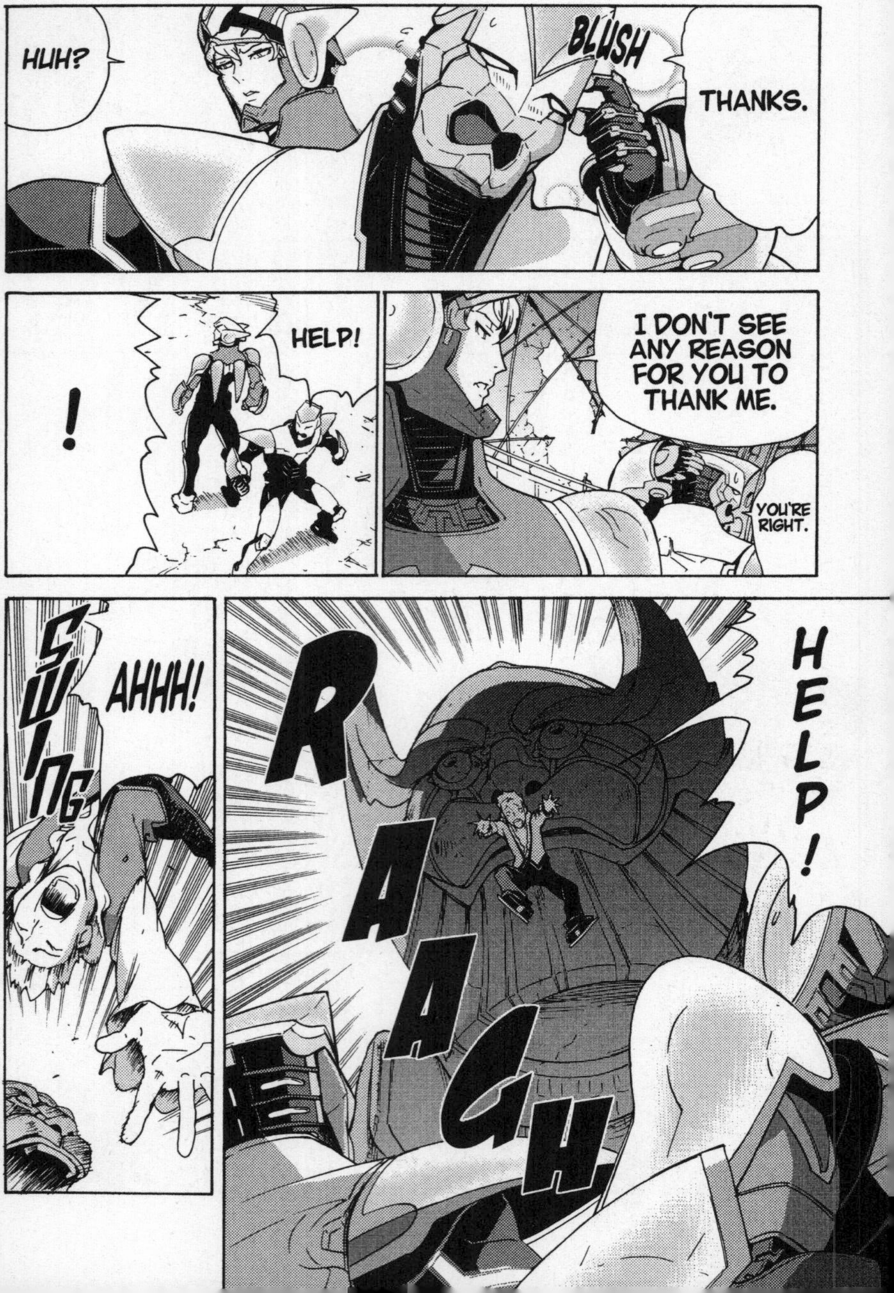
THANKS.
BLUSH
HUH?
I DON'T SEE ANY REASON FOR YOU TO THANK ME.
YOU'RE RIGHT.
HELP!
!
HELP!
RAAAGH
AHHH!
SWING

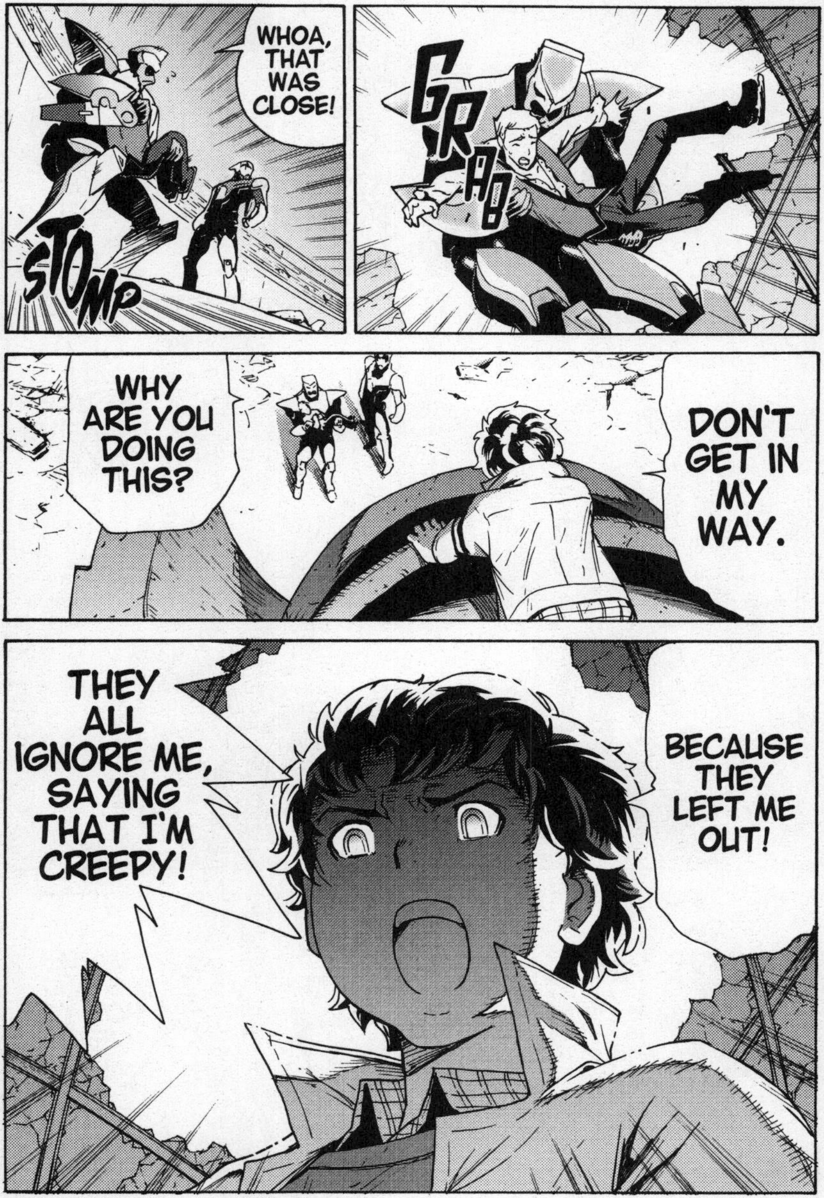
GRAB
WHOA, THAT WAS CLOSE!
STOMP
DON'T GET IN MY WAY.
WHY ARE YOU DOING THIS?
BECAUSE THEY LEFT ME OUT!
THEY ALL IGNORE ME, SAYING THAT I'M CREEPY!

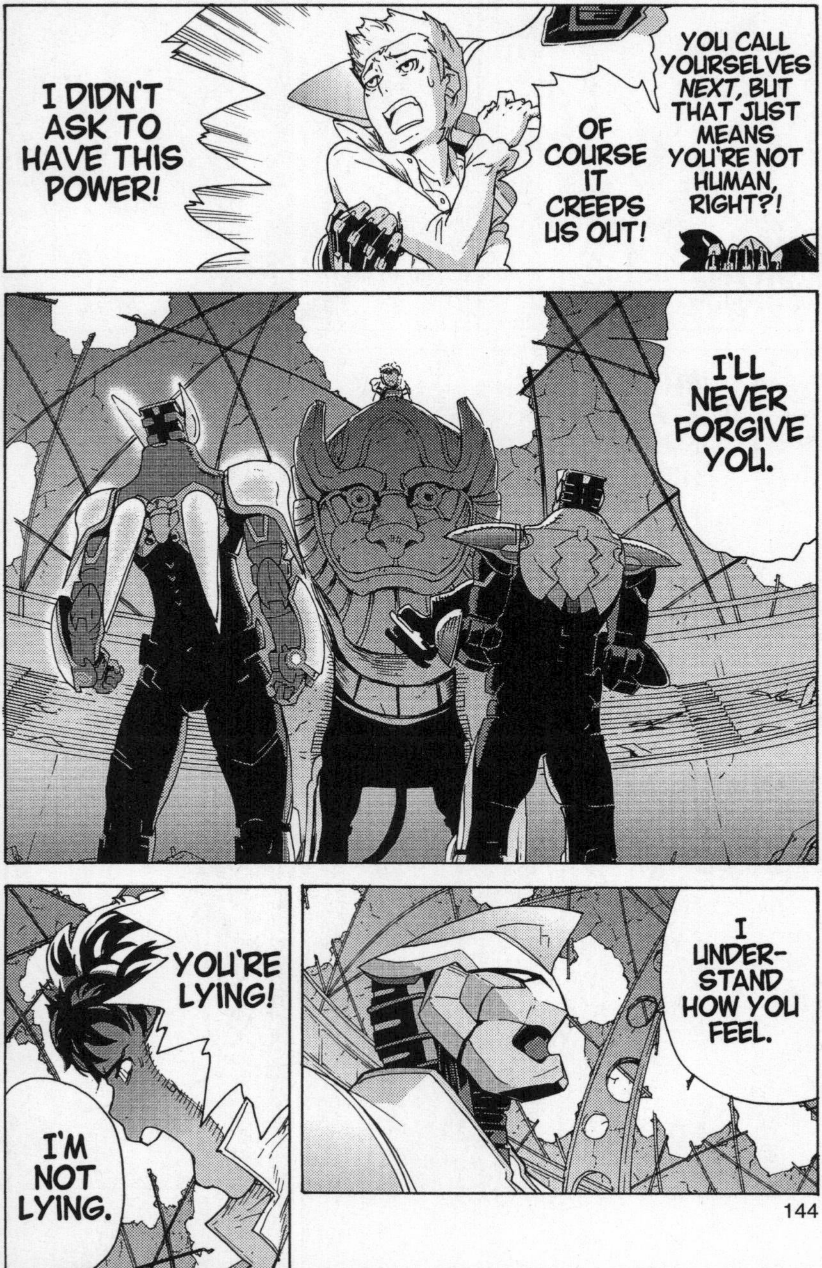
YOU CALL YOURSELVES NEXT, BUT THAT JUST MEANS YOU'RE NOT HUMAN, RIGHT?!
OF COURSE IT CREEPS US OUT!
I DIDN'T ASK TO HAVE THIS POWER!
I'LL NEVER FORGIVE YOU.
I UNDER-STAND HOW YOU FEEL.
YOU'RE LYING!
I'M NOT LYING.

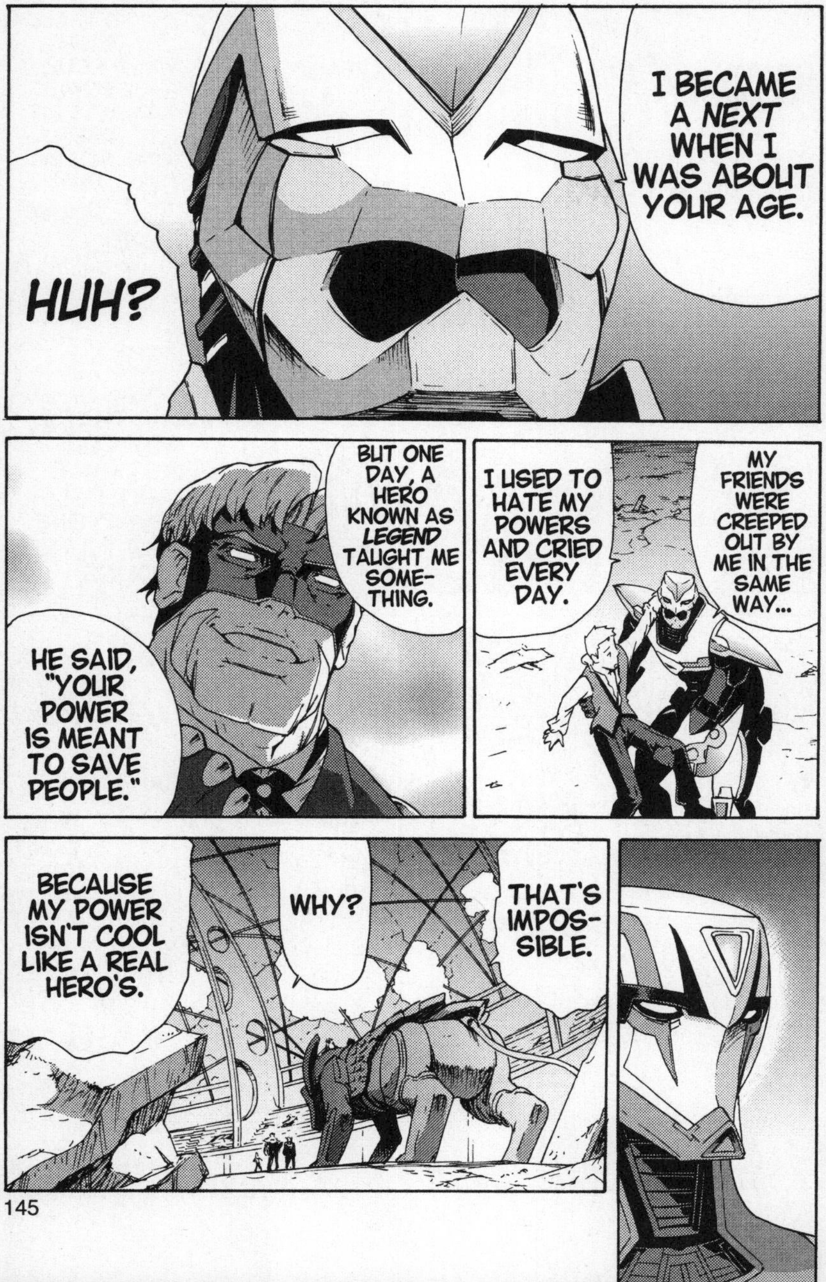
I BECAME A *NEXT* WHEN I WAS ABOUT YOUR AGE.
HUH?
MY FRIENDS WERE CREEPED OUT BY ME IN THE SAME WAY...
I USED TO HATE MY POWERS AND CRIED EVERY DAY.
BUT ONE DAY, A HERO KNOWN AS *LEGEND* TAUGHT ME SOME-THING.
HE SAID, "YOUR POWER IS MEANT TO SAVE PEOPLE."
THAT'S IMPOS-SIBLE.
WHY?
BECAUSE MY POWER ISN'T COOL LIKE A REAL HERO'S.

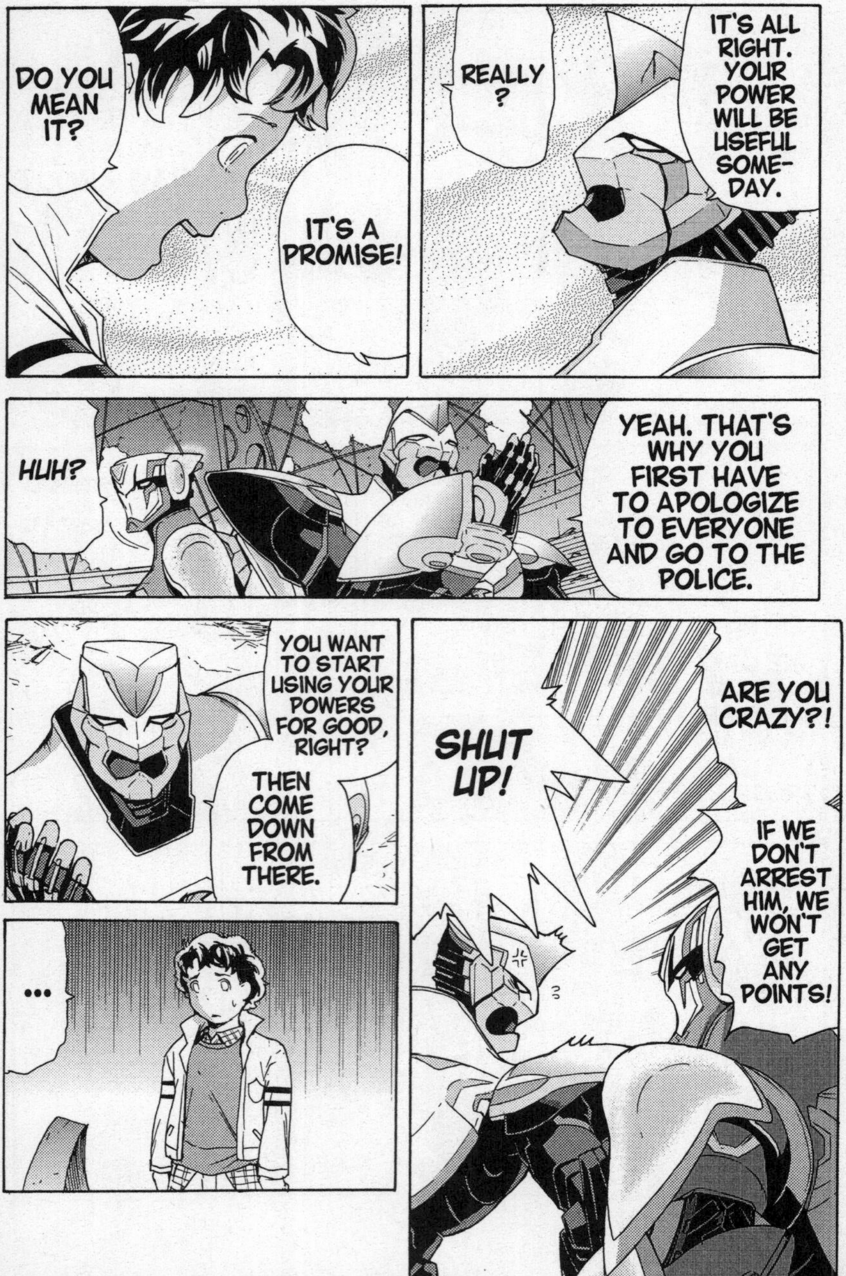
IT'S ALL RIGHT. YOUR POWER WILL BE USEFUL SOME-DAY.
REALLY?
DO YOU MEAN IT?
IT'S A PROMISE!
YEAH. THAT'S WHY YOU FIRST HAVE TO APOLOGIZE TO EVERYONE AND GO TO THE POLICE.
HUH?
ARE YOU CRAZY?!
SHUT UP!
IF WE DON'T ARREST HIM, WE WON'T GET ANY POINTS!
YOU WANT TO START USING YOUR POWERS FOR GOOD, RIGHT?
THEN COME DOWN FROM THERE.
...

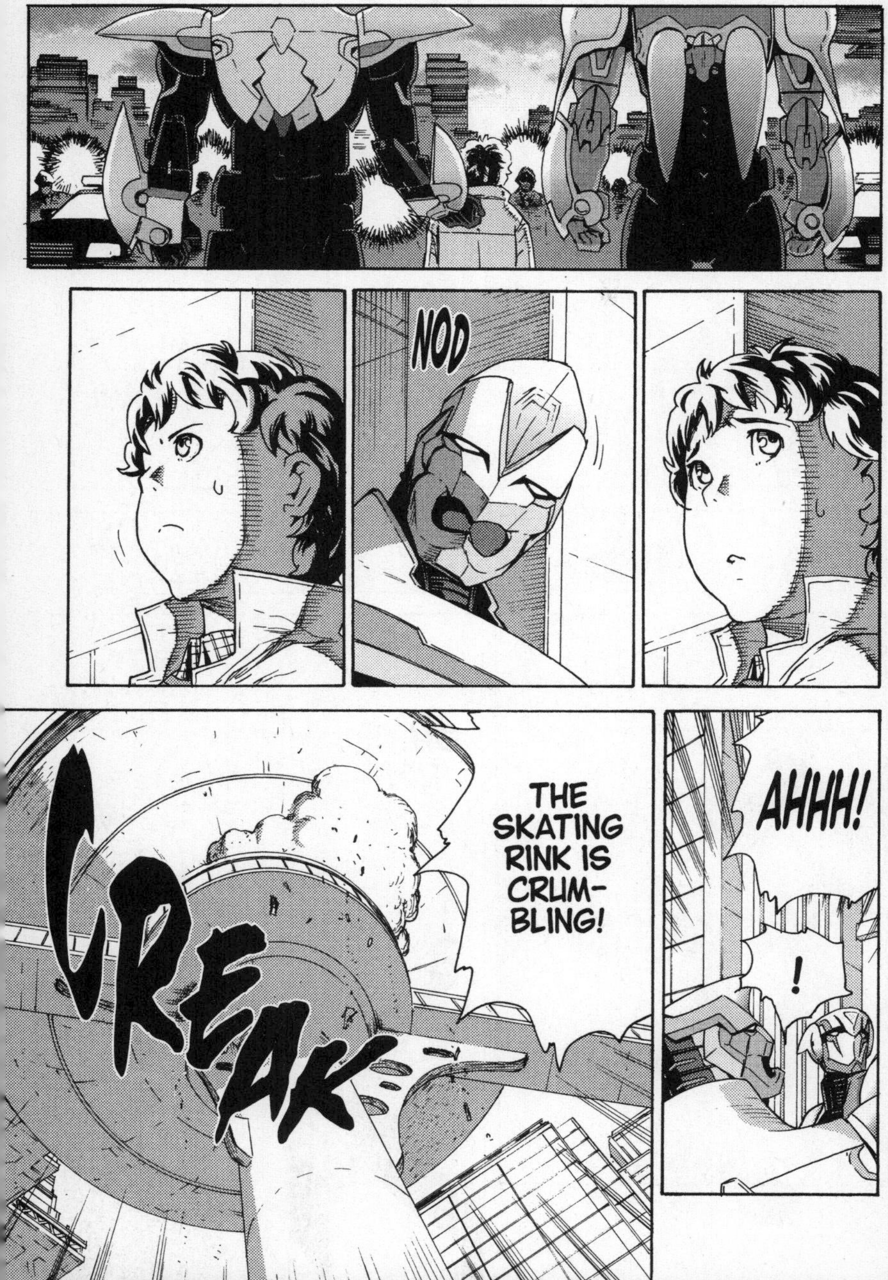
NOD
AHHH!
!
THE SKATING RINK IS CRUM-BLING!
CREAK

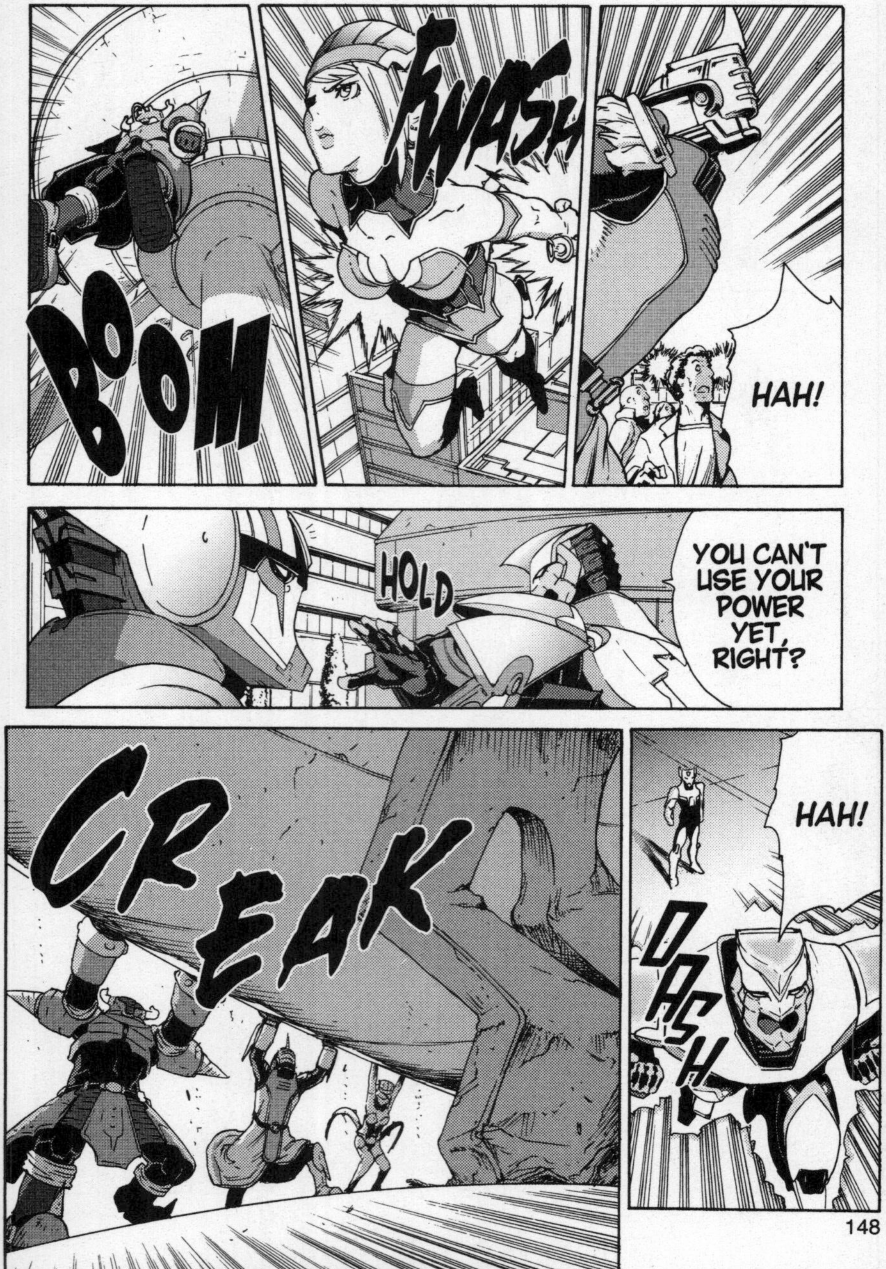
HAH!
FWASH
BOOM
YOU CAN'T USE YOUR POWER YET, RIGHT?
HOLD
HAH!
DASH
CREAK

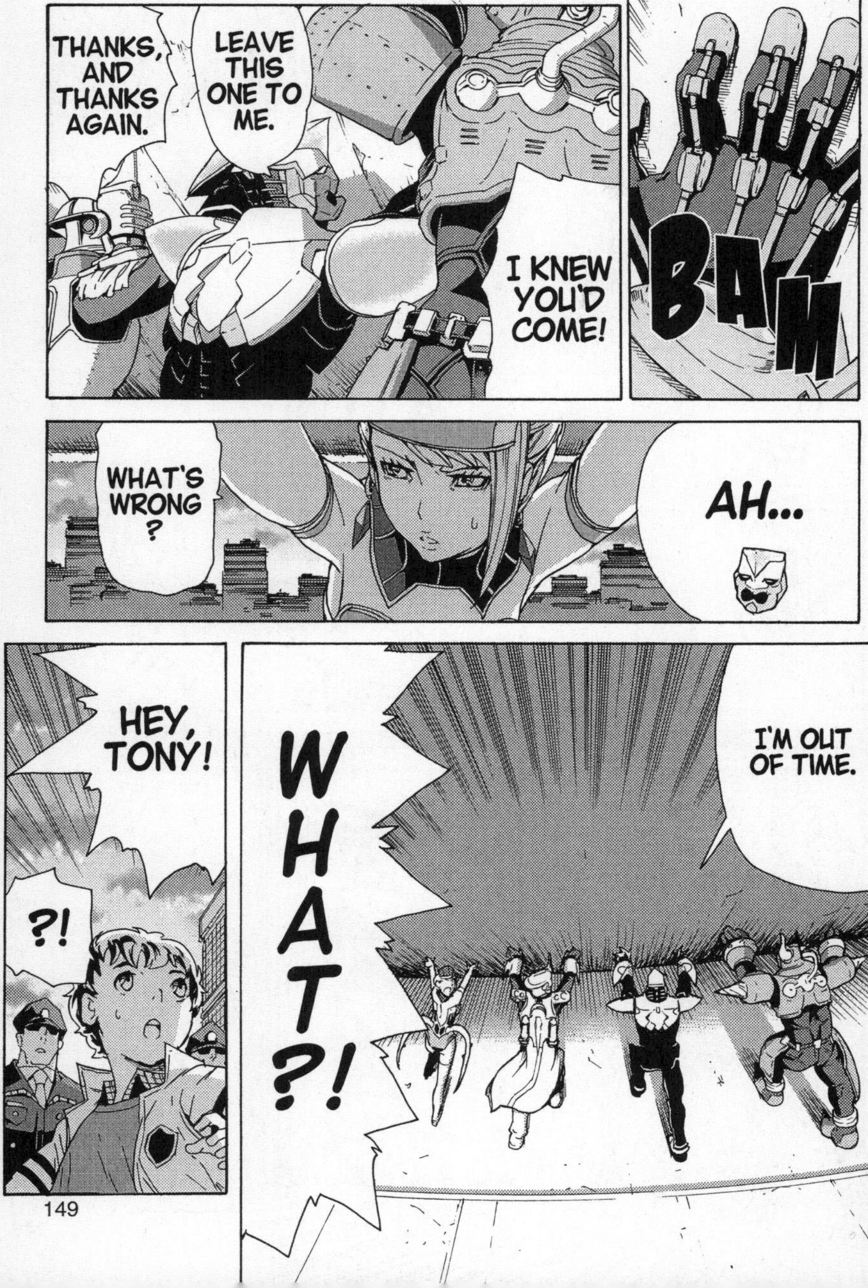
BAM
LEAVE THIS ONE TO ME.
THANKS, AND THANKS AGAIN.
I KNEW YOU'D COME!
AH...
WHAT'S WRONG?
I'M OUT OF TIME.
WHAT?!
HEY, TONY!
?!

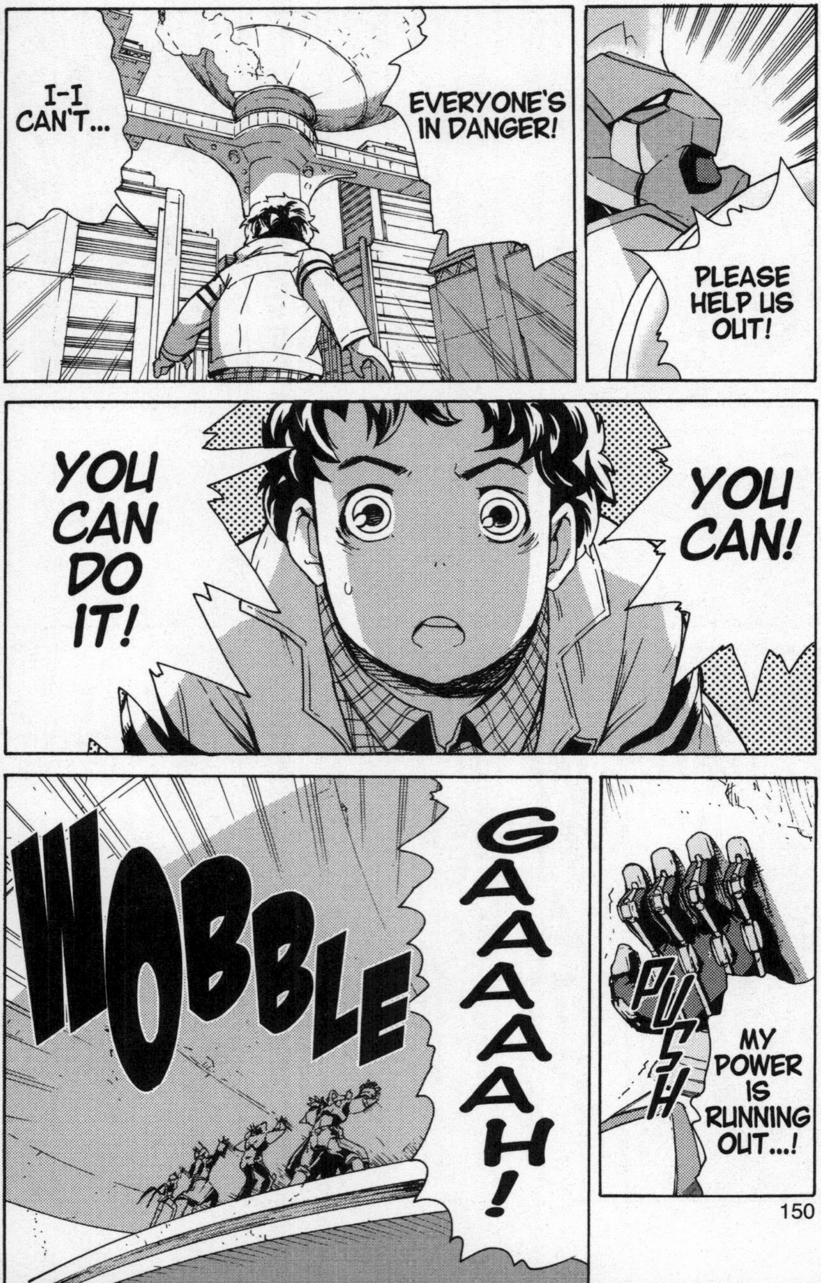
PLEASE HELP US OUT!
EVERYONE'S IN DANGER!
I-I CAN'T...
YOU CAN!
YOU CAN DO IT!
PUSH
MY POWER IS RUNNING OUT...!
GAAAAAH!
WOBBLE

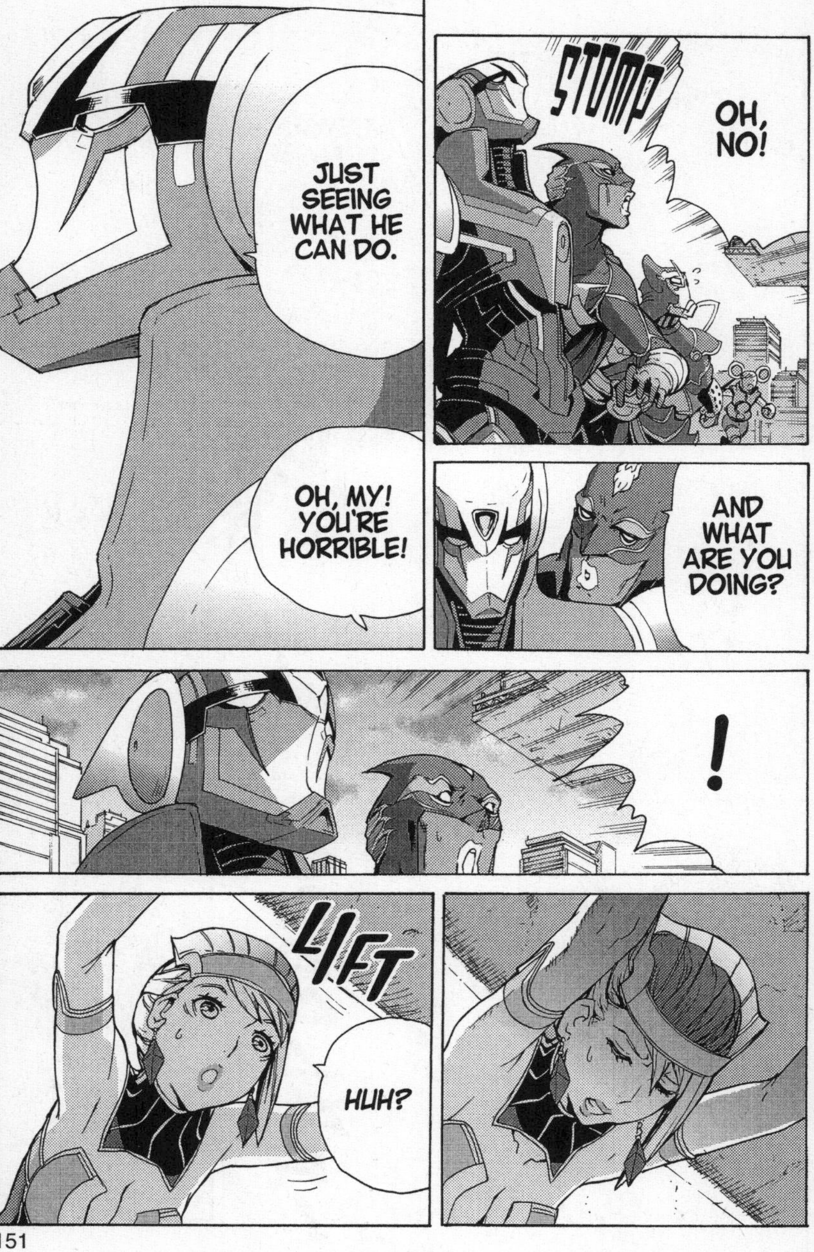
STOMP
OH, NO!
AND WHAT ARE YOU DOING?
JUST SEEING WHAT HE CAN DO.
OH, MY! YOU'RE HORRIBLE!
!
LIFT
HUH?

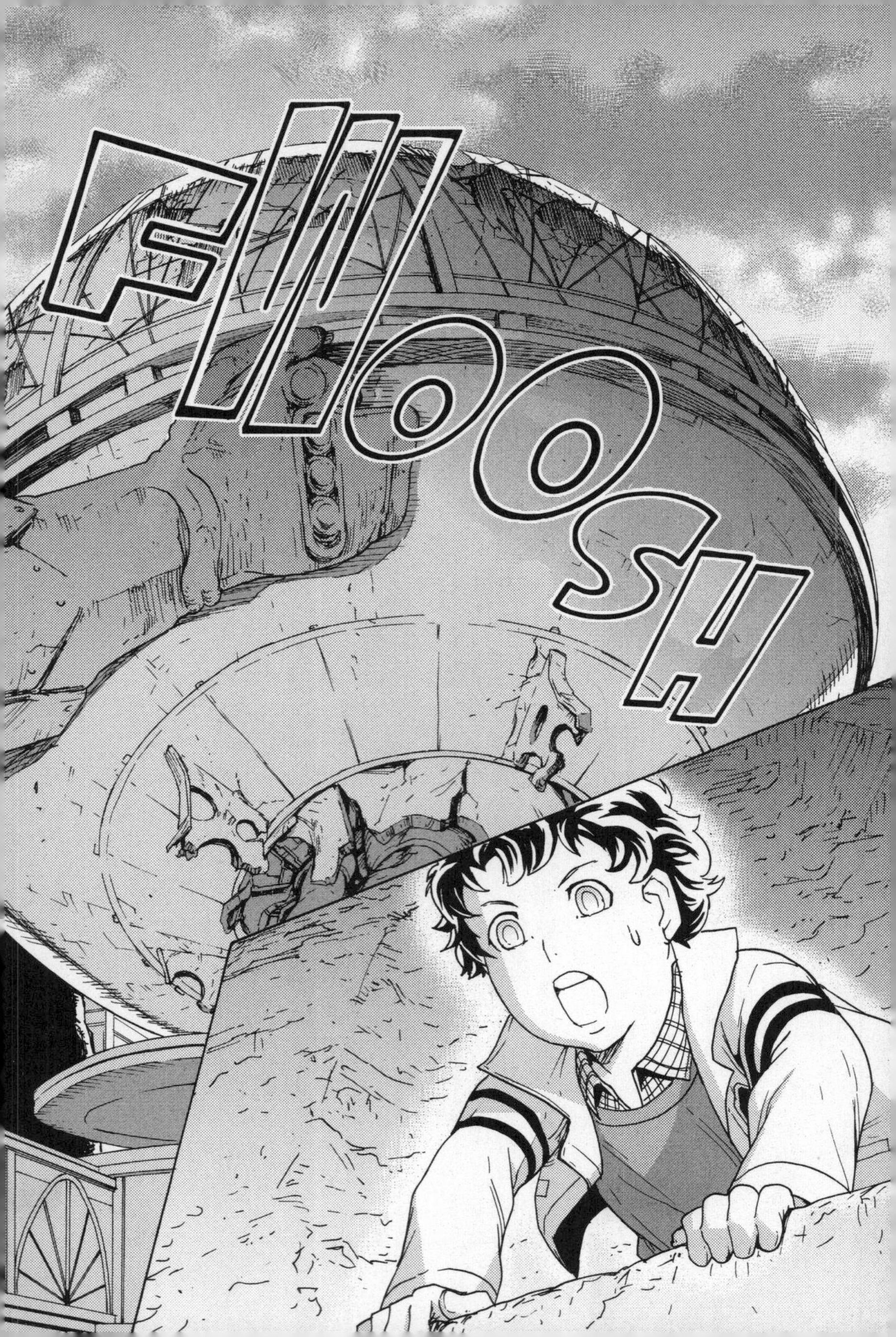
FWOOSH

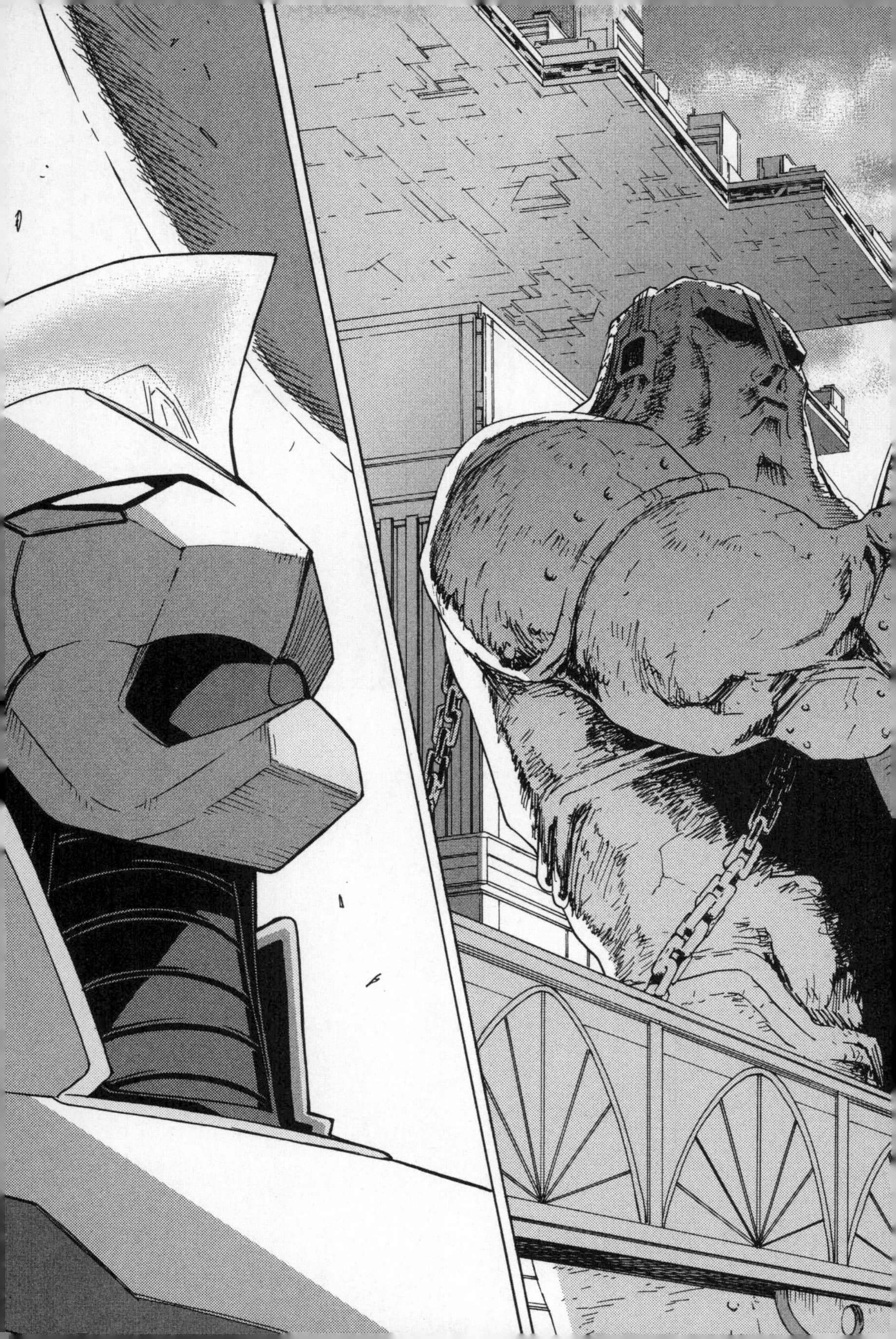

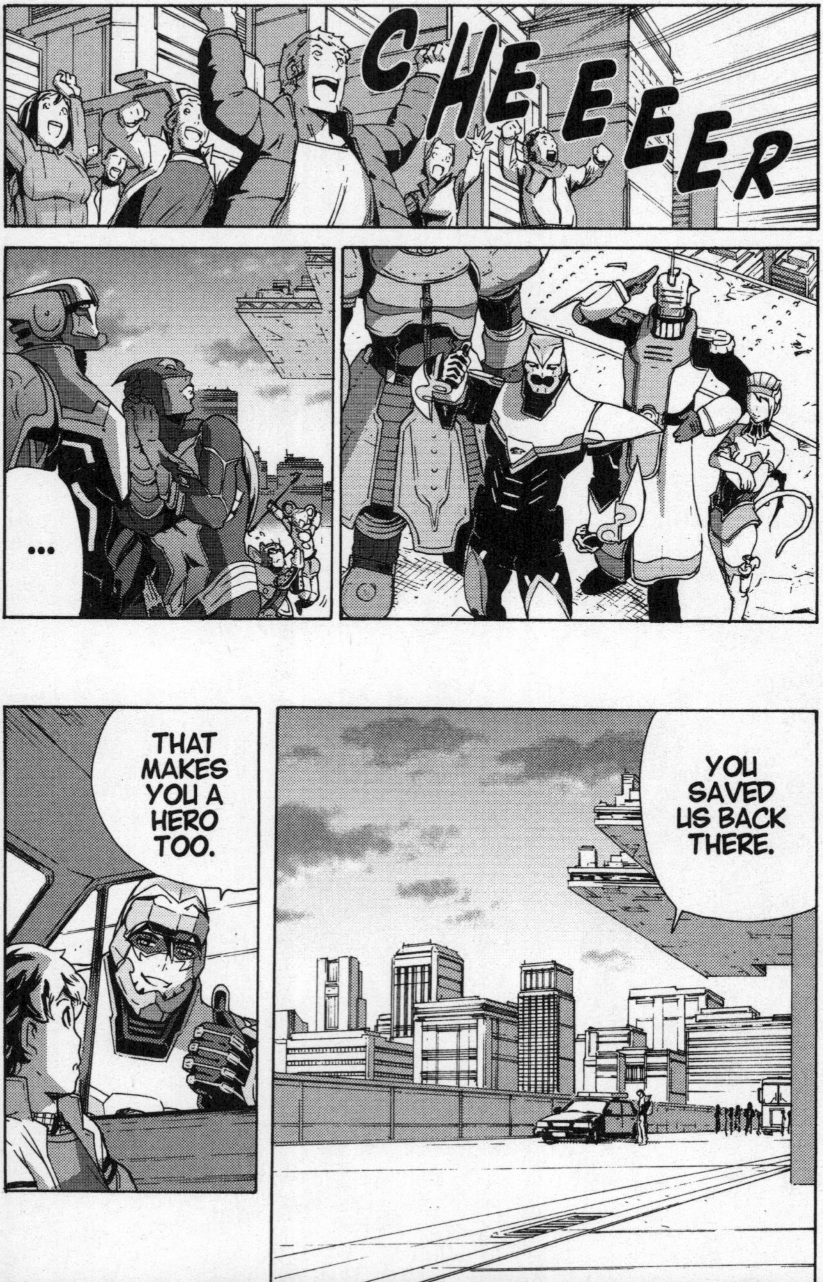
CHEEEER
...
YOU SAVED US BACK THERE.
THAT MAKES YOU A HERO TOO.

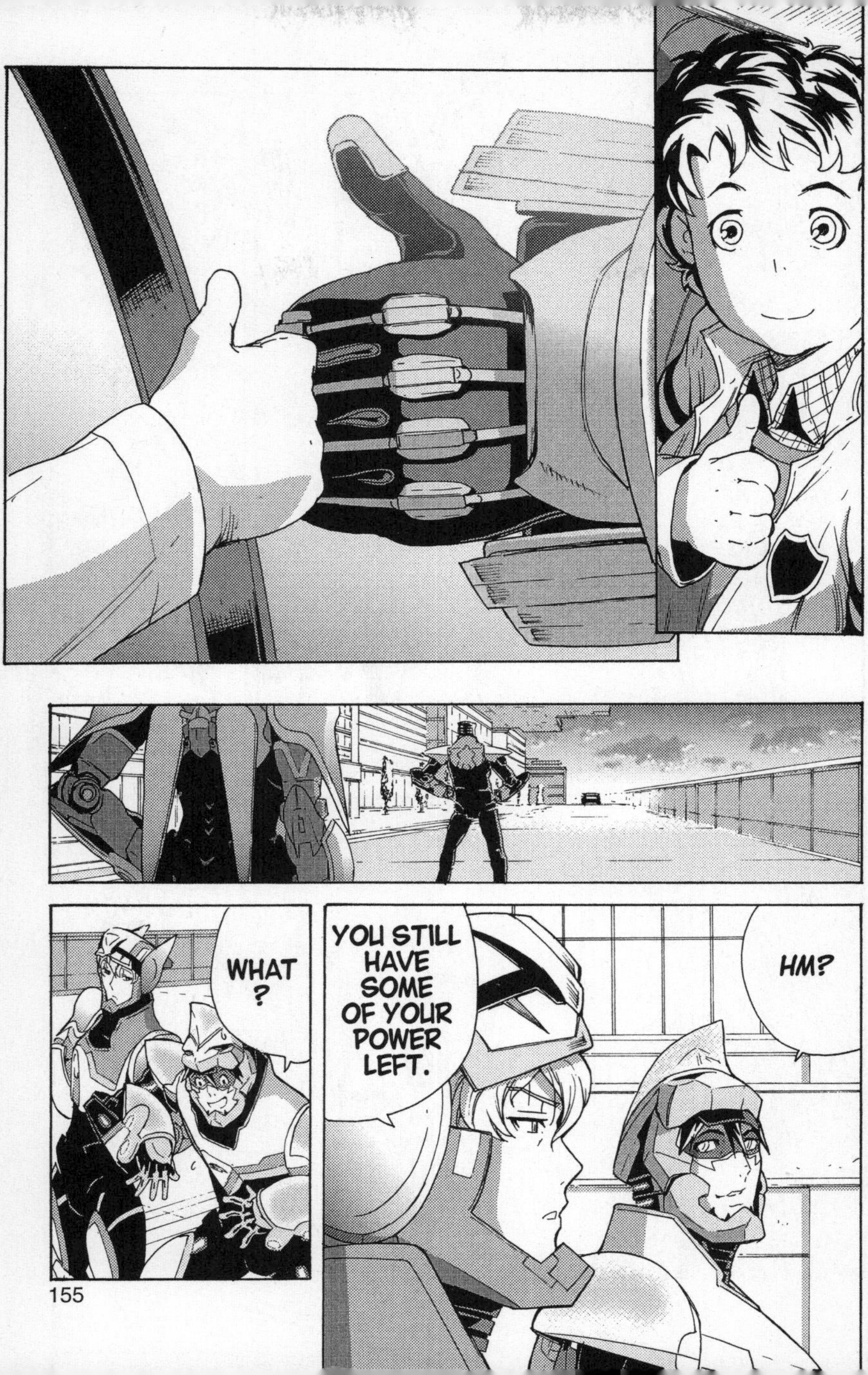
HM?
YOU STILL HAVE SOME OF YOUR POWER LEFT.
WHAT ?

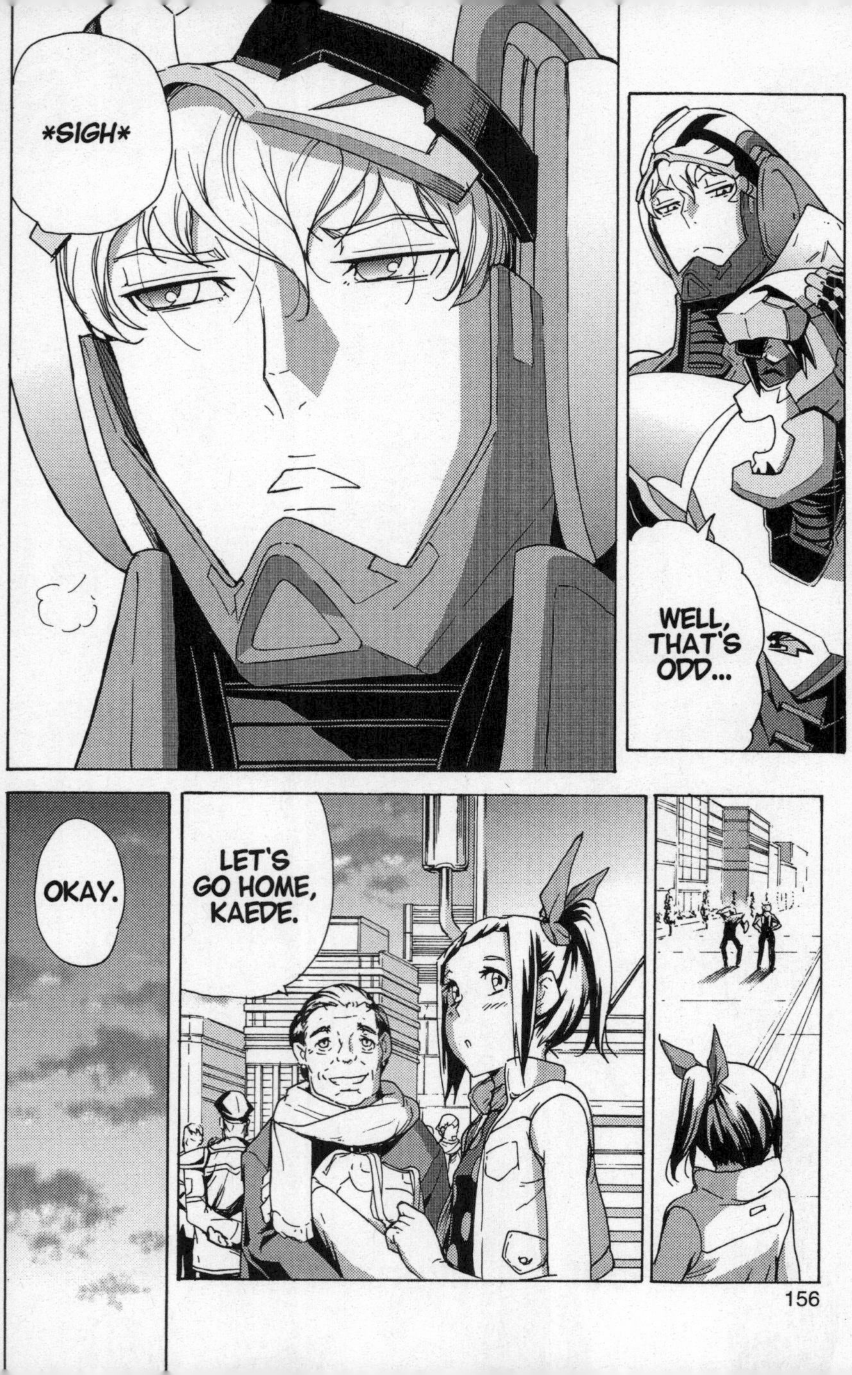
WELL, THAT'S ODD...
SIGH
LET'S GO HOME, KAEDE.
OKAY.

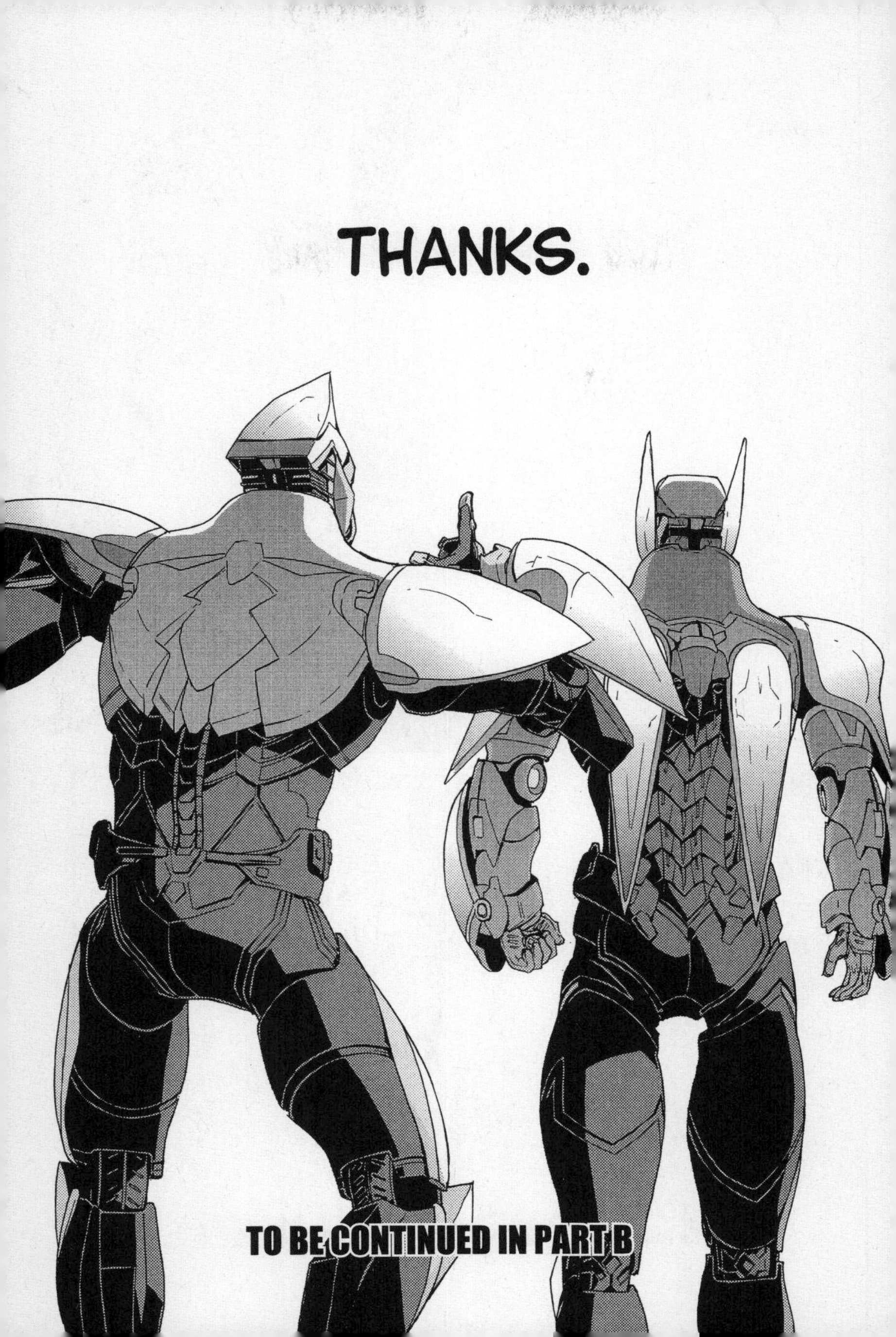
THANKS.
TO BE CONTINUED IN PART B

TIGER & BUNNY: The Beginning
Side A
VIZ Media Edition

Art by **TSUTOMU OONO**
Planning/Story **SUNRISE**
Original Script **MASAFUMI NISHIDA**
Original Character and Hero Design **MASAKAZU KATSURA**

TIGER & BUNNY –The Beginning- SIDE:A
© Tsutomu OONO 2012
© SUNRISE/T&B MOVIE PARTNERS
First published in Japan in 2012 by KADOKAWA SHOTEN Co.,Ltd., Tokyo.
English translation rights arranged with KADOKAWA SHOTEN Co.,Ltd., Tokyo.

Translation & English Adaptation **LABAAMEN & JOHN WERRY, HC LANGUAGE SOLUTIONS**
Touch-up Art & Lettering **STEPHEN DUTRO**
Design **FAWN LAU**
Editor **MIKE MONTESA**

Printed in the U.S.A.

Published by VIZ Media, LLC
P.O. Box 77010
San Francisco, CA 94107

10 9 8 7 6 5 4 3 2 1
First printing, October 2013

viz
MEDIA
www.viz.com

STOP!
YOU'RE READING IN THE WRONG DIRECTION!
This is the END of the graphic novel

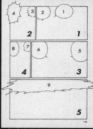

To properly enjoy this VIZ graphic novel, please turn it around and begin reading from **RIGHT** to **LEFT**. Unlike English, Japanese is read right to left, so Japanese comics are read in reverse order from the way English comics are typically read.

This book has been printed in the original Japanese format in order to preserve the orientation of the original artwork. Have fun with it!

⇐ Follow the action this way.